MAXIMIZE *Your* INHERITANCE

MAXIMIZE *Your* INHERITANCE

FOR *WIDOWS, WIDOWERS & HEIRS*

Jarratt G. Bennett

DEARBORN™
A **Kaplan Professional** Company

This publication is designed to provide accurate and authoritative information in regard to the subject matter covered. It is sold with the understanding that the publisher is not engaged in rendering legal, accounting, or other professional service. If legal advice or other expert assistance is required, the services of a competent professional should be sought.

Editorial Director: Cynthia Zigmund
Managing Editor: Jack Kiburz
Project Editor: Trey Thoelcke
Interior Design: Lucy Jenkins
Cover Design: Salvatore Concialdi
Typesetting: the dotted i

Library of Congress Cataloging-in-Publication Data

Bennett, Jarratt G.
    Maximize your inheritance : for widows, widowers & heirs / Jarratt
G. Bennett.
        p.   cm.
    Includes bibliographical references and index.
    ISBN 0-7931-3330-0 (pbk.)
    1. Widows—Finance, Personal.   2. Widowers—Finance, Personal.
3. Inheritance and succession.   4. Finance, Personal.   I. Title.
HG179.B397 1999
332.024'0654—dc21   99-30539
                                                                            CIP

Dearborn books are available at special quantity discounts to use as premiums and sales promotions, or for use in corporate training programs. For more information, please call the Special Sales Manager at 800-621-9621, ext. 4514, or write to Dearborn Financial Publishing, Inc., 155 N. Wacker Drive, Chicago, IL 60606-1719.

Contents

Foreword   vii
Preface   xi
Acknowledgments   xiii

PART ONE Immediate Concerns

1.   The Financial Aspects of Inheritance   3
2.   First Things First: Immediate Concerns   7
3.   Claiming Everything That's Yours—Private Sources   27
4.   Claiming Everything That's Yours—Government Sources   47
5.   Getting Organized: Bringing Order to Your Financial House   65
6.   Settling the Estate   81

PART TWO A Look at the Big Picture

7.   Retirement Planning: Making the Money Last   105
8.   The Inheritor's Guide to Taxes   123
9.   Insurance: Understanding the Great Mystery   139

PART THREE Ensuing Concerns

10.   You and Your Home   165
11.   Funding College Education   183
12.   Long-Term Care   201

PART FOUR Prosperous Transitions

13. Giving: How, When, to Whom, and How Much   219
14. Estate Planning: Passing Along Your Wealth   233
15. The Financial Aspects of Remarriage   251
16. Choosing Professional Advisers   263
17. Frauds and Scams: Protecting Yourself   277
18. Preparing for Incapacity   283

Appendix A: Telephone Number Resource Directory   291
Appendix B: Second Singlehood   295
Bibliography   297
Index   299

Foreword

As a long-time financial adviser, Jerry Bennett has doggedly pursued academic and professional training and certifications. He is a Certified Financial Planner (CFP), a Chartered Life Underwriter (CLU), and Chartered Financial Counselor (ChFC). He obtains 30 or more credit hours of continuing education every year.

Education is important to the learning process. But the vicissitudes of daily living are what seasons an adviser and counselor. And the experience that hits close to home is usually the most powerful, painful, and impressionable of life's lessons.

Jerry has been counseling widowed persons and heirs since 1966. However, it wasn't until 11 years ago, when a 46-year-old friend and neighbor died suddenly—on his own kitchen floor—that Jerry truly realized the in-depth needs of loved ones left behind.

There had been no warning, no previous illness. For Jerry's seemingly healthy neighbor, who everyone later agreed was "too young to go like that," his heart attack that day was his first and last. He and Jerry had discussed financial matters but they never looked closely at what would be needed in the aftermath of his death.

"His wife was suddenly widowed," Jerry recalled, "with two children in college and young twin boys who were still living at home. She faced raising those boys alone, providing their living expenses and their eventual college educations, as well as her own support. Fortunately, her husband had a life insurance policy, issued years before his death. Still, there were a number of problems to resolve.

"There were critical issues the widow had to face: immediate cash flow, continuing income over a long period of time, finishing the older children's college, building a reserve for the twins' college education, and, eventually, planning for her own retirement.

"In addition to all of this, she was concerned about investing her money." Experience has taught Jerry that when widowed people, as well as heirs, have a substantial amount of money with which to work, they always worry about making a mistake with it.

Maximize Your Inheritance is not just about money; it's also about having quick access to answers about money problems. It's a book for people who have been widowed or lost a parent, whether the loss was recent or not.

Many books provide general consumer financial information, while others have been written about the grieving and recovery process. Yet, there is no definitive resource book that deals with the financial questions asked by widowed persons and heirs, either about initial money decisions or long-term financial planning.

The few books that have attempted to approach this subject suffer from two major flaws: 1) they require readers to review most or all of the book to answer specific financial questions, and 2) while their authors may be experienced personal counselors, they have little background in financial planning, strategies, and procedures.

Thankfully, *Maximize Your Inheritance* covers the full range of financial concerns that widowed people and heirs have to face—everything from immediate money needs through the survivor's retirement and estate plan. Jerry has avoided technical terms, references to confusing regulations, and psychobabble, and has kept language reader-friendly. Moreover, the book has been organized so that you don't have to read everything to get specific information.

While part of an integrated whole, each section can stand alone. If you have a particular problem, you can find potential solutions by reading just the section dealing with that issue. What you need to know has been streamlined to the essence; you can get information easily and act on it immediately.

Once you get started, you will find yourself taking sound, giant steps forward. I encourage you to make notes, photocopy pages, use the helpful forms, and even call Jerry. After all, nothing less than your financial health is at stake.

I commend Jerry Bennett for the dedication and diligence required to produce this most useful work and I commend you, the reader, for seeking guidance from one of the top financial planners in America.

Lewis J. Walker, CFP
President,
Institute for Certified Investment Management Consultants
Past President,
The Institute of Certified Financial Planners

Preface

This book is not about death or dying, grief or bereavement. It is about money—your money—and your stewardship of the assets left by your deceased spouse or parent.

We start with the premise that the funeral is over, that you've begun to realize the large number of tasks facing you, and that you've started some tentative planning. You're now at the point of paying bills, keeping daily financial activities on track, worrying about estate settlement, and wondering how to make your money last. Is it possible to take charge of your financial life? While you may not feel like doing so while you're in mourning, there are decisions that must be made.

Many bereavement counselors suggest that organizing and restructuring the family finances is therapeutic and aids in the grieving process. Melba Colgrove, Ph.D., and Peter McWilliams, authors of *How to Survive the Loss of a Love*, note that when an emotional injury takes place, the body begins a process as natural as the healing of a physical wound.

Let the process happen; trust that nature will do the healing and the pain will ease. When it does, you will be stronger, happier, and more sensitive and aware. A similar process will work for you as you come to grips with your financial future.

People who have lost a spouse or a parent face one of life's greatest challenges. They must somehow make sense out of the death of a mate, while handling a huge array of financial problems, making mind-boggling adjustments, and building a new life.

I've structured *Maximize Your Inheritance* so you can quickly find the answers you need without being overwhelmed with information. Building a sound financial future is a step-by-step procedure, so you can read what you need to know now and leave the rest for another time.

Jarratt G. Bennett

Acknowledgments

I am fortunate to be in a business I love. Over the past 32 years I have learned much from my clients and hope they have profited from my relationship with them. This book is dedicated to those I have had the privilege to serve.

It takes more than one person to make a book a reality. Without the individuals listed below this book would not exist.

Thanks to Gregory P. Seal, CFP; Lewis J. Walker, CFP; Douglas G. Hesse, CFP, Lee D. Pennington, CFP; David G. Hoffman, Attorney at Law; and Ken Hill for their support, insights, and technical reviews. To Jeffrey P. Davidson goes a special thanks for initially bringing order to the manuscript and adding his professional writing insights throughout its development.

Especially, my thanks go to my Executive Assistants, Sarah B. Murphy and Julie Essman, who labored, unrelentingly, during the whole process and organized the manuscript into a polished, professional format.

And finally, thanks to my wife, whose patience, encouragement, and support helped give me the strength to bring this book to publication.

Immediate Concerns

CHAPTER 1

The Financial Aspects of Inheritance

*I*t was bad. Nothing in Nancy's life had ever ached as much and, now, on top of the unrelenting anguish and bone-deep sadness, she needed to deal with financial problems. Where would she find the answers?

Jim was dead—gone and buried. God, how the loss hurt. Nancy watched the ceiling begin to take on the colors of sunrise. Another day to face; could she get through it? What would she do for income over the next few weeks? How would her son continue college? What about Jim's pension and 401(k)? Would she ever have enough money to retire? What about probate, estate settlement, finding an attorney, investments? The endless questions raced through her mind.

Every year hundreds of thousands of husbands and wives lose their spouses. It is the most stressful event of their lives. For most it is also a nerve-wracking financial ordeal. Only a few are fortunate enough to have highly competent advisers on whom they can rely to share in financial decision making.

Most widowed persons are not so lucky. They have neither the training nor the temperament to handle the assets left in their care, and they fear making a financial mistake. Their fear is not without substance: most widows and widowers suffer a substantial loss in asset value in the first two years.

TYPICAL WIDOWS: YOU ARE NOT ALONE

Death does not respect age or social status. There are widowed people in every conceivable life situation, at every age, and in every financial bracket.

Consider Bob and Sarah who were married in 1950. They met in college, married in their mid-twenties, and were together almost 43 years. Bob worked for several companies during his lifetime. They bought their first house for $42,000 and, 12 years ago, purchased their dream house for $195,000. Their home is worth approximately $300,000 today.

Today Sarah, who has two children and five grandchildren, is alone. Bob handled most of the money matters in the family and although it has been a couple of years since his passing, Sarah is still apprehensive about making financial decisions.

Elaine is a young widow with two small children. When her husband Russell was killed in a car crash, Elaine's world was shattered. After four months, she is beginning to come to grips with the financial aspects of widowhood.

Bill, 51, is a middle-aged widower. One of his sons attends a top Ivy League school, and the other will start college soon—if Bill can afford it. His wife Nancy was a substantial contributor to the family income before her untimely death.

Mary Jo's father Don collapsed on the ski slopes of the Pocono Mountains and died two days later. Don was a highly paid corporate executive who had many company benefits and large insurance policies.

Sarah, Bill, and Mary Jo share some common concerns, yet each has to approach the problems from a different stage of life. Each has to handle immediate concerns, get financially organized, file claims, make investment decisions, and consider strategies to solve the dilemmas unique to his or her individual situation.

THE BIG TWENTY

In working with widowed persons and heirs from all walks of life, there are 20 financial issues that routinely arise after the loss of a spouse or parent. Here's a list of 20 concerns that you will likely face:

1. Do I have enough money for immediate needs?
2. Will there be enough money to last if I need long-term health care at some point?
3. Will the rising cost of living adversely affect me?
4. Will I have enough for retirement?
5. What about medical insurance coverage?
6. How should I invest life insurance proceeds?
7. What should I do with 401(k), IRA, and company pension funds?
8. Should I sell the home and buy a smaller, less expensive home?
9. Can I use the capital gains tax exclusion for the home to my advantage?
10. Will I have to file quarterly estimates for income taxes?
11. Can I afford to help my children or grandchildren with college expenses?
12. Should my will be changed?
13. Should I have a living will?
14. Will I have enough income to live without working?
15. (If there are young children) How will I finance day care if I return to work?
16. Have claims been filed for everything that's coming to me?
17. When can I expect the Social Security check to arrive?
18. Should I choose a financial advisor? How?
19. Who should I contact right now?
20. What should I do first?

TAKE CHARGE

The decision to take responsibility for your financial life requires making intelligent, ongoing financial decisions by:

- collecting the information you will need;
- assembling and organizing this information; and
- using the information to make correct or corrective decisions.

You will no doubt feel a strong temptation to continue deferring all but the most immediate judgments. If you surrender to the desire to postpone taking control, things will coast along as the years drift past. Eventually, you'll reach a point of no return and the opportunity to make those vital, long-term decisions will be lost forever.

    This book begins with what you must do first, and gradually takes you into the future of your financial life. Let's begin the journey.

CHAPTER 2

First Things First
Immediate Concerns

As a newly widowed individual or inheritor, you will immediately be faced with a profusion of financial details. Your need to pay attention to these urgent matters coincides with a time of great emotional upheaval, and you may think, "Decisions, decisions, decisions. Why must I deal with them now?"

You might feel uninformed and ill-prepared to deal with these issues in the aftermath of your loved one's death. Nevertheless, it's important to set your emotions aside and face up to your finances.

If you're lucky, you and your spouse or parent discussed finances before his or her death. If this is the case, you will find this chapter easier to go through. If you did not have that discussion, press forward; this chapter will help you deal with what needs to be done now and in the weeks ahead.

DOS AND DON'TS DURING MOURNING

Put off making long-term money decisions until you're able to face them unemotionally. You may think that you're functioning normally, but your behavior may be erratic and you may not realize it. That's normal after suffering a major loss.

You will also have a tendency to want to take action. While taking action may be therapeutic, in some case it can be a major mistake. Don't take any action that you can't reverse later.

Do you have someone you know and trust to help you organize your papers and help you with your initial decisions? To the extent possible during the early part of the mourning period, you'll want to take certain actions while avoiding others. At this stage you need time to let reality seep in and allow the healing process to begin. When you start to feel the ground more firmly under your feet, you'll be in a better position to make decisions that will serve you well over the long term.

- *Do* keep your money in a safe place—for example, money market accounts, certificates of deposit for three- or six-month terms, and passbook savings accounts. Accounts in any one bank are insured only up to $100,000, so put your money in more than one institution if it is above the $100,000 limit.
- *Do* protect yourself from financial problems that can result from illness or accident by making sure you're covered by medical insurance and, if you are employed, disability insurance.
- *Do* be wary of impulse spending, especially on large-ticket items. You may later regret the money you spend quickly now.
- *Do* recognize that you are in mourning and are especially vulnerable to pressures. Hold back; be cautious with your funds.

- *Don't* make any major money decisions now that can be deferred to a later time.
- *Don't* remodel your house or buy a new car.
- *Don't* buy life insurance.
- *Don't* invest with well-meaning friends or relatives.
- *Don't* put your funds where they can't be accessed quickly and at little or no cost.
- *Don't* borrow money, or lend it.
- *Don't* make major money decisions for the good of the kids, unless the decisions are also good for you. Give it a little time.
- *Don't* give away money, even to friends or relatives, until you've had time to determine how far your money will take you.

Over the next several months, and in the years to come, it may be appropriate to do some or all of the actions listed above. However, right now is too soon to do so. You need time to learn more about your financial status and define the financial course you wish to steer.

WHAT TO DO RIGHT AWAY

When the funeral is over and all the relatives have gone back to their own lives, you may find yourself alone. This is a good time to face the financial details that require prompt attention.

The actions recommended in this section may contradict the dos and don'ts listed earlier because circumstances in your life might require you to do some things during the mourning period that cannot be avoided. The two lists are intended to make you aware of what's important, so that you can act wisely in accordance with the time pressures of your own situation.

Set up an area to work specifically on your financial affairs. You may want to have a desk and file cabinet with file folders for each important topic in your financial life. See Chapter 5 for suggestions on how to organize your files. If you already have many of the files in various locations throughout your home, it will be helpful to put them all in one central location. Eventually, some files will no longer be needed while others will become permanent and will serve you for the rest of your lifetime.

Keep notes and make lists; doing so will help you handle the shock and grief of losing a loved one. When people give you information, they will expect you to understand and remember it. However, it is unlikely that you will be able to remember the details of the vast amount of information you will receive. The forms at the end of this chapter will help you with this task.

Some of the terms in the following list will be familiar and some will be new to you. The inclusion of strange-sounding terms is not intended to create anxiety, but to ensure thoroughness. In fact, some of the words will help you deal with various agencies so you can determine exactly what your assets are. Don't be concerned if you don't understand every one of these terms right now; their meanings will become clear as we proceed.

Right-Away Activities

Set Up

- *Child care.* If small children are involved, arrange child care so you can concentrate on the logistics of what you need to do.
- *Accurate records.* Record all the money you spend on the funeral and other costs associated with your spouse's or parent's death. These figures may be needed for income tax returns and may entitle the estate to income tax deductions.
- *Phone log.* Maintain a written log of everyone you talk to on the phone concerning business, legal, and financial matters. Include in the log a summary of important facts, and answers to any questions you asked.
- *Incoming mail system.* Collect mail and sort into important categories—i.e., bills, life insurance matters, and health insurance forms.
- *Outgoing mail system.* Keep photocopies of everything you mail or deliver to someone else, and develop an appropriate filing system.
- *Checking and savings accounts.* Examine all accounts and make a list of the totals in each. Doing so will help you determine whether you have enough available cash for the short term.
- *Immediate cash requirements.* Get a clear short-term picture of whether the money will last by completing the Immediate Cash Requirements form in Figure 2.1.
- *Death certificates.* If you haven't done so already, order certified death certificates. The number of certificates you need will depend on the number of claims you have—as a general rule, 10 to 20 copies are required. You may need death certificates for life insurance policies (one for each policy); Social Security benefits; veteran survivor's benefits; retirement or pension plan survivor's benefits; financial accounts at banks, savings and loan institutions, and brokerage firms; safe-deposit boxes; property insurance proceeds; automobile registration; health insurance policy proceeds; credit card companies; real estate title transfers; and stock and bond title transfers.

  The funeral director can order as many certified copies as you need. If you need additional copies at a future date, ask the funeral provider for assistance, or order them yourself from your state's vital statistics or health agency.

Organize

- *Checkbooks.* Make sure all checkbooks balance. Bounced checks will only add to your burdens.
- *The will.* Find your spouse's or parent's will and any trusts. Call your attorney and arrange a meeting to discuss these items. If you don't have an attorney, see Chapter 16, Choosing Professional Advisers.
- *Important papers.* Go through your loved one's desk and files. Look for important papers, especially, unpaid bills.
- *Outstanding debts.* Make a list of all outstanding bills, debts, and installment payments. If you anticipate a delay in meeting obligations, especially if you are waiting for life insurance proceeds to handle bills, call the creditors, explain the circumstances, and ask for an extension.
- *Employee benefit information.* If your spouse or parent was employed, notify the company and request a list of benefits. For example, insurance, vested retirement benefits, 401(k), stock option plans, stock purchase plans, deferred compensation, supplemental insurance, medical benefits, vacation pay, sick leave pay, and any disability benefits due to illness before death.

Note: If you were covered by your deceased spouse's medical plan, you should immediately check with the employer to see if you and your family will automatically be covered. If not, apply for continuation of coverage under Federal COBRA conditions within 60 days. Under COBRA you must pay the premiums.

Take Care of These Insurance-Related Matters

- *Life insurance.* Contact the insurance companies that issued policies on the life of your spouse or parent. Once you've received the proper instructions, submit the death claim forms along with certified death certificates. (See Chapter 3 for details). Benefits may take up to six weeks to receive. In addition, if your loved one was killed on the job or while traveling on company business you will probably be entitled to worker's compensation survivor benefits. Contact the employer to process worker's compensation claims.

- *Accidental death benefits.* If death was accidental, look for accidental death and dismemberment policies. If death was due to a car crash, check with your insurance agent about the death benefits and medical coverage provisions of the automobile insurance policy. Also, if the deceased belonged to an automobile club, check to see if accidental death benefits were included as part of membership.
- *Credit and mortgage life insurance.* Determine whether there was any mortgage life insurance and credit life insurance on each installment contract and credit card. Such coverage will pay off, respectively, the balance of the mortgage on your home or the entire installment contract and credit card debt.
- *Insurance and taxes.* Check to ensure that your health, homeowners, and automobile insurance policies, and income and property taxes are all up to date and paid.

Take Care of These Bank-Related Matters

- *Safe-deposit box.* If your safe-deposit box is jointly owned and you have the key, open it and review the contents. Make a list of anything that requires your immediate attention. Put aside items for your children and others, and plan to deal with them later. In some states, even safe-deposit boxes that are jointly held are sealed after the death of one of the owners. In that case, consult your attorney about getting a court's permission to get access to the box.
- *Certificates of deposit.* Determine whether there are any certificates of deposit that are ready to mature. You may not want them to roll over for another investment period if you need the cash to pay bills. However, if a jointly owned certificate of deposit has recently rolled over, your bank may allow you take the funds without penalty because one of the owners has died.
- *IRAs.* Determine whether your spouse or parent owned one or more IRA accounts, where the money is located, and who the beneficiaries are.

Determine Government Benefits

- *Social Security benefits.* You must apply to receive any Social Security funds to which you're entitled; the money will not be sent to you automatically. Set up an appointment with your local Social Security office to apply for death and survivor's benefits.

  If you are a surviving spouse you will need to bring with you a certified copy of the death certificate, proof of marriage, and the Social Security numbers of your spouse and yourself. When you call to set up an appointment, ask if you will also need your children's birth certificates and Social Security numbers, and W-2 forms of the most recent tax year for both you and your spouse. If you are a surviving heir, be aware that there is a death benefit available.

- *Department of Veterans Affairs.* If your spouse or parent served in the armed forces, contact the Department of Veterans Affairs. There may be burial or survivor's benefits to which you're entitled. Some funeral directors may be able to supply the necessary forms.

Contact

- *American Legion.* If your loved one belonged to the American Legion, contact the local branch. The War Orphans and Widows Educational Assistance Act may provide benefits to a child who is 18-25 years old for 36 months of schooling.

- *Labor unions.* If your spouse or parent was a member of any labor union, contact the union to determine if any death benefits are available.

- *Other membership organizations.* Notify any organizations of which your spouse or parent was a member and inquire whether you are entitled to any benefits or income as a survivor. Membership organizations include credit unions, trade unions, fraternal orders, college alumni groups, and military service organizations.

Notify

- *Financial institutions.* Notify all financial institutions, stock brokerage firms, insurance carriers, and investment companies of the death. Request that account registrations be changed as appropriate.

- *Attorney.* Contact your attorney to set up a time to review the will and/or living trust. If there is no will, talk to an attorney for instructions on estate settlement issues regarding intestate (dying without a will).
- *Insurance agent.* Call both the life and automobile insurance agents to set up claims procedures for those policies.
- *Accountant/CPA/tax preparer.* If you and your spouse used a tax preparer contact that person. Eventually you will need to meet to determine your overall tax picture and how it may change in the future.
- *Bank.* Reposition accounts you held in joint with the deceased into your name. Open your own checking account if you don't have one. If your spouse or parent was receiving direct deposit checks have the bank return them to the sender (i.e., Social Security). Open your own safe-deposit box. Find out if there are any benefits such as credit life insurance to pay off loans.

Take Care of These Other Matters

- *Foreign death certificates.* If the death occurred abroad, immediately notify the nearest U.S. diplomatic or consular mission. The staff will assist you with the logistics of transporting the decedent's remains to the point of burial. A local funeral director will then prepare the body for shipment to, and burial in, the place you select.
- *Filing forms.* Check with your attorney, accountant or financial planner about filing the following documents: federal estate tax returns, inheritance tax report, federal individual income tax returns, state tax returns, and state tax returns for other states where property is owned.
- *Beneficiary changes.* If your spouse or parent was the beneficiary of your insurance policies, annuities, IRAs, or other retirement accounts, request beneficiary change forms to protect your heirs.
- *Funeral home disputes.* If you have a problem regarding your funeral home bill, first discuss it with the funeral director. If you still have problems, contact your state licensing board; the Con-

ference of Funeral Service Examining Boards, PO Box E, Huntsville, AR 72740, 501-738-1915.

- *Your will.* Review your own will and discuss with your attorney any changes you wish to make.
- *Outside pressure.* For now, disregard unsolicited advice and pressure from others, especially about financial matters. Resolve not to make any major decisions now, particularly about business ventures with friends or relatives.

IMMEDIATE DEMANDS FOR CASH

In the first few days there are likely to be many demands for cash—usually, about $2,500 is needed within the first five to ten days, and more shortly thereafter. If savings and checking funds are insufficient, more money must be found or an arrangement worked out with creditors.

In the event you need emergency cash before insurance claims are paid, you can try to negotiate a cash advance from the insurance company against the full amount of life insurance benefits due you. However, this may slow down the process of issuing the total face amount of the policies.

Do not ignore debt. If your creditors—funeral home, hospitals, physicians, nursing homes—hound you for payment of bills and you cannot pay them all at once, call each creditor, explain the situation, and offer to set up a payment schedule. Your attorney, accountant, or financial adviser can do this for you if you can't face it yourself.

When Hilda was coping with the loss of her husband, the reaction of his elderly parents, and pressure from her boss, she didn't want any more problems so she placed all her bills in a large cardboard box. She meant to go through them, but never found time to deal with them. Fortunately, her oldest son realized the situation and stepped in before there were serious problems. Debts won't go away and creditors can be nasty if they feel you may not pay.

When you receive money from insurance companies or your spouse's or parent's estate you may wonder what to do with it. There will probably be many suggestions from friends and relatives about how you should invest the money. Unless you need the funds to pay immediate bills, or cover an emergency, don't do anything. Set up a money market fund at your local bank (FDIC insured, of course), and wait until you feel less overwhelmed or confused. You need a game plan to invest the money. When you're ready, find an objective financial adviser who understands your position and situation. Then, make whatever investment decisions you deem appropriate.

SECONDARY CONCERNS

Housing

You may feel pressure to decide what to do with the house. Well-meaning friends and relatives may insist you'd be better off in a place without so many memories, others may think a smaller home requiring less upkeep would be an improvement for you, or you may feel guilty living alone in a large house. You may even hear from real estate agents with generous offers for your property.

When George's wife passed away George's sister suggested several times that he sell the family house and live in a small condominium. George's grown children were also anxious to know if he was moving. But George was content to remain in his home for the foreseeable future. He was comfortable there and wanted time to consider all the aspects of moving.

George was wise to wait. Moving is one decision that can be deferred until you're sure it's what you want. Remember that the house also may have an important psychological meaning for you. As a surviving spouse, remaining in your home may be instrumental in helping you work through your grief. Thus, unless the house is your only source of money, do nothing with it now. If housing is a pressing issue for you turn to Chapter 10 You and Your Home.

Credit

You may be wondering about the status of bank cards such as VISA, MasterCard and American Express, as well as retail store and gasoline credit cards. If the cards were in both names or you used your spouse's card, you're probably concerned about using them.

There are no specific rules about how your credit will be affected by the death of your spouse. Some companies will permit you to retain their credit card, but may lower the credit limit, while others may cancel the card. Either way contact creditors to inquire whether there is credit life insurance.

As a surviving spouse, it is to your advantage to apply for credit in your own name. Some widowed people never notify credit card companies of their spouse's death. They go on using the same credit cards and paying the bills as they did prior to their mate's death. There are two problems with this approach. The first is that any credit life insurance will remain uncollected. The second is that the good credit rating may continue to accrue to your deceased spouse, and not to you.

Other Secondary Concerns

Here are several general topics that will need to be addressed eventually:

- Bank
- Real estate taxes
- College financial aid
- Health club
- Magazines
- Utilities
- Credit cards (expired)
- State Department of Motor Vehicles
- Stockbroker/financial planner
- Real estate title
- Mortgage holder

FIGURE 2.1   Immediate Cash Requirements

Item	Due Date	Amount Due
Household Operation (1 month estimate)	_____	$ _____
Funeral Expenses:		
1. _____	_____	$ _____
2. _____	_____	_____
3. _____	_____	_____
4. _____	_____	_____
5. _____	_____	_____
6. _____	_____	_____
Totals		$ _____
Outstanding Bills Now Due:		
1. _____	_____	$ _____
2. _____	_____	_____
3. _____	_____	_____
4. _____	_____	_____
5. _____	_____	_____
6. _____	_____	_____
7. _____	_____	_____
8. _____	_____	_____
Totals		$ _____
Total Expenses		$ _____

FIGURE 2.2   Immediate Cash Resources

0–30 Days

Name/Source	Amount Available
Checking Accounts:	
1. _____	$ _____
2. _____	_____
3. _____	_____
Total	$ _____
Money Market Funds:	
1. _____	$ _____
2. _____	_____
3. _____	_____
Total	$ _____
Savings Accounts:	
1. _____	$ _____
2. _____	_____
3. _____	_____
Total	$ _____
Certificates of Deposit:	
1. _____	$ _____
2. _____	_____
3. _____	_____
4. _____	_____
5. _____	_____
Total	$ _____
Investment Income:	
1. Dividends_____	$ _____
2. Interest_____	_____
Total	$ _____
From Your Spouse's Employer:	
1. Wages Due	$ _____
2. Vacation Pay	_____
3. Sick Leave Pay	_____
4. Miscellaneous Accrued Pay	_____
5. Disability Payments	_____
Total	$ _____
From Your Employer:	
1. Wages	$ _____
2. Bonuses	_____
Total	$ _____
Total Immediate Cash (0–30 Days) _____	$ _____

FIGURE 2.2 (Continued)

Expected Within 30–90 Days	
Name/Source	**Amount**
Life Insurance Proceeds:	
1. _____	$ _____
2. _____	_____
3. _____	_____
4. _____	_____
Total	$ _____
Retirement Survivor Benefits:	
1. 401(k) or Thrift Savings Plan	$ _____
2. Pension/Profit Sharing Plan	_____
3. IRA Account(s)	_____
4. Social Security/Government Benefits	_____
5. Previous Employer Pension Plan	_____
Total	$ _____
Cash Values of *Your* Life Insurance Policy(ies) Available as Loan or Withdrawal:	
1. _____	$ _____
2. _____	_____
Total	$ _____
Spouse's Medical Payment Reimbursements:	
1. Medicare	$ _____
2. Private Medical Insurance	_____
Total	$ _____
Miscellaneous:	
1. _____	$ _____
2. _____	_____
3. _____	_____
Total	$ _____
Total Cash (30–90 Days)	$ _____
Total Cash (0–30 Days)	$ _____
Total Cash (30–90 Days)	$ _____
Grand Total Cash (0–90 Days)	$ _____

FIGURE 2.3   Checklist of Important Documents to Locate

_____ Wills

_____ Trusts

_____ Life Insurance Policies

_____ Retirement Plans:

       _____ 401(k)

       _____ IRA's

       _____ Self-Employment Plans

       _____ Pension

       _____ Profit-Sharing

       _____ ESOP

_____ Business Agreement, Book and Records

_____ Uniform Donor Card

_____ Final Instructions Letter

_____ Birth Certificate

_____ Military Discharge papers of your spouse

_____ Marriage License

_____ Prenuptial Agreement

_____ Divorce Papers

_____ Birth Certificate and Adoption Papers for your children

_____ Deeds

_____ Title to burial plot

_____ Vehicle registrations to all vehicles

_____ Bank accounts

_____ Securities statements and certificates

_____ Last two years tax returns and related information

_____ Loan documents (including all mortgage information)

_____ Other insurance policies (auto, homeowners, flood, travel and accident, health).

_____ Credit Card information

_____ Membership club information, auto clubs, etc.

_____ Citizenship papers

_____ Property appraisals

_____ Social Security cards

FIGURE 2.4   Telephone Log

Date	Name of Person	Company	Summary of Discussion

FIGURE 2.5 Important People and Organizations

Date	Item	Contact Person/ Organization	Phone Number	Action Required or Completed

FIGURE 2.6   Information Needed to Apply for Benefits

Information About Your Spouse

Name: _____

Date/Place of Birth: _____

Marriage History:

Name(s) of Spouse(s)	Dates of Marriage(s)	Name(s) of Children	Children's Birth Date(s)
_____	_____	_____	_____
_____	_____	_____	_____
_____	_____	_____	_____
_____	_____	_____	_____

Soc. Sec. # _____   Military ID # _____

Branch of Service: _____

Dates of Service: _____

Discharge Date: _____

Employment History:

Name of Organization	Address	Employment Dates
_____	_____	_____
_____	_____	_____
_____	_____	_____
_____	_____	_____
_____	_____	_____

College/Alumni Groups: _____

Fraternal/Membership Organizations: _____

Extended Family History:
   List parents, grandparents, siblings, grandchildren. If none are living, your attorney may require identification of other relatives, depending on the terms of the will.

Name	Relationship	Address	Date of Birth/Death
_____	_____	_____	_____
_____	_____	_____	_____
_____	_____	_____	_____
_____	_____	_____	_____

FIGURE 2.6　(Continued)

Information About You

Name: _____　Soc. Sec. # _____
Date/Place of Birth: _____

Marriage History:

Name(s) of Spouse(s)	Dates of Marriage(s)	Name(s) of Children	Children's Birth Date(s)
_____	_____	_____	_____
_____	_____	_____	_____
_____	_____	_____	_____
_____	_____	_____	_____

Employment History:

Name of Organization	Address	Employment Dates
_____	_____	_____
_____	_____	_____
_____	_____	_____
_____	_____	_____
_____	_____	_____

Extended Family History:
　List parents, grandparents, siblings, grandchildren. If none are living, your attorney may require identification of other relatives, depending on the terms of the will.

Name	Relationship	Address	Date of Birth/Death
_____	_____	_____	_____
_____	_____	_____	_____
_____	_____	_____	_____
_____	_____	_____	_____
_____	_____	_____	_____
_____	_____	_____	_____
_____	_____	_____	_____
_____	_____	_____	_____
_____	_____	_____	_____
_____	_____	_____	_____

FIGURE 2.7 Credit Card Master List

Credit Card Name	Account Number	Outstanding Balance	Interest Rate	Phone Number	Remarks
		$	%		
		$	%		
		$	%		
		$	%		
		$	%		
		$	%		
		$	%		
		$	%		
		$	%		
		$	%		
		$	%		
		$	%		
		$	%		
		$	%		
		$	%		

CHAPTER 3

Claiming Everything That's Yours— Private Sources

Almost all widowed persons, and heirs in certain cases, are eligible for some type of death and/or survivor benefits through insurance policies, pensions and profit sharing plans, self-employment plans, IRAs, and other benefit programs. This chapter will show you how to file for benefits correctly and in a timely fashion, and offers a way to track your claims.

The first rule is to photocopy and file every piece of paper—each letter, form, policy, and any other document—you give or mail to anyone. Keeping complete and accurate records makes good sense no matter what kind of business you're conducting.

Note:

Do not think of filing claims as seeking handouts, but as receiving benefits to which you're entitled. The best approach is to assume you qualify for everything, and apply even if there is only a remote chance you are eligible. Remember that these programs were paid for by your spouse or parent, provided by his employer, or are available through the government. View them as your legal and just entitlements, not as handouts.

LIFE INSURANCE

One of the first money concerns of many newly widowed persons or inheritors is how to get the proceeds of life insurance. Life insurance claims are not paid automatically following a death; you have to file the forms to get the benefits. A Master Insurance Claims Tracking Form is provided in Figure 3.1 to help you keep track of your various policies.

1. Locate the Policies

If you followed the procedures outlined in Chapter 2, you've most likely found the policies already. If so, move on to step 2. If not, look for the policies among your spouse's important papers. If you can't locate them, look through your spouse's checkbook register to find the name of the insurance companies to which payments were sent.

If you are unable to find the actual policy, call the insurance company and ask for a lost policy form. Most insurance companies have toll-free phone numbers which you can find by calling 800 Information at 800-555-1212. If not, contact the local office of the insurance carrier for information.

Sometimes insurance forms can be confusing. When you're looking for a life insurance policy, the key word on the insurance papers is the word *Life*. There are several kinds of life insurance under which your spouse or parent may have been covered:

- *Personally, individually owned policies* issued by regular life insurance carriers.
- *Group life policies issued through the deceased's employer.* Often there will be a certificate of coverage, rather than a policy. If you don't find it, ask the employer.
- *Travel accident policies,* which often are issued by major gasoline credit card companies, and sometimes by banks and automobile club associations. Accidental death policies fall under this heading.
- *Credit life policies* typically pay off the outstanding balance owed on an installment debt.
- *Mortgage life insurance* will pay off a mortgage, leaving the house free and clear. Your mortgage lender will know if your spouse or parent had this type of policy.

- *Group coverage offered through associations.* There are many professional, business, religious, and other types of associations in the United States, and your spouse or parent may have belonged to several. Examples are the Professional Engineers Society of America, the National Association of Female Executives, and B'nai B'rith. The Yellow Pages has an extensive listing of types of associations.

  When you determine the name of the insurance carrier providing association coverage under which life insurance was provided, call the company directly.
- *Group coverage offered through fraternal orders.* If your spouse or parent was a member of an organization such as the Elks, Lions, Moose, Kiwanis, Masons, or Woodmen, you should check with them about benefits.
- *Cancer care policies* may include death benefits.
- *Guaranteed issue policies* cover individuals with health problems. This coverage offers reduced benefits in the early years, paying only 10 or 20 percent of the face amount if death occurs in the first year or two. The percentage increases for each year the insured remains alive, until the coverage reaches 100 percent of face value.
- *Survivorship life or "second-to-die" policies* insure two parties, typically both spouses, but pay the proceeds only when the survivor dies. If you are covered by such a policy, notify your insurance agent; some survivorship policies offer options to the survivor upon the death of the first insured.
- *Automobile insurance.* If your loved one was killed as a result of an auto collision, contact your automobile insurance carrier to see if any death benefits were included in the policy.
- *Worker's compensation.* Contact your spouse's or parent's employer if his or her death was work related.

2. Contact the Insurance Company

Check to be sure that no premiums were paid on life insurance policies after the date of death. If, in the confusion of the moment, premiums were paid, ask for reimbursement.

Then write letters to the insurance company using the sample letter in Figure 3.2. Include with the claim letter the policy number, the

FIGURE 3.1 Master Insurance Claims Tracking Form

Policy No./ Description	Co. Name, Address	Contact Person/ Phone No.	Date Submitted	Follow-Up Dates	Date Acknowledged	Notes	Final Action

---

FIGURE 3.2   Sample Insurance Company Claim Letter

Date: _____

ABC Life Insurance Co.
Claims Department
Street Address
City, State, Zip Code

RE: (Policy No.)

Dear Claims Department:

My husband/wife/father/mother, John/Jane Doe, died on
(date). His/her Social Security number is _____. I
wish to file a claim for the life insurance benefits from the
above-referenced policy.

I am enclosing the policy/lost policy form and a certified
copy of the death certificate. Please provide me with a
detailed account of how you determine payment, as well
as the various settlement options available. I am/am not
subject to backup withholding. My Social Security number
is provided on the enclosed IRS Form W-9.

I appreciate your prompt attention to this matter.

Sincerely,

Your Name

---

actual policy, and a certified copy of the death certificate. Some companies also like to have a copy of the obituary notice.

Many companies will permit you to start the claims procedure with a phone call in advance of formal filing. This process helps to expedite things once the company receives the claim forms. If you cannot find the policy, call the insurance company or your agent and ask for a lost policy form. Once it arrives, follow the claims procedure above, substituting the lost policy form for the policy.

Where there is more than one primary beneficiary under a specific policy, each beneficiary needs to file a claim form. Insurance companies will provide additional claim forms at no charge.

The face amount of the policy accrues interest from the date of death until the date the check is cut to you. Thus, if you're owed $100,000 and the insurance company pays 20 days following the date of death, you should receive 20 days' worth of interest.

Note that if your spouse or parent named a trust as beneficiary, then the trustee will be the person to complete the claims information, sign the forms, and submit all the documents to the insurance company.

Provide your Social Security number on IRS Form W-9 (Request for Taxpayer Identification Number and Certification), a copy of which appears in Figure 3.3.

The W-9 form provides information the insurance company needs to notify the Internal Revenue Service of the interest paid to you; while the face amount of the life insurance is not subject to federal taxes, the interest paid is taxable. Any IRS office can provide a W-9 form. A facsimile will do in most cases, or the insurance company may have a form of its own. The most important thing is to make sure the insurance company has your Social Security number.

Most insurance carriers do not require that you notarize claim forms. However, photocopies of death certificates are not acceptable. Certified (raised seal) copies are required.

Carefully read the beneficiary provisions of the life insurance policies. If the primary beneficiary on the policy—the first person named to receive the proceeds—is deceased, a certified copy of that primary beneficiary's death certificate will be required. For example, suppose your father had a $10,000 policy and named your mother (now deceased) as primary beneficiary and you as contingent beneficiary—the person to receive the proceeds if the primary beneficiary has died. The proceeds will not be released to you, the contingent beneficiary, until the insurance company has proof that the primary beneficiary is deceased.

Sometimes after a death the cash on hand is so limited that all or part of the proceeds from life insurance must be assigned to a funeral home to cover funeral expenses. The funeral home can supply an assignment form, which must be signed by funeral home officials and by all those who are named to receive equal shares of the policy proceeds.

FIGURE 3.3 IRS Form W-9

Form **W-9** (Rev. December 1996) Department of the Treasury Internal Revenue Service	**Request for Taxpayer Identification Number and Certification**	Give form to the requester. Do NOT send to the IRS.

Please print or type

Name (If a joint account or you changed your name, see **Specific Instructions** on page 2.)

Business name, if different from above. (See **Specific Instructions** on page 2.)

Check appropriate box: ☐ Individual/Sole proprietor   ☐ Corporation   ☐ Partnership   ☐ Other ▶ ....

Address (number, street, and apt. or suite no.)   Requester's name and address (optional)

City, state, and ZIP code

Part I **Taxpayer Identification Number (TIN)**   List account number(s) here (optional)

Enter your TIN in the appropriate box. For individuals, this is your social security number (SSN). However, if you are a resident alien OR a sole proprietor, see the instructions on page 2. For other entities, it is your employer identification number (EIN). If you do not have a number, see **How To Get a TIN** on page 2.

Note: *If the account is in more than one name, see the chart on page 2 for guidelines on whose number to enter.*

Social security number

OR

Employer identification number

Part II **For Payees Exempt From Backup Withholding** (See the instructions on page 2.)

▶

Part III **Certification**

Under penalties of perjury, I certify that:

1. The number shown on this form is my correct taxpayer identification number (or I am waiting for a number to be issued to me)**, and**

2. I am not subject to backup withholding because: **(a)** I am exempt from backup withholding, or **(b)** I have not been notified by the Internal Revenue Service (IRS) that I am subject to backup withholding as a result of a failure to report all interest or dividends, or **(c)** the IRS has notified me that I am no longer subject to backup withholding.

Certification Instructions.– You must cross out item **2** above if you have been notified by the IRS that you are currently subject to backup withholding because you have failed to report all interest and dividends on your tax return. For real estate transactions, item **2** does not apply. For mortgage interest paid, acquisition or abandonment of secured property, cancellation of debt, contributions to an individual retirement arrangement (IRA), and generally, payments other than interest and dividends, you are not required to sign the Certification, but you must provide your correct TIN. (See the instructions on page 2.)

Sign Here   Signature ▶   Date ▶

Purpose of Form.– A person who is required to file an information return with the IRS must get your correct taxpayer identification number (TIN) to report, for example, income paid to you, real estate transactions, mortgage interest you paid, acquisition or abandonment of secured property, cancellation of debt, or contributions you made to an IRA.

Use Form W-9 to give your correct TIN to the person requesting it (the requester) and, when applicable, to:

1. Certify the TIN you are giving is correct (or you are waiting for a number to be issued),

2. Certify you are not subject to backup withholding, or

3. Claim exemption from backup withholding if you are an exempt payee.

Note: *If a requester gives you a form other than a W-9 to request your TIN, you must use the requester's form if it is substantially similar to this Form W-9.*

What Is Backup Withholding?– Persons making certain payments to you must withhold and pay to the IRS 31% of such payments under certain conditions. This is called ™backup withholding. Payments that may be subject to backup withholding

include interest, dividends, broker and barter exchange transactions, rents, royalties, nonemployee pay, and certain payments from fishing boat operators. Real estate transactions are not subject to backup withholding.

If you give the requester your correct TIN, make the proper certifications, and report all your taxable interest and dividends on your tax return, payments you receive will not be subject to backup withholding. Payments you receive **will** be subject to backup withholding if:

1. You do not furnish your TIN to the requester, or

2. The IRS tells the requester that you furnished an incorrect TIN, or

3. The IRS tells you that you are subject to backup withholding because you did not report all your interest and dividends on your tax return (for reportable interest and dividends only), or

4. You do not certify to the requester that you are not subject to backup withholding under 3 above (for reportable interest and dividend accounts opened after 1983 only), or

5. You do not certify your TIN when required. See the Part III instructions on page 2 for details.

Certain payees and payments are exempt from backup withholding. See the Part II instructions and the separate **Instructions for the Requester of Form W-9.**

Penalties

Failure To Furnish TIN.– If you fail to furnish your correct TIN to a requester, you are subject to a penalty of $50 for each such failure unless your failure is due to reasonable cause and not to willful neglect.

Civil Penalty for False Information With Respect to Withholding.– If you make a false statement with no reasonable basis that results in no backup withholding, you are subject to a $500 penalty.

Criminal Penalty for Falsifying Information.– Willfully falsifying certifications or affirmations may subject you to criminal penalties including fines and/or imprisonment.

Misuse of TINs.– If the requester discloses or uses TINs in violation of Federal law, the requester may be subject to civil and criminal penalties.

Cat. No. 10231X   Form **W-9** (Rev. 12-96)

3. *Contestable Periods*

Most life insurance policies reserve to the company the right to challenge claims filed for deaths that occur within one or two years after the policy was issued, and/or in the event the death was a suicide. Unless the policy states that no benefits will be paid in the case of suicide, survivors of a suicide may be eligible for full death benefits as long as the policy was in force longer than one or two years. However, any accidental death benefits that are part of the policy will not be paid because suicide is not considered an accident.

Once you've submitted claim forms, the insurance company will conduct its own investigation to determine if there's any reason not to pay the claim. Aside from suicide, the primary reason not to pay a claim would be fraud, for example if the insured knowingly had cancer when the policy was issued and didn't inform the insurance company. If the insured had cancer and did not know about it when the policy was issued, you may still be able to collect on the claim. The same procedures for filing a claim apply whether the policy is contestable or not.

4. *What to Expect*

Most life insurance claims take five to ten working days from the date the death notification reaches the company until the initial claims handling is complete. During this time the claims department orders all applications from the company's files, sets up and reviews a claims file, checks for incontestability, prepares a letter to you, and mails it.

Normally you will be assigned a claim number and given the phone number of a claims examiner, who handles your claim personally. In the event of a financial emergency, some companies will advance up to $10,000 to a beneficiary before completing the claims requirements. If you need to apply for emergency funds, you must state the amount needed; the beneficiary's name, address, date of birth, and Social Security number; and the nature of the emergency. You will not be able to apply for emergency funds if your coverage is contestable.

Once you've sent all the documentation to the insurance company's claims department, you can expect a check to be approved and mailed within five to seven working days. However, if your claim is contested, it will take two to three months before the claims investigation is complete. Check with the insurance carrier every two weeks to determine the progress of a contested claim.

5. Form of Payment

Many companies automatically set up an interest-bearing checking account in your name, and mail you a checkbook drawn on that account for the life insurance proceeds. This method is superior to lump sum payments because it gives you options not otherwise immediately available.

For instance, you can close the account by writing a check for the entire amount and placing the funds elsewhere; because the funds are earning interest every day, the insurance company often provides a toll-free number so you can find out the exact amount to the penny. Alternatively, you can leave the funds in the account established by the insurance company, writing periodic checks for smaller amounts while the balance continues to earn interest, or leave the entire amount at interest until you decide what to do with the funds.

At some point in the claims process you will be asked to choose whether you want the life insurance proceeds in a lump sum or in an annuity. Here's what they're talking about:

1. *Lump sums.* You receive the entire death benefit payment in full as described above. In other words, if the policy was for $100,000, you get $100,000, and the insurance company has no further dealings regarding that policy. This is the most popular payout and one that makes the most sense for most individuals.

2. *Annuity options:*
   - *Non-refund life annuity.* You would receive payments, usually monthly, during your lifetime. All payments cease when you die. Use this option only in the extreme case that you're young, have no dependents, and want to be assured of regular, monthly payments for the rest of your life. However, most people—who usually have dependents and cannot predict how long they're going to live would be better advised to take the lump sum payment.
   - *Period certain only annuity.* In this case you would receive payments for the specified period—5, 10, 15, or 20 years—whether you live or die, but there are no payments after that specified time period.
   - *Life annuity with guaranteed, time-specified payments.* You, or your estate, would receive guaranteed payments for a specific period of time—5, 10, 15 or 20 years—whether you live or die.

If you live longer than the guaranteed period of time, payments continue for the rest of your life. This is particularly beneficial if you need a lifetime guaranteed income. The payments in this case would be slightly lower than the payments of a period certain only annuity because they are allocated for a longer period of time.

- *Installment Refund.* You would receive a periodic payment for life. If there are any unused funds left in the policy at your death, they go to a person or persons previously designated by you. The payments here would be lower than the previous options, which permits some funds to remain for beneficiaries after your death.

Although there are others, the annuity options summarized above are the most popular. Once you've selected an annuity option, regardless of how your financial situation may change in the future, you're stuck with it. Therefore, it makes sense for most people to choose the lump sum payment because they can put those funds into other types of financial vehicles, and maintain their flexibility in the years to come.

Life insurance proceeds paid to a named beneficiary are not taxable income for federal or state tax purposes. If the proceeds of a life insurance policy are taken in installment payments the non-taxable portion of each installment equals the total amount payable at death divided by the number of installments to be paid. Anything paid to you over this amount in each installment would be considered taxable income.

Note:

Your insurance proceeds check may arrive through your insurance agent, who may have some suggestions as to investments. Do not make any decisions at this time that you can't change in the near future. Ask that any recommendations be put in writing so you will have time to carefully consider them once you are in a better frame of mind to make investment decisions. At the same time, you should ask for an update on your own insurance policies, especially in regard to naming a new beneficiary if your spouse or parent was the named beneficiary on your policies.

ANNUITY CLAIMS

Annuity claims are handled in the same way as life insurance claims. The annuity company or the employer can help you determine if your spouse or parent was receiving periodic payments from an annuity. Depending on the provisions of the plan, you may be entitled to benefits in the form of continued payments or a lump sum. If you have an annuity claim, you need to be aware of the four most popular types of annuities.

1. *Single premium deferred annuity.* A lump sum annuity with an interest rate that is guaranteed for a specific period of time. Once the time period is completed, a new rate is guaranteed for a new term. The principal is also guaranteed by the insurance carrier.
2. *Tax sheltered annuities (TSAs).* Often available through school systems to county or municipal employees, periodic contributions to TSAs are made—usually by employees—to a fixed yield or to a variable yield fund.
3. *Variable annuities.* An annuity offering many different investments, ranging from money market to speculative growth stocks or real estate. Contributions may be made monthly or in a lump sum. The principal or the value of the annuity, whichever is greater, is guaranteed to the named beneficiaries upon the death of the annuity holder.
4. *Indexed annuities.* These are relatively new and provide a minimum guaranteed interest rate, but can earn more if an index, for example the S&P 500, does well.

If you are the beneficiary of your spouse's annuity you have several options depending on the date of issue of the annuity:

- If the annuity was issued after January 8, 1985, you become the new owner with the option to:
  - continue the tax deferral,
  - select an annuity settlement option, or
  - take a lump sum distribution, at which time all the tax-deferred income will be taxed.
- If the annuity was issued prior to January 9, 1985, you must take the proceeds in a:
  - lump sum, or
  - settlement option.

If you are the beneficiary of your parent's annuity, you can:

- annuitize the annuity using any of the settlement options (see page 27), or
- withdraw the money by the end of the fifth year, either in a lump sum, or withdrawals spread over the five-year period.

Income taxes on the gain will be due in either case as you withdraw the money.

Whether you are dealing with an annuity or life insurance, you may find the policy language difficult to follow. Feel free to call the company that issued the policy and ask for an explanation. Staff members will go through the language line by line, and lay out the options available to you.

Note:

Insurance company employees have no interest in keeping you from funds you're entitled to receive, but because they may not understand your particular situation, the information you receive may be general.

It makes good sense to have advisers—financial, insurance, banking, and others—on your side in advance. More about professional advisers is discussed in Chapter 16.

EMPLOYMENT BENEFITS: STARTING THE CLAIMS PROCESS

Contact the personnel department of your deceased spouse's or parent's employer. Do this whether your spouse or parent was still working or had already retired. They will help you determine what benefits you are eligible to receive in the form of pension income, life insurance proceeds, and health insurance. Send a letter similar to the one in Figure 3.4 to the employee benefits department. A Master Employer Benefits Tracking Form can be found in Figure 3.5.

Note:

If your spouse or parent was still working at the time of death, you and your family are entitled to receive health insurance benefits at group insurance rates for the 18-month period following his or her death.

FIGURE 3.4   Sample Employee Benefits Claim Letter

Date: _____

ABC Corporation
Employee Benefits Department
Street Address
City, State, Zip Code

RE: (Your Spouse's or Parent's Name)

Dear Employee Benefits Department:

Please be advised that my (husband/wife/father/mother), _____,
Social Security number _____, died on _____. Please provide
me with full information regarding all employee benefits I am eligible for as
his/her beneficiary. In particular, please provide information on the following:

1. Life insurance benefits
2. Continuation of health insurance for 18 months
3. Payments of unused vacation time and/or unpaid payroll
4. Pension benefits, 401(k) plan, stock options
5. Payout options on available retirement plans

I may be reached at the address and phone number below. Thank you for your
prompt attention.

Sincerely yours,

Your Name
Your Address
Your Phone Number

UNDERSTANDING PENSION BENEFIT CLAIMS

The terms *pension* and *qualified plans* are used to refer to a variety
of investment benefit programs to which your loved one, and perhaps
the employer, made regular contributions. These plans can include
pension, profit sharing, stock option, 401(k), target benefit, stock pur-

FIGURE 3.5 Master Employer Benefits Tracking Form

Benefit	Company	Contact Person	Phone No.	Date Contacted	Notes
Pension					
Profit Sharing					
Thrift Savings					
401(k)					
Medical Insurance					
Vacation					
Unpaid Payroll					
Life Insurance					

chase, thrift savings, and 403(b) plans. In addition, a person who was self-employed may have had a form of profit sharing plan known as a Keogh (HR10) plan.

You may not know what all these terms mean, but recognizing them will allow you to ask questions that will help you determine what is rightfully yours. Call the employer and find out what benefits are available through retirement plans, and whether they are available in a lump sum or periodic payouts.

If you are a surviving spouse, every lump sum held by your spouse in a qualified plan of which you're the named beneficiary can be rolled over to an IRA in your name. You may receive the proceeds yourself. You will have 60 days to place them in your own IRA, or the proceeds can be transferred directly from the custodian of your spouse's account to the custodian of your IRA. In most cases, the best format will be what is called a self-directed IRA which allows you to place the funds in a variety of investments.

Any after-tax dollars your spouse contributed to company plans are available to you tax-free, but this only applies to after-tax contributions. When you receive the after-tax dollars invested in a qualified plan, a sheet will accompany the check showing both the before-tax and after-tax contributions made by the employer and by your spouse.

Here are some related issues to consider:

- If you're receiving periodic pension benefit payments, do they have a provision for cost of living increases? If so, how often are the adjustments made?
- If your mate's previous marriage ended in divorce, the former spouse may qualify through the divorce decree for part of your partner's pension benefits. Check the divorce papers if you're not sure.
- If your spouse was already retired at the time of death, and was receiving pension benefits, what are the terms of the survivor provisions? For example, if the benefits are available to you, will they be smaller than what your spouse received? Or are survivor benefits available to you, but not until a certain age? If so, when can you begin receiving the payments and approximately how much will they be?
- If the deceased had a pension through a previous employer no longer in business, you can find out if there are any benefits by

contacting the Pension Search Program of the federal Pension Benefit Guaranty Corporation (PBGC). The PBGC has names of thousands of people owed money from old pension plans. You can write them at 1200 K Street, N.W., Washington, D.C. 20005, or check the internet at www.pbgc.gov.

If IRA accounts are paid directly to you as the beneficiary, you will have to declare the IRA payments—whether lump sum or periodic—as ordinary income because they are received as though you were the original owner of the IRA. The IRA distributions are considered income. If you take the IRA account as a lump sum distribution, be aware that you may have to pay income taxes as well as estate taxes on those proceeds.

If you are a surviving spouse under age 59½, the deceased spouse's IRA can be taken without the 10 percent IRS penalty. There is no penalty after age 59½ on your IRA.

As an IRA spousal beneficiary, you may elect to roll the funds over into your own IRA, avoiding current taxes. (You can also make your own deductible IRA contributions to that IRA account if you qualify.) You also have the option of leaving the funds in your spouse's name. Distributions from that IRA account do not have to begin until your spouse would have reached the age of 70½. If your deceased spouse was already receiving payments according to a schedule and you are the beneficiary you must receive distributions at least as rapidly. If you are a non-spousal heir, then no IRA options are available to you.

A rollover IRA means taking receipt of the assets for up to 60 days before reinvesting them into a new retirement IRA plan. A transfer means moving the assets from one IRA custodian to another IRA custodian. Rollovers are allowed once a year. Transfers can occur as often as you wish. Losses that are incurred in an IRA account are not deductible.

There are two types of rollovers for IRAs. One is an IRA-to-IRA rollover. In this case, all or a portion of the existing funds are withdrawn and checks come to you. The funds are not subject to current income taxes as long as they are deposited into another IRA within 60 days. Each IRA can be rolled over once every 12 months.

For surviving spouses, the other type of rollover is from a qualified retirement plan to an IRA. If your spouse was a participant in a company retirement plan, such as a pension or profit sharing plan, you may take the proceeds from that plan and roll them into an IRA. Again you may receive those proceeds yourself and then have 60 days in which to roll that money into an IRA. If you use the rollover, at least 50 percent of the amount in the company retirement program must be rolled over into an IRA. Also be aware of the IRS ruling that requires 20 percent withholding on rollovers. Use a direct custodian-to-custodian transfer to avoid the 20 percent withholding.

There are different tax treatments of IRA withdrawals depending upon your age:

- *Before age 59½*—Withdrawals are taxable as ordinary income plus a 10 percent penalty for early withdrawal. Withdrawals from a deceased spouse's IRA escape the 10 percent penalty.
- *Age 59½ to 70½*—Withdrawals are taxable as ordinary income and there is complete flexibility on amounts and timing of withdrawals.
- *Age 70½ and later*—Withdrawals are taxed as ordinary income. Minimum distributions must begin by age 70½ and are based on life expectancy. A 50 percent penalty is imposed if minimum distributions are not withdrawn. Distribution can exceed the minimum requirement.

TAXES ON LUMP SUM DISTRIBUTIONS

As a surviving spouse, you normally have two choices when a lump sum distribution is received from your deceased spouse's retirement program: (1) you can roll over part or all of it into an IRA (as already discussed) or (2) pay tax on the distribution. If you elect to pay taxes, the lump sum distribution may qualify for a five- or ten-year averaging. If your spouse made non-deductible contributions to a company pension or annuity plan, those parts of the distributions will be considered nontaxable. Five-year averaging will not be available after December 31, 1999.

If you wish to use averaging, all five of the following requirements must be met for a lump sum distribution:

1. The lump sum distribution must represent the entire account balance from the employer's plan.
2. Your spouse must have been 50 or older on January 1, 1986. If so, you have the option of choosing the ten-year averaging

using 1986 tax table rates. The ten-year averaging tax table is shown in Figure 3.6.

3. The plan must have been a qualified pension plan, profit sharing plan, or stock bonus plan.

4. Your spouse must have participated in the plan at least five years before the year of the distribution, or the distribution is to be paid to a named beneficiary at death.

5. Also, one of the following conditions must be true:

   • The distribution is to be paid to a beneficiary of the employee who died.

   • The employee quit, retired, or was laid off or fired before receiving a distribution.

   • Your spouse was self-employed or an owner-employee and became disabled, or was age 59½ or older at the time of distribution.

Finally, besides the above requirements, note that averaging can only be used once. If you choose the averaging method you have to use it for all qualifying lump sum distributions you receive in that year.

ROLLOVER OR FORWARD AVERAGING?

Should the lump sum distribution from your spouse's retirement plan be rolled over into an IRA or should you elect the 10-year averaging on the lump sum distribution? Here are some issues to consider when making the choice.

Consider the current tax rate and the fact that future tax rates may change. Also, realize that if you pay the tax now you have unrestricted after-tax use of the funds in the future. This eliminates the uncertainty about any future tax laws and possible tax problems for you and for your heirs. If you pick the IRA rollover you will effectively be deferring paying taxes until a future date. More wealth will be available to accumulate without taxation during that period. Higher taxes in the future may be offset by the investment values accumulated in the IRA over the intervening years. An additional consideration would be to roll the funds to a regular IRA, then roll them again to a Roth IRA.

FIGURE 3.6 Ten-Year Averaging (available only to persons born before 1936)
Tax Computation at 1986 Rates

Taxable Lump-Sum Distribution	Multiply by This %	Subtract This Amount	= the Tax
$ 0 to 20,000	× 5.5%	− $ 0 =	Tax
20,001 to 21,583	× 13.2%	− 1,540 =	Tax
21,584 to 30,583	× 14.4%	− 1,799 =	Tax
30,584 to 49,417	× 16.8%	− 2,533 =	Tax
49,418 to 67,417	× 18.0%	− 3,126 =	Tax
67,418 to 70,000	× 19.2%	− 3,935 =	Tax
70,001 to 91,700	× 16.0%	− 1,695 =	Tax
91,701 to 114,400	× 18.0%	− 3,529 =	Tax
114,401 to 137,100	× 20.0%	− 5,817 =	Tax
137,101 to 171,600	× 23.0%	− 9,930 =	Tax
171,601 to 228,800	× 26.0%	− 15,078 =	Tax
228,801 to 286,000	× 30.0%	− 24,230 =	Tax
286,001 to 343,200	× 34.0%	− 35,670 =	Tax
343,201 to 423,000	× 38.0%	− 49,398 =	Tax
423,001 to 571,900	× 42.0%	− 66,318 =	Tax
571,901 to 857,900	× 48.0%	− 100,632 =	Tax
Over 857,900	× 50.0%	− 117,900 =	Tax

SUMMARY

Although applying for claims may seem burdensome and unnatural to you, remember that your spouse or parent contributed to these programs so that some day you would receive the promised benefits. Think of it as your money—it just hasn't been transferred to you yet. If you don't fill out the forms, file the claims, and follow the procedures, what is rightfully yours will just sit there, maybe forever.

CHAPTER 4

Claiming Everything That's Yours— Government Sources

In addition to the benefits obtained through private sources discussed in Chapter 3—such as insurance policies, pensions and profit sharing plans, self-employment plans, and IRAs—it's likely that you're entitled to a variety of government related benefits through Social Security, veterans programs, and, if applicable, your spouse's or parent's government employment. This chapter will show you how to file with Uncle Sam to get everything that's yours from the government.

SOCIAL SECURITY BENEFITS

The term *Social Security* conjures up all sorts of misinterpretations. As dispensed by the Social Security Administration, four basic areas of survivor benefits may be available to you:

1. Survivor insurance benefits
2. Disability insurance benefits
3. Supplemental income benefits
4. Medicare

Let's explore each one in order.

Survivor Insurance Benefits

If your spouse or your parent paid into Social Security, then you, and perhaps other family members, may qualify for survivor's benefits. Eligible family members include the surviving spouse, children, dependent parents and, in certain circumstances, surviving divorced spouses.

Benefits could include a one-time funeral payment, monthly survivor's benefits, retirement income, disability income, and Medicare. It may be possible for a widowed person of any age to qualify for Social Security benefits. Keep in mind that benefits are never sent to you automatically—you must apply for them.

General Eligibility for Benefits

Benefits are available to those who qualify under one of the following circumstances:

- As the surviving spouse, you can receive full benefits—100 percent—at age 65 or older. Between ages 60–64, benefits range from 71 to 94 percent. If you are disabled, you can start receiving benefits as early as age 50.
- As the surviving spouse, you can receive benefits at any age, as long as you are caring for your children who are under age 16 or disabled. You will receive 75 percent of full benefits for each child.
- Surviving children up to age 18.
- Surviving children age 18–19, if they attend school full time.
- Surviving children over age 18 who became disabled before age 22.
- Surviving divorced spouses age 60 or older, if married to the deceased spouse for ten years or longer provided the surviving spouse has not remarried before age 60.
- The surviving parents of the deceased age 62 or older, if they were being supported by the deceased. Any qualifying children are entitled to a percentage of the deceased's age-65 benefit, even if he or she did not live to age 65.

There is a limit to the amount that can be received from Social Security. It can vary but it is usually between 100 and 180 percent of the full benefit rate. The amount paid in total is limited to what is called a family maximum benefit. Currently, this can range from \$667/month to \$2,836/month. Your Social Security office can give you an accurate determination of your family maximum.

If you are an adult heir, you are not entitled to survivors' benefits from Social Security.

As a surviving spouse, children's benefits are not affected if you remarry, even if your new spouse adopts them and contributes to their support. No adoption of a surviving child by any other person causes benefits to stop. Your children's benefits stop when they marry or they reach the age of 18. When your youngest surviving child marries or reaches age 16, your benefits also stop, but you can restart them again at age 60 (or age 50 if you are disabled). Note that payments received from Social Security for children are considered the child's income, not yours.

You can receive survivor's benefits only if your spouse accumulated enough credits for work done as an employee or in self-employment; most workers earn four credits per year. The number of credits needed to receive benefits as a survivor depends on the age of your spouse at death, but the average number of credits is 40. However, under a special rule, benefits can be paid to you and your children even if your spouse had only 1½ years of credit accumulated within the three years prior to death.

Credit for work under Social Security had to be earned by your spouse before he or she was eligible for benefits. Social Security credits are earned during employment that is covered by the law after 1936 and for self-employment after 1950. Social Security coverage is measured by quarters of coverage. As of 1998, both wage earners and self-employed people are credited with one quarter of coverage for every \$700 earned.

It does not matter when the income is earned during the year and no more than four quarters of coverage may be credited during a calendar year. One quarter of coverage is credited for each dollar amount listed up to a maximum of four quarters per year. Once your spouse has earned 40 quarters of coverage he or she is considered to be fully covered. The term fully insured means that your spouse, you, and your dependents are all eligible for most Social Security benefits. This does not govern the amount of those benefits, only that you qualify for benefits.

Also, if your spouse was fully covered when he or she died, a one time $255 lump sum death benefit can be collected. However, the benefit can only be paid to you if you were living with your spouse at the time of death, or to you as the widow or widower if you were not living with your spouse, but you can demonstrate eligibility on your spouse's earnings records. As with all Social Security benefits, you need to apply for the one-time death benefit in order to receive it. They won't just send it to you!

Any Social Security checks addressed to your spouse or parent that arrive after his or her death should be returned to the Social Security Administration. If the checks were directly deposited to a bank account, notify the bank to return them. The law requires that such checks be returned, and it's an important factor in establishing a legitimate basis for your own claims.

Staking Your Claim

The following list summarizes what you need to do as a surviving spouse in order to receive benefits from the Social Security Administration:

1. If you are not currently receiving Social Security benefits, act promptly. In some cases, benefits are not retroactive. Visit any Social Security office or phone the toll-free number, 800-772-1213, from 7 AM to 7 PM Eastern time, to find the office nearest you. You can also check their web site at www.ssa.gov.
2. Have the following information handy, but apply even if it's not all available. You will need to submit original documents, or copies certified by the proper issuing office. You can mail or bring them to the Social Security office; the staff will make copies for you and return the documents if you request that they do so.
   • Your Social Security number and your spouse's Social Security number
   • A death certificate
   • Proof of your spouse's worker earnings from the last year before death—W-2 forms are usually sufficient
   • Your birth certificate
   • A marriage certificate, if you're applying for benefits as a widowed individual or a divorced spouse

- A divorce decree if you are a divorced spouse
- Children's birth certificates and Social Security numbers, if you are applying for benefits for your offspring
- Your checking or savings account information if you want direct deposit of Social Security benefits made to one of those accounts

3. If you're already receiving Social Security benefits from your spouse's account, report your spouse's death to the Social Security office; your payments will be changed to survivor's benefits.

4. If you're receiving Social Security benefits from your own account, you'll need to fill out an application to receive survivor's benefits. The Social Security office will calculate whether you will receive more as a widowed individual than you received under your own primary benefit, and will give you the plan that provides the highest payout.

Figure 4.1 is a sample letter you can use to file a claim with the Social Security Administration. Feel free to photocopy it and adapt its language to your situation.

If you are divorced and your deceased ex-spouse was covered under Social Security you may still be eligible for Social Security benefits. To be eligible you must be at least 60 years old, or 50 and disabled, and have been married for at least 10 years. You can be any age if you are caring for a child that is eligible for benefits. Another qualification is that you cannot be currently married, unless the remarriage occurred after age 60, or 50 if you are disabled.

The easiest way to reach the Social Security Administration is to call their toll free number, 800-772-1213. You can call anytime from 7:00 AM to 7:00 PM, on any business day. If you would prefer to talk to someone in your area, call the 800 number and ask for the location of the closest office.

You can obtain a detailed document from the Social Security Administration which gives an accurate estimate of your Social Security benefits by calling 800-772-1213 and asking for Form SSA-7004. This form requests some personal information such as your name, Social Security number, date of birth, previous year's earnings, estimate of current year's earnings, planned age of retirement, and projected earnings until retirement. However, you can get the estimate of your benefits as a result of your spouse's or parent's death by just giving that

FIGURE 4.1   Sample Letter to Social Security Administration

Date: _____

Social Security Administration
Department of Health and Human Services
Washington, DC 20201
RE: Name of Deceased _____
Social Security No. _____
Claimant: _____

Dear Staff:

The person whose Social Security number appears above passed away on (Date) in (City/State).

As a claimant under this Social Security account, I hereby request that you send the necessary forms to initiate a Clearance Claim and a Survivor's Claim.

Listed below are the names and dates of birth of our children:
(Name) _____ (Date of Birth) _____
(Name) _____ (Date of Birth) _____
(Name) _____ (Date of Birth) _____

Sincerely,

(Your signature)
(Your Street Address)
(Your City/State/Zip Code)

same information on the deceased, that is if the death occurred in the same calendar year.

Disability Insurance Benefits

If you are a disabled widow or widower, 50 years of age or older, you may also qualify for disability coverage from Social Security. Your disability must have started before your spouse's death or within seven years after it if you are a surviving spouse and you are 50 years or older and your marriage lasted 10 years or longer. In addition, if you have dependent children they may be eligible for disability benefits if they are under age 18.

Call Social Security and ask for the following publication that covers disability: Social Security and SSI Benefits for Children with Disabilities, Publication 05-10026 or Publication 05-11000.

It is important for you to understand the definition of disability that the Social Security Administration uses. You are considered disabled only if you are unable to do any kind of work for which you are suited, and if your inability to work is expected to last for at least one year or result in death. Physical evidence from a physician or other source should show how severe the condition is and to what extent it prevents you from working.

If you become disabled you should file for disability benefits as soon as possible. Do this by calling or visiting your local Social Security office. It may take as long as five or six months before disability benefits begin, so you need to plan accordingly.

Note:

If you can do any other job that provides substantial gain you would not be considered disabled under Social Security law.

Supplemental Income Benefits

Supplemental security income, called SSI for short, is another program administered by the Social Security Administration. SSI makes monthly payments to people who have low incomes and very few assets. To obtain SSI you must be living in the United States or the Northern Mariana Islands, and you must be a U.S. citizen or living in the United States legally. In addition, you must be 65 or older, blind, or disabled.

Your children also can qualify for SSI benefits if blind or considered disabled under Social Security rules. To qualify for SSI, your income and the value of your possessions must be below the poverty level for your state. Income here means any kind of income that you receive, such as Social Security or government checks, pensions, etc. Also noncash items such as the value of free food and shelter may be counted.

Most people who receive SSI also get food stamps and Medicaid assistance. Medicaid, a different program than Medicare, helps pay doctor and hospital bills. (See Chapter 12 for more details about Medicaid). For more information, call Social Security and ask for Publications 05-10026, 05-10100, or 05-10095.

Correct Monthly Payments

How can you determine if you are receiving the correct monthly payment from Social Security? William M. Mercer, Inc., the world's largest compensation/employee benefits consulting firm, publishes a pamphlet titled *Guide to Social Security and Medicare,* which describes how Social Security benefits are computed. It includes worksheets for you to make calculations for yourself; however, the calculations are complex and you'll need accurate records of your annual earnings before starting these calculations.

To get a copy of the Mercer pamphlet, write to William M. Mercer, Inc., 15 Hunter Meidinger Tower, Louisville, KY 40202-3415. If you calculate your earnings yourself, check your records against the Social Security Administration's figures. If their figures are wrong notify them immediately. You will need copies of your statements showing what your records state.

Medicare

The rising cost of health care has become a critical concern throughout our country. The ability to obtain quality health care service at cost-effective prices is a dilemma for many people. National statistics cite that senior citizens, of which widowed persons make up a large segment, are the fastest growing population segment in our country. Medicare is the health care alternative available for senior citizens through the government.

Offered for over 20 years, the Medicare health program is ministered under the Social Security Administration. There are two major parts to the program: (1) Hospital Insurance, and (2) Medical Insurance.

Hospital Insurance

Also known as Medicare Part A, Hospital Insurance pays for inpatient hospital and certain follow-up care. Medical Insurance helps pay for doctor's and many other medical services.

If you are 65 or older and receive either Social Security or Railroad Retirement benefits, you are automatically eligible for the Medicare Hospital Insurance. Surviving spouses are eligible if your spouse qualified under Social Security. The Medical Insurance is currently available for eligible Medicare recipients for a monthly premium of $31.80. These premiums can be deducted automatically from your Social Security check.

If you have Medicare and have little income or assets you should know about a program that will help save you money. It is called the Qualified Medicaid Beneficiary or QMB program. If you qualify for help from the QMB program, your state will pay your monthly Medicare premiums, deductibles, and co-insurance. The rules vary from state to state, but in general you may qualify for the QMB program if your income is limited and your resources do not exceed certain limitations. Contact the Medicaid Agency, Social Security office or Welfare office for additional information.

Medical Insurance

Also known as Medicare Part B, Medical Insurance pays 80 percent of the reasonable and customary charges for doctor's and other medical services after a $75.00 per year deductible. Often there is a discrepancy between what Medicare pays and what you are charged. For example, the charges for a major operation and Medicare's payment may look like this:

Doctor's charge for operation	$40,000
Medicare's definition of reasonable payment	25,000
Medicare pays 80% of the $25,000	20,000
You pay	20,000

In this case Medicare pays only 50 percent of the total charges and you pay the difference. To protect yourself, consider buying a Medicare supplemental insurance policy. (See Chapter 9 on insurance.) This can be purchased after you turn 65. Coverage and cost vary so you should shop around for these Medigap policies.

With the hospitalization part of Medicare (Part A), Medicare pays hospitals according to what are called diagnosed illnesses. Each illness has a predetermined hospital charge, which Medicare is willing to pay to the hospital, regardless of how long you use a facility. For example, if the predetermined cost of a heart operation is $30,000 and the hospital can get a patient out at a cost of $15,000, the hospital will make a $15,000 profit.

New Medicare options are slated to go into effect in 1999 and may particularly affect participants in Medicare HMOs. Check with your local Medicare office if you think you may be affected. As a result you may be forced to leave the hospital before you should, and you will have to find supplemental nursing care. Medicare will not pay for supplemental custodian nursing home care, and these costs can be very high. Consider buying long-term health care insurance to cover such unusual costs unless you have substantial assets.

CLAIMS FROM THE FEDERAL GOVERNMENT

Here's a list of government employee benefits and programs for which you may be eligible:

1. Federal Employees Group Life Insurance (FEGLI) Claims

Federal Employees Group Life Insurance is provided with various options for coverage including:

- *Basic insurance amount.* This is coverage equal to the greater of (a) the employee's annual basic pay (rounded to the next $1,000) plus $2,000, or (b) $10,000. For employees age 35 or younger the basic benefit is double; beginning with age 36, the extra benefit decreases 10 percent each year, until age 45 when the extra benefit disappears.
- *Accidental death.* This feature doubles the amount payable under the basic insurance amount if the employee died as a result of bodily injury received solely through violent, external, or accidental means.
- *Option A—standard.* If your spouse or parent enrolled in FEGLI, then this option, in the amount of $10,000, could have been purchased. Accidental death benefits are available also on this coverage, thereby doubling it in the event of accidental death.

- *Option B—additional.* This option makes available amounts equal to one, two, three, four, or five times the basic insurance amount.

A more complete description of insurance benefits is available in the *Federal Personnel Guide,* published by Key Communications Group Inc., Post Office Box 42578, Washington DC 20015-0578. The cost is $12.95 per copy.

Filing a Claim: Contact the employment office where your spouse's or parent's official personnel folder, or its equivalent, is maintained. A claim form and instructions will be furnished to you.

2. Survivor Claims Procedures after Death for Civil Service Retirement System (CSRS) or Federal Employees Retirement System (FERS) Annuities

- Return any uncashed annuity checks to the return address shown on the envelope in which the check was delivered. If annuity payments have been sent directly to the bank or other financial institution, promptly notify that institution of the date of death. Ask that any payments received after the date of death be returned to the Treasury Department.
- Notify the Office of Personnel Management, Employee Service and Records Center, Boyers, PA 16017, of the death so they can send an application (Standard Form 2800) for survivor benefits. Use of this address will expedite your claim.
- Obtain a certified copy of the death certificate to enclose with the application that the Office of Personnel Management will send. OPM prefers that the applicant wait for the official application, and that it be completed and returned promptly after receipt. While awaiting return of the application, OPM will have completed certain preliminary actions so that the application can be expedited.

VETERANS BENEFITS

If your spouse or parent was a veteran, you may qualify for veteran's benefits. These include burial in a national cemetery (there are over 100 throughout the country), an allowance for burial expenses, transportation of the remains to the nearest national cemetery, a head-stone or grave marker, and an American flag to drape the casket.

In the event the deceased has been buried in a private cemetery, either by preference or because you were unaware of the veterans benefits, you can still apply for burial reimbursement and other benefits, but you must do so within two years of the date of death.

Veterans Life Insurance

There are several life insurance programs under which a veteran may be covered. If you wish to file a claim, or receive information about a veteran's life insurance benefits, be sure to provide the insured's full name, policy number, date of birth, and Social Security number.

For those who served prior to 1965, there are five plans listed below, administered by the Department of Veterans Affairs regional office and insurance centers in St. Paul, Minnesota, and Philadelphia, Pennsylvania:

1. *United States Government Life Insurance*
2. *National Service Life Insurance*
3. *Veterans Special Life Insurance*
4. *Service-Disabled Veterans Insurance*
5. *Veterans Reopened Insurance*

For more specific information, call the Department of Veterans Affairs at 800-827-8244, or write directly to the VA office that is closest to you.

Also, here are two life insurance programs for those who were on active duty:

1. *Servicemen's Group Life Insurance* (SGLI), set up in September, 1965, to provide group coverage to members on active duty. Benefits have since been extended to ready reservists, retired reservists, and National Guard members. The maximum coverage is $50,000. If your spouse or parent was covered under one of these policies, call your local VA office, not the Philadelphia or St. Paul offices.
2. *Veterans Group Life Insurance* (VGLI), established in August, 1974, to provide for the conversion of SGLI to five-year, non-

renewable term coverage. If your spouse or parent owned a VGLI policy, call the VA office closest to you to make a claim.

These two types of coverage are administered by the Office of Servicemen's Group Life Insurance, 213 Washington Street, Newark, New Jersey 07102, to which you can write if you have questions about either of these programs.

Educational Assistance for Dependents

If you are a surviving spouse and your spouse's death was service-connected, or if death occurred while your spouse was completely disabled from service-connected causes, the Department of Veterans Affairs will pay a monthly allowance to help educate you or your children. Payments are usually provided for children 18–26 years of age. The benefits to your children are not canceled if they marry, but your remarriage would terminate educational benefits to you.

Dependency and Indemnity Compensation

Payments are available for surviving spouses and/or the surviving children due to veterans dying on or after January 1, 1957 from:

- A disease or injury incurred or aggravated in line of duty while on active duty or active duty for training
- An injury incurred or aggravated in line of duty while on inactive duty training

There are many possible ways to obtain payments and the subject should be followed thoroughly to see if benefits apply.

Nonservice-Connected Death Pension

Death pension may be paid to eligible surviving spouses and children of veterans who had 90 days or more of wartime service or who had less than 90 days of wartime service but were separated from such service for a service-connected disability who have died of causes not related to their service.

Making a Department of Veterans Affairs Claim

If your spouse or parent was in the military and you believe you have a valid claim in one or more areas, assemble the following information before contacting the VA office.

1. Certified copy or original Form DD214, Enlisted Record, and Report of Separation
2. Certified copy of your original marriage certificate, if applicable
3. Certified copy of the death certificate
4. The amount of life insurance proceeds you expect to receive as a result of death
5. Paid receipts for funeral and cemetery expenses
6. Paid receipts for hospital and doctors' bills incurred during the last illness
7. Social Security numbers for yourself and your dependent children
8. If your spouse was previously married, an original or certified copy of the divorce decree, or the former spouse's death certificate
9. If you have dependent children under age 18 or children who are over 18 but still in school, originals or certified copies of their birth certificates; if your children are over 18 and still in school, a form for possible benefits for them
10. If you are currently receiving Social Security benefits, show the exact amount of benefits you receive
11. Your VA claim number, if you already have one

Gathering these documents is an essential part of your overall strategy to secure your financial future. You may not like doing it—few people do—but once you're armed with the proper documents it's much easier to claim what's rightfully yours.

SOCIAL SECURITY AND RETIREMENT

Disturbed by the high rate of inflation in 1975, the United States Congress passed a law that allows Social Security benefits to rise automatically with inflation. The adjustment for next year is the rate of inflation based on the consumer price index in the third quarter of the previous year. It is announced in October and begins in January. In 1997 the adjustment for 1998 was set at 2.1 percent. This is an important feature of your benefits—without it, your benefits could be diminished substantially due to inflation.

The usual retirement age in America remains age 65. The Social Security Administration regards this as the age at which those qualifying may receive full retirement benefit. In the year 2000, retirement age will be moved up to 67 and will affect people born in 1938 and thereafter. The table below shows the ages that full retirement Social Security benefit is available.

Year of Birth	Age When Full Benefits Available
1938	65 years, 2 months
1939	65 years, 4 months
1940	65 years, 6 months
1941	65 years, 8 months
1942	65 years, 10 months
1943–1954	66 years
1955	66 years, 2 months
1956	66 years, 4 months
1957	66 years, 6 months
1958	66 years, 8 months
1959	66 years, 10 months
1960 & later	67 years

Taking Early Benefits

You can start your Social Security benefits as early as age 62 but the benefit amount you receive will be permanently less than your full retirement benefits. Early retirement reduces your monthly benefit by ⅝ of 1 percent per month prior to age 65. For example, at age 62 you would currently receive 80 percent of your age 65 benefit; at age 63 you would receive 86.68 percent; at age 64 you would receive 93.33 percent.

Note:

When the phase-in to normal retirement age of 67 is complete, early retirement at age 62 will yield only 70 percent of what the full benefit would generate.

As a general rule, early retirement gives you about the same total Social Security benefits over your lifetime, assuming you live to your life expectancy. The smaller amount at early retirement takes into account the longer period you would receive benefits. Assuming everything remains constant, if you wait until age 65 to receive normal retirement benefits, you will be 77 years old before you reach a break-even point.

If you take the retirement benefit at age 62 and invest that money for the 3-year early retirement period, the interest earned on that money would more than offset the money lost due to drawing early retirement benefits. In other words, by waiting until age 65 until you start receiving benefits, you would never catch up. Hence, if you have the discipline to invest the early benefits, you'll fare better.

Delaying Your Benefits

If you delay taking your full retirement benefit by a year or more, you can increase your Social Security benefit in two ways:

1. If you are working, you could be adding a year of high earnings to your Social Security record. Your higher lifetime average earnings may result in higher benefits.
2. Your benefits will be increased by a certain percentage for each year you delay retirement. These increases are added automatically from the time you reach your full retirement age until you begin taking your benefits up to age 70. The percentage varies depending on your date of birth. For example, if you were born in 1935, 6 percent will be added to your benefit for each year you delay Social Security retirement benefits.

Note:

Should you decide to delay your retirement, make sure you sign up for Medicare at age 65. In some cases the medical insurance costs more if you delay applying for it.

If you're under age 70, there is a limit on the amount you can earn and still collect full Social Security retirement benefits. As of 1999, under age 65 your benefits are reduced by $1 for each $2 earned over $9,600. Between the ages of 65 and 69 you will lose $1 of Social Security for every $3 earned above $15,500.

CHAPTER 5

Getting Organized
Bringing Order to
Your Financial House

key to maximizing your inheritance is developing a well-thought-out approach to financial management. Your first step to building a plan is to organize your finances according to a step-by-step procedure. Right now your future is full of financial questions. The secure feeling you had when your spouse or parent was with you is probably gone. One way to begin alleviating your concerns is to determine where you stand financially.

Like most people, you've probably thought you'd be in better financial shape if you had a workable financial plan. However, just the thought of where to start and how to do it was enough to make you shudder. Developing a plan was something you'd do later, but later never came. Now, your lack of planning might mean that you will run out of money before you run out of life.

As mentioned in Chapter 2 you should set up a filing system to keep everything organized. Figure 5.1 lists suggested file topics.

It takes motivation, time, and effort to put your financial house in order. The method and the worksheets in this chapter will guide you, but first you must learn about, and generate, two important documents:

1. *A net worth statement.* Sometimes called a balance sheet, this is a listing of all the assets you own or are about to receive and their established or estimated value, your liabilities, or what

FIGURE 5.1 Suggested File Headings

Bank statements	Certificates of deposit
Automobile insurance	Real estate titles and deeds
Charge accounts statements	Mortgage statements
IRA statements	Investment statements
Health insurance information	Income tax information
	Title insurance
Life insurance information	Auto registrations, etc.
Wills	
Living wills	Property and casualty insurance information
Powers of attorney	Mutual fund info
Trusts agreements	Prenuptial/Postnuptial agreements
Social Security records	
Divorce agreement	Stock option plans
Birth certificates	Pension accounts
Death certificates	Partnership information
Marriage certificate	401(k) accounts
Military discharge papers	Business real estate
Stock brokerage statements	Safe deposit box information

you owe, and your net worth, which is determined by subtract-
ing your liabilities from your assets.

Your net worth is an important statement about you. It re-
veals crucial financial information to which you will refer again
and again for future planning. Your net worth indicates what
you and your spouse accomplished financially during your
lives, and is now the critical amount you have available to plan
for your future.

2. *A cash flow statement.* This is simply a list of all the incoming funds
from every source, along with a record of all your expenses,

usually by category. The cash flow statement will show you how much money is coming in, where it is going, and the impact of taxes on your cash flow resources.

DETERMINING YOUR NET WORTH

The first step in determining your net worth is difficult but important—assembling and organizing all your financial data. A sample net worth statement of Martha Young appears in Figure 5.2.

Your net worth statement can be general or very detailed. Figure 5.3 is a blank net worth form that is simplified and Figure 5.4 is a detailed net worth form. Which form you use depends on the complexity and variety of your assets and your level of financial sophistication. Whichever form you use, be sure you include everything. If you don't know the exact value of an asset, estimate its worth.

As you can see in Figures 5.2–5.4, the basic factors that make up your net worth statement include:

- *Cash reserves,* or money set aside for use in an emergency. These are liquid funds that can be obtained on very short notice.
- *Investment assets* that are all the assets you set aside to generate long-term streams of income, or build toward a particular financial goal, such as your retirement, inflation hedges, college for children, and travel.
- *Personal use assets* that are resources you use every day—your home or your car, for example—or assets you use for enjoyment, such as a boat or a camper.
- *Liabilities* that are simply what you owe.

If you are a widowed person, you're likely to have need for liquidity and safety. Often the dollars left to you represent all the money you have, and those funds have to last your lifetime. Your desire for liquidity and safety is counterbalanced by your need for inflation-fighting growth in some of your assets. There is really no correct formula to determine how much cash you should have available for emergencies, but the following approach has worked well for many:

- Retain, in an interest-bearing checking account, sufficient cash to cover one month's expenses. This means that after you have

FIGURE 5.2 Net Worth Statement of Martha Young

Assets		Totals
Cash Reserves (less than 12 months maturity)		
Checking accounts	$ 20,000	
Money market funds	20,450	
Life insurance proceeds	125,000	
Other: Series EE bonds	7,000	
		$172,450
Invested Assets		
Tax deferred annuities	$ 90,000	
Municipal bonds	86,000	
Individual stocks	22,500	
Stock mutual funds	150,000	
Investment real estate	150,000	
401(k) proceeds	17,500	
		516,000
Personal Use Assets		
Home @ market value	$200,000	
Household furnishings	40,000	
Automobiles	15,500	
		255,500
Total Assets		$943,950
Liabilities (Debts)		
Mortgage on residence	$ 12,500	
Mortgage on rental unit	70,000	
		$ 82,500
Net Worth		
Total assets less total liabilities		$861,450

paid all your expenses for one month, you will have the equivalent of one month's funds left in your checking account.

• Keep a minimum of five additional months' expenses in a money market account, or other fairly liquid investment. For example, if your monthly expenses are $3,000, you would keep $15,000 in an easily accessible account. Many widowed persons keep up to a year's equivalent in this type of account.

FIGURE 5.3 Simplified Net Worth Statement

A. What You Own:	Current Value	% of Total Assets
Liquid assets		
Checking accounts	$_____	
Savings accounts	_____	
Money market funds	_____	
Cash value of your life insurance	_____	
Other	_____	
Total Liquid Assets	$_____	_____%
Investment Assets		
Stocks	$_____	
Bonds	_____	
Mutual funds	_____	
Certificates of deposit	_____	
Retirement plans:	_____	
IRAs	_____	
401(k)	_____	
Pension plans	_____	
Other	_____	
Miscellaneous	_____	
Total Investment Assets	$_____	_____%
Personal Assets		
Residence	$_____	
Vacation property	_____	
Jewelry	_____	
Art/antiques	_____	
Other	_____	
Total Personal Assets	$_____	_____%
B. What You Owe (Liabilities):		
Credit cards	$_____	
Banks	_____	
Car loans	_____	
Personal installment loans	_____	
Education loans	_____	
Mortgages	_____	
Other	_____	
Total Liabilities	$_____	_____%
Total assets	$_____	
Less total liabilities	−_____	
Your Net Worth	$_____	

FIGURE 5.4   Detailed Net Worth Statement

	Current Est. Value	Total		Current Est. Value	Total
Assets			**Personal Use Assets**		
Cash Reserves			Home (market value) $ ____		
Checking accounts	$ ____		Household furnishings ____		
Credit union shares			2nd residence	____	
Savings accounts	____		Motor vehicles	____	
Money market funds	____		Camper/RV	____	
U.S. savings bonds	____		Jewelry/furs	____	
Treasury bills	____		Art/antiques	____	
Life insurance cash	____		Time share	____	
Values	____		Other	____	
Other	____	$ ____	Total Assets	____	$ ____
Investment Assets					
Stocks	$ ____		**Liabilities**		
Bonds			Home mortgage	$ ____	
Stock mutual funds	____		Other mortgages	____	
Bond mutual funds	____		Auto loans	____	
Bond unit trust	____		Credit cards	____	
Certificates of deposit	____		Installment loans	____	
Notes receivables	____		Private loans	____	
Deferred annuity	____		Taxes owed	____	
Series E bonds	____		Brokerage margin		
Investment real estate	____		accounts		
Limited partnerships	____		Education loans	____	
Collectibles	____		Retirement plan loans	____	
Business value	____		Other	____	$ ____
IRA accounts	____				
Keogh accounts	____		Total Liabilities	$ ____	___%
401(k)/403(b)	____				
Pension/profit sharing	____		Total assets		$ ____
Other	____	$ ____			
			Less total liabilities		– ____
			Your Net Worth		$ ____

- If you have other assets to which you have quick access, such as certificates of deposit, insurance, or securities, you can reduce the five-month reserve in a money market account. However, it is wise to stay within your comfort zone; this is intended to be peace-of-mind money.

Analyzing Your Net Worth Statement

First, look at what you have. If you have a high percentage of your assets in easily accessible cash reserves, they may not be producing enough growth for the long term.

If your assets are largely in speculative stocks—perhaps those you inherited—you may be fighting inflation, but risking the loss of principal.

Next, take a look at your liabilities. How do your liabilities compare to your overall assets on a percentage basis? For example, Joan has $90,000 in debts and only $140,000 in assets, mostly in her home. Her debt-to-asset ratio is $90,000 to $140,000, or 64 percent. One of Joan's goals might be to restructure her debts and build up her assets by refinancing her home, using the savings generated from lower mortgage payments to reduce debts or build investments.

Your assets may contain a large amount of cash reserves because of the lump sum life insurance payment resulting from your spouse's or parent's death. This should be a temporary situation because a portion of those funds should be invested to provide growth and income to you in future years.

DEVELOPING A CASH FLOW STATEMENT

Most of your cash inflows will be what is usually considered income. The term *inflows* is used because it's all encompassing and includes, for example, a loan that someone is repaying that might not necessarily represent taxable income. The same applies for the term *outflows*. Everything you pay out over a given year is an outflow. Some are deductible expenses on your federal and state income tax returns and some are not. For purposes of tracing what's happening to your cash, the term *outflows* yields a more useful picture of where you stand.

For inflows, check your most recent pay stubs if you work outside the home, as well as brokerage accounts, tax returns, bank statements, and retirement survivor statements. Include any rents you receive on real estate, as well as tax refunds and proceeds of any stocks. If you know the monthly amounts from pensions, annuities, Social Security, or other benefits, enter them. If not, you may need to make a few calls to come up with a close estimate.

Total all these items so you will have a total cash inflow figure for the year. Figure 5.5 is a simplified cash flow worksheet; Figure 5.6 is a detailed cash flow worksheet. Use the one that's best for your situation to plot the cash that's coming in versus the cash that's going out on an annual basis.

FIGURE 5.5   Simplified Annual Cash Flow Planning Sheet

	Amount	Total
Cash Inflows		
Wages, salary, commissions	$_____	
Dividends and interest	_____	
Annuities, Social Security, pensions	_____	
Rents	_____	
Other	_____	$_____
Cash Outflows	$_____	
Housing	_____	
Food	_____	
Clothing	_____	
Transportation	_____	
Utilities	_____	
Taxes	_____	
Insurance	_____	
Education	_____	
Child care	_____	
Entertainment	_____	
Vacations/travel	_____	
Gifts/donations	_____	
Other	_____	$_____
	Net Cash Flow	$_____

Subtract your estimated cash outflows from your estimated annual cash inflows. If the result is a plus, you'll likely finish the year in a positive cash flow situation. If the result is a minus, you are spending more than your income and you are headed for trouble.

FIGURE 5.6   Detailed Annual Cash Flow Planning Sheet

	AMOUNT		AMOUNT
Income			
Salary	$_____	Housing expenses (Cont.)	
Self-employment income	_____	Other	_____
Interest:		Total Housing Expenses	$_____
Savings	_____		
Money market funds	_____	**Household Expenses**	$_____
Credit union	_____	Gas	_____
Certificates of deposit	_____	Electricity	_____
Bonds	_____	Phone	_____
Other	_____	Water/sewer	_____
Dividends:		Trash/garbage pickup	_____
Stocks	_____	Groceries/supplies	_____
Bonds	_____	Cleaning costs	_____
Mutual funds	_____	Water softener service	_____
Rental income	_____	Gardening/lawn service	_____
Partnership income	_____	Cable TV	_____
Annuity income	_____	Home maintenance	_____
Pension income	_____	Home improvements	_____
IRA income	_____	Appliance repair	_____
Civil service benefits	_____	Major purchases: rugs	
Social Security income	_____	furnishings, etc.	_____
Veterans benefits income	_____	Other	_____
Child support/alimony	_____	Total Household Expenses	$_____
Tax refunds	_____		
Bonuses, gifts	_____	**Personal Expenses**	
401(k) or 403(b) income	_____	Miscellaneous &	$_____
Other	_____	pocket cash	
		Clothing	_____
Total Income	$_____	Dry cleaning/laundry	_____
		Cosmetics/hair care	_____
Expenses		Entertainment/hobbies	_____
Housing expenses		Vacations/travel	_____
Rent/mortgage condo fee	$_____	Education	_____
Property taxes	_____	Dues/membership fees	_____
Homeowner's fees	_____	Pets/pet care	_____
Insurance: fire, liability	$_____	Charity	_____
homeowners, theft		Gifts/religious instruction	_____
Assessments,	_____	Other	_____
Special taxes		Total Personal Expenses	$_____

FIGURE 5.6 (Continued)

	AMOUNT		AMOUNT
Children's Expenses		**Insurance Expenses**	
Tuition	$_____	Life	_____
Room/board at school	_____	Disability	_____
Travel to/from school	_____	Group	_____
School visitations	_____	Accident	_____
Books & supplies	_____	Health	_____
Summer camp	_____	Other	_____
Lessons: music, dance	_____	Total Insurance Expenses	$_____
Sports activities	_____		
Lunch money	_____	**Taxes (If Not Included Elsewhere)**	
Allowance	_____	Federal income taxes	$_____
Entertainment	_____	FICA (Social Security)	_____
Child care/babysitters	_____	State income taxes	_____
Other	_____	State sales taxes	_____
Total Children's Expenses	_____	City/local taxes	_____
		Personal property tax	_____
Medical Expenses		Other	_____
Doctors	$_____	Total Tax Expenses	$_____
Dentists	_____		
Specialists	$_____	**Category Expense Totals**	
Prescription drugs	_____	Housing	_____
Lab fees	_____	Household	_____
Glasses	_____	Personal	_____
Other	_____	Children	_____
Total Medical Expenses	$_____	Medical	_____
		Transportation	_____
Transportation Expenses		Taxes	_____
Car loan/lease	_____	Miscellaneous	_____
Car insurance	_____		
Gas/oil	_____	Total Expenses	$_____
Maintenance	_____	List Your Total Income	$_____
Tires	_____	Subtract Total Expenses	$_____
Tolls, fares	_____		
License fees/tags	_____	Net Cash Flow Remaining	$_____
Other	$_____	For Savings and Investment	
Total Transportation Expenses	$_____		

What you want from your cash flow worksheet is a representative snapshot of your best *guesstimate* for the coming year. Outflows have a way of escalating so be sure to include a healthy guesstimate in each area.

After you have the figures, look for categories or expenses that can be controlled. Can you cut back, or is there an unusual expense that won't recur? Will some expenses drop or increase dramatically? High costs in certain areas may indicate that you need to consider a financial step, such as refinancing your home, consolidating loans, or streamlining insurance costs.

Actual Versus Estimate

Your net cash flow can be either positive or negative. As you receive the inflows and spend the outflows, your actual experience may—and in all likelihood *will*—differ from what you put on the planning sheet. If the planning sheet indicates that you will have a surplus of $5,000 at the end of the year and it's clear by May that you've fallen behind, perhaps you understated one or more of your outflow items or overstated one or more of your inflow items.

Examine your checkbook, looking especially at the amount of cash you're withdrawing every week for spending money; perhaps there's seepage somewhere such as an outflow that you did not include in your planning. In any case, continue to revise your cash flow plotting sheets so that they more closely reflect reality and you always have the latest figures to use in financial planning.

If you have a serious cash flow shortage consider these nine suggestions:

1. *Rearrange debt payments.* Consider talking with your creditors informally about reducing your debt and/or creating a payment schedule you can manage.
2. *Sell your life insurance policies.* You can sell a life insurance policy for cash (called a vintical settlement), often for much more than the cash value. This money can then be used to reduce debt or be invested to provide income.
3. *Create rental property.* Consider turning your residence into an assisted-living home, or taking in boarders.
4. *Move in with a friend or family member or rent a less expensive space.*

5. *Review your assets and consider selling those that produce little or no income.*

6. *Review your retirement assets to see if you are maximizing the income to increase cash flow.*

7. *Consider a reverse mortgage if there is equity in your house and you are over age 62.*

8. *Review your house mortgage to see if a lower interest rate may be available by refinancing.* This may lower your monthly payments.

9. *Determine which expenses are necessary and which are discretionary.* Some of the discretionary may be unnecessary once you examine them more closely.

A Cash Flow Control Plan

One way to put yourself in control of your cash flow is to establish two separate checking accounts. The first account can be a money market fund or traditional checking account. This account is to handle all the expenses that always seem to come at the wrong time or in the wrong amounts. These expenses are usually ones that do not recur monthly but can still be programmed. Examples are once-a-year or occasional expenses such as auto insurance, travel and leisure activities, real estate taxes, and estimated tax payments.

One of the first steps in setting up this approach is to identify all these occasional expenses. Most widowed persons feel comfortable with keeping a six-month or one-year reserve in this account to cover these occasional programmed expenses. If you don't have an interest-bearing checking account, you can place some of the funds in a money market fund so that temporarily idle funds are earning some interest. As expenses are covered from this account, replenish the account to always keep the reserve intact.

The second checking account—a traditional checking account or regular account—will be used to pay most of your regular bills and recurring monthly expenses, including cash you withdraw to spend on incidentals.

This system is simple and effective because it helps you separate monthly living costs from occasional expenses and money used for savings and investments. Meanwhile, the programmed account is drawing interest while you are writing fewer checks on it, and the regular account is also drawing interest while you are drawing more checks against it. In this way, you're optimizing the use of your checking accounts.

VALUABLE DOCUMENTS AND SAFE STORAGE

Another aspect of getting organized is physically securing valuables and important documents. These items should be sorted and kept in a fireproof safe or safety-deposit box. A safety-deposit box is the best choice for storage outside your house, though it's wise to keep photocopies of original papers in a file at home.

In general, store only those documents and valuables which are irreplaceable in the safe-deposit box; if they're replaceable, they can be covered by insurance. Figure 5.7 is a list of items to keep in a safe-deposit box.

If you have a power of attorney agreement, which gives someone else the right to act in your behalf should you become incapacitated, don't keep it in your safe-deposit box. It's better for the person to

FIGURE 5.7 Items to Keep in a Safe-Deposit Box

Adoption papers	Jewelry
Automobile titles	Valued letters
Original birth certificates	Original marriage certificates
Valuable books	Military discharge papers
Certificates of deposit	Mortgages
Citizenship papers	Naturalization papers
Coin collections	Patents
Contracts	Pension certificates
Copyrights	Treasured photo negatives
Court decrees	Promissory notes
Death certificates	Savings certificates
Deeds and titles	Social Security card
Divorce decrees	Stock or bond certificates
Employment contracts	Trust agreements
Household inventory for insurance purposes	Veterans Administration papers
	Videotape of household contents
List of life and disability insurance policies	Copies of your will

whom you grant the power to retain one copy of the power of attorney
and for you to retain another in your personal files at home. Figure 5.8
provides a checklist so you can keep track of the location of all your important documents.

FIGURE 5.8   Location of Important Documents

	Safe-Deposit Box	Office	Residence
Wills	___	___	___
Trust agreements	___	___	___
Powers of attorney	___	___	___
Burial instructions	___	___	___
Cemetery deeds	___	___	___
Safe combination	___	___	___
Employment benefits	___	___	___
Employment contracts	___	___	___
Pension records	___	___	___
Social Security records	___	___	___
Life insurance policies	___	___	___
Home & car insurance	___	___	___
Birth certificates	___	___	___
Passports	___	___	___
Naturalization papers	___	___	___
Military discharge	___	___	___
Marriage certificates	___	___	___
Partnership agreements	___	___	___
Checking accounts records	___	___	___
Savings accounts	___	___	___
Credit card records	___	___	___
Certificates of deposit	___	___	___
Record of investments	___	___	___
Stock & bond certificates	___	___	___
Tax returns	___	___	___
Real estate titles and deeds	___	___	___
Mortgage papers	___	___	___
Notes payable/receivable	___	___	___
Ownership records:	___	___	___
Auto	___	___	___
Boat	___	___	___
Recreational property	___	___	___

If you've computed your net worth, determined your cash flows, and safely stored what needs to be stored, you can take a deep breath and relax a bit now. The preliminary planning is a great deal of work, but it's done and out of the way.

Estate Income/Expenses Record Book

Any income received that was due your spouse or parent prior to death should be deposited in a separate bank account (also see Chapter 6 Settling the Estate). This could include dividends and work related income.

Discuss with your bank what is involved in setting up an estate account. Until then, keep track of any checks you receive, including date, amount, and who the payer is. Also keep receipts for expenses incurred to settle the estate and record them.

CHAPTER 6

Settling the Estate

*T*he burden of settling your spouse's or parent's estate may rest entirely with you, but don't let that scare you. Following the death of a loved one, the surviving spouse or adult child is most often named executor or personal representative and is responsible either for carrying out the terms of the will or for settling the estate according to the laws of the state in which you live.

The term *settling the estate* describes the process of collecting assets, filing inventories of accounts, paying claims, completing administrative details, and distributing any remaining assets. More broadly defined, settling the estate is the process of legally transferring title to property currently in the deceased person's estate to the heirs or confirming title to property the heirs already have in their possession.

Note:

Don't be intimidated by the phrase settling the estate, or by the tasks involved. When you have taken care of the basic items discussed here, in essence, you will have settled the estate.

Estate administration can be extremely complex or relatively simple—it largely depends on how many assets and what type of assets are involved. It is not the purpose of this book to teach you to prepare a complete estate administration by yourself, although that may be possible if the estate is simple and has few assets. However, few heirs have the training or temperament to settle an estate, especially in the aftermath of their loss. In many cases, the best advice is to seek competent legal assistance. Even if an expert does most of the work, you need to be familiar with estate administration so you will know what your attorney is doing and you won't feel threatened by the process.

Whether you bring in professionals or initiate the proceedings yourself, you'll need to collect certain information about the deceased, about the estate, and about yourself. Much of this information is described in Chapter 2, but the following is a brief list to aid you. All official documents—for example, birth, marriage and death certificates; military papers; and deeds—should be originals or certified copies.

- Your spouse's or parent's will. Find it and read it right away. Studying a copy of the will is okay, but you'll need the original to start the settlement process.
- Any trusts established by your spouse or parent or any trust for which they may have acted as trustee
- Retirement plan information, including pension, profit sharing, 401(k), IRAs, and self-employment plans
- Any business agreements and accompanying company books and records
- Birth certificates for you, your spouse or parent, and other beneficiaries
- Military discharge papers
- Marriage certificate
- Any existing prenuptial agreements
- Divorce papers
- Adoption papers for you or other beneficiaries
- Deeds to property owned or co-owned by you and your spouse or parent
- Registration papers for motor vehicles, boats, etc.
- Bank account statements
- Securities certificates and account statements
- Tax returns for the last two years, the most recent W-2 forms from your spouse's or parent's employer, and 1099 forms

- Any loan documents, including mortgages
- Life insurance policy information, both those on the life of your spouse or parent's and any he or she may have owned on the lives of others
- Health, travel and accident, disability, property, and auto insurance policy information
- Membership statements and benefit descriptions for all clubs and organizations
- Credit card information
- Citizenship papers, if applicable
- Social Security cards
- Death certificates
- Inventory of all assets in the estate
- Inventory of safe-deposit box, if available (also covered in Chapter 2)

SIMPLIFIED PROCEDURE ONCE THE WILL IS READ

- Determine who is the executor or personal representative.
- File the will with probate court.
- Have the court issue letters of appointment certifying the authority of the personal representative.

Helpful Pointers

1. Prepare yourself to answer a lot of questions, even some that may seem pointless. You can expect questions about:
   - property owned individually or jointly by your spouse;
   - how to contact your legal or financial advisors; and
   - Social Security numbers for you, your spouse or parent, and other beneficiaries including your children.
2. If you think your spouse or parent had life insurance but cannot find the policy, search through canceled checks to see to what company payments were made. Also, if the company paid dividends, you may find annual statements from the company.
3. Contact the state Office for Inheritance Tax, usually listed under state agencies in the phone book. If your state imposes

an inheritance tax—a tax on people receiving property from a decedent—ask for the release forms.

4. If you can't locate the decedent's will, perhaps you can find the attorney who drafted it. The attorney's name may be in an address book, a pile of business cards, the personal papers in your spouse's or parent's office or desk, the checkbook register, or on a canceled check. Original wills are often kept in the safe of the attorney who prepared them.

If the will is in a safe-deposit box, you may be permitted to open the box if you have the key and you were a joint signer on the box. If state law requires that the box be sealed upon death, you will probably have to file a petition with the probate court for permission to open the box and search for the will.

Professional Advisers

Once you've found the will and have read it, you may want to hire an attorney or other professionals to help you settle the estate and get your legal and financial affairs in order. If you follow the steps already outlined, you will be giving your advisors a head start and you will probably reduce the time they will need to spend thus reducing the cost of their services. Chapter 16 specifically discusses the qualifications of various advisers, but here is a synopsis of the types of professionals you may need to hire:

- *Lawyers* can do everything required to settle an estate, including probate. They also can help collect survivors' benefits, deal with creditors, prepare or modify your own will, and draft other estate planning documents.
- *Accountants* can prepare estate and income tax returns, advise about financial matters, minimize taxes, and help with financial decision making.
- *Financial planners* can assist you in choosing financial goals, develop strategies to reach them, and help invest insurance proceeds to achieve your financial objectives.

A major factor in hiring an expert—one that will be essential to your working relationship—is trust. You also need to feel comfortable asking questions and voicing your concerns, and secure that your advisers can provide answers, educate you if necessary, and not push you to take actions about which you feel ill at ease. If you're not happy with a professional adviser, say so. If changes aren't made to satisfy your concerns, change advisers.

Understanding Probate

Probate is the process of law that proves the authenticity of your spouse's or parent's will (or establishes that there is no will) and oversees the distribution of probate property to the creditors and rightful heirs. It is usually handled by the office of the registrar of wills or the clerk of the court. Assets may be considered probate or nonprobate. Nonprobate holdings are those that pass to survivors independently of the will, and, with the possible exception of federal and state death taxes, are not subject to claims of your spouse's creditors.

You do not need to report nonprobate assets to the court. If your spouse's entire estate is composed of nonprobate assets and there are no minor children to consider, no probate is required and the assets may be distributed. However, if there was any property held in the decedent's own name, it is necessary to submit the will for probate.

Here are some examples of nonprobate property:

- Property owned by you and your spouse or parent in joint tenancy with right of survivorship (JTWRS).
- Property owned by you and your spouse in tenancy by the entirety, a designation used only for real estate and spouses. The property in this case will pass to you as surviving spouse.
- Life insurance proceeds. Almost all life insurance proceeds are received federal-income-tax-free at the death of the insured (unless the proceeds are payable to the estate or the named beneficiary has died). Thus, you normally don't have to file any federal income tax forms on life insurance proceeds.
- Property held by a trust established during your spouse's or parent's lifetime, known as a living trust or an *inter vivos* trust.
- Qualified plan benefits of which there are named beneficiaries (unless the estate was named as beneficiary, or the beneficiary has died). These may include IRA, pension, 401(k), or similar plans.

- Savings bonds co-owned by you and your spouse or parent, or those that are payable to a named beneficiary.
- Wages, vacation pay, sick leave pay, and the like, earned by the decedent but not paid at the time of death can be paid without having to go through probate in many states.
- Totten trusts—joint bank accounts that are set up with your spouse or parent, or set up by your spouse or parent with you as beneficiary.
- Transfer on death accounts. This is a relatively new type of registration mainly used with mutual funds to avoid probate.

INFORMATION NEEDED WHEN PROBATING A WILL

- The will
- The contents of the safe-deposit box
- A listing of all real estate
- A listing of all securities, government bonds and bills, certificates of deposit, or other financial instruments
- A listing of all corporations owned in whole or in part, especially closely held corporations
- A listing of all money accounts such as checking, savings, money market, and wrap accounts
- A listing of all judgments (whether owed or owing), accounts receivable, notes receivable, and notes payable
- A copy of all insurance policies, including life, health, disability, and property and casualty
- A listing of all limited partnerships and partnerships
- A listing of all personal property
- A listing of all business and governmental benefits
- A listing of all debts and claims against the estate
- A listing of the last five years' tax returns
- A listing of all pension funds, IRAs, or other retirement accounts
- A listing of medical and funeral expenses
- A copy of any buy-sell agreements
- A copy of all trusts, revocable and irrevocable

Suppose the estate of George's wife, Jane, was comprised of the following assets:

- the family house, held as joint property in tenancy by the entirety;
- pension and 401(k) plans, and IRAs, which all name George as beneficiary;
- three life insurance policies, including a company group policy naming George as beneficiary;
- securities owned by Jane and George as joint tenants with right of survivorship; and
- three stocks that Jane owned in her name only.

The only assets requiring probate in this case are the three stocks owned in Jane's name. The entire balance of the estate, amounting to more than $500,000, passes to George outside of probate.

Some states require any will to be filed with the proper court; but, if there is no probate estate to settle, administration may not be necessary. Also, probating the will is a separate procedure from the administration and settlement of the estate and is separate from the payment of inheritance or estate taxes.

A GLOSSARY OF ESTATE PLANNING TERMINOLOGY

The average surviving spouse or adult child can feel overwhelmed by the complexities of our legal system. Many of the terms are in Latin or have special meanings in the context of settling an estate that is different from their usual definitions. The following is a glossary of *legalese* you may encounter.

Administrator (Male) or Administratrix (Female)

The person named by the court to handle an estate if no one was named in the will, or if the person named in the will cannot serve.

Assets

Money or value in any form owned by the deceased.

Beneficiary

A person named in the deceased's will to receive assets and who is entitled by law to receive them.

Bequest

A gift of personal property given through a will; a legacy.

Codicil

A supplement, amendment, or addition that modifies an existing will or possibly revokes only a portion of the will.

Crummy Power

A right given to a beneficiary of an irrevocable trust. It allows the contribution to qualify for the present-interest test and also for the annual exclusion.

Decedent

The person who has died.

Devise

To give real estate through a will.

Disclaimer (Qualified)

A complete refusal to accept property where one is entitled to receive it. It must be made timely and no direction as to ultimate disposition may be made. No receipt of property can be made previous to a qualified disclaimer and it must be made within nine months of death.

Estate

All the assets and the liabilities left by the person at death.

Executor (Male) or Executrix (Female)

The person, or sometimes institution, named in a will to handle an estate. The executor of an estate has four major duties:

1. Listing, assembling, and safeguarding the deceased's assets
2. Managing the estate while the settlement is being processed
3. Paying taxes and debts of the estate
4. Distributing the assets to the proper beneficiaries

An individual can serve as executor and also be a beneficiary of a will.

Fair Market Value

Value at which estate assets are measured for calculating the gross estate tax and gift tax; price at which a willing buyer and a willing seller will transfer property.

Fiduciary

Person who is in a legally defined position of trust.

Gift

Property transferred for less than adequate and full consideration; a gratuitous transfer from one individual to another either in trust or outright.

Gift Splitting

Spouses' ability to split a gift to an individual with the assumption half the gift is made by each spouse.

Guardian

Person named to represent the interests of minor children or incompetent individuals. Also known as a conservator, he or she may represent financial interests or caretaking interests.

Insurance Trust

Irrevocable trust created to hold life insurance policies for estate planning purposes.

Intestate

Died without a will. Each state has specific laws as to how an estate is to be divided when there is no will.

Legacy

A bequest.

Liabilities

Money owed.

Marital Deduction

May be made outright or through a trust; either a marital deduction trust or a qualified terminable interest property (QTIP) trust. All assets transferred from one spouse to another either while alive or at death are free of transfer taxes.

Probate

The process by which property is transferred in accordance with the terms of a will.

Power of Appointment

A right created by the donor enabling the donee to designate the ultimate owner of the property; can be general or limited. General power of appointment gives the donee the ability to transfer the property to anyone, including himself. Limited power of appointment allows the assets to be transferred to a certain class of individuals, typically not the donee. This power can be testamentary or created while the donor is alive.

Principal

The assets making up the estate or property inside the trust; otherwise known as corpus.

Qualified Domestic Trust (QDOT)

A trust that meets the requirement for a marital deduction for property left to a surviving resident noncitizen spouse. The trust must have at least one U.S. trustee who approves of distributions.

Qualified Terminable Interest Property Trust (QTIP)

A trust that allows property to be transferred to the surviving spouse in trust and qualifying for the marital deduction. The surviving spouse must be given the exclusive right to all the income derived from the property in the trust at least annually during the surviving spouse's remaining life.

The deceased spouse's executor must make the irrevocable election on the decedent's federal estate-tax return to qualify the property for the marital deduction. An affirmative election must be made. All property remaining in the trust will be included in the surviving spouse's estate at their death. Property will be distributed according to the deceased spouse's wishes.

Reciprocal Wills

When spouses have mirror-image wills.

Right of Dower

A widow's interest, for the remainder of her life, in the property of her deceased husband.

Shrinkage

The amount of property that will be reduced due to estate settlement costs at the first or second death.

Step-up in Basis

Property held in a revocable trust or outright at the time of death will receive a tax basis equal to fair market value. This will cause no capital gains to be recognized on the sale of the assets immediately following the death. Gifted property does not receive a stepped-up basis.

Testate

Died with a will.

Trust

The legal instrument set up to hold property or money for a particular person or persons, and managed by a trustee.

Trustee

The person or institution attending to the management and distribution of a trust.

Unified Credit

A credit to which every individual is entitled either at death as a credit against estate taxes or during the life of the individual with a credit against gift taxes. The credit in 1999 is $211,300 which is equal to $650,000 worth of property.

Will

A legal instrument providing for an orderly distribution of property from one individual to many individuals. It has provisions choosing an executor to administer all aspects of the estate, including the postmortem period. Each state varies the requirements necessary for executing a valid will, but most require witnessing the signature.

NO WILL OR NO EXECUTOR NAMED IN THE WILL

If your spouse or parent died intestate (i.e., without a will) or did not name an executor, you will probably be appointed as personal representative of the estate. You do not have to accept the appointment but being involved will help speed settlement and protect your interests and future needs.

Again, it is recommended that you retain an attorney for these procedures. However, if you choose to do it on your own, you can call the clerk of the probate court or the clerk of the circuit court for guidance.

Their numbers are listed in the white pages or in the city or county directory section of the phone books in most cities.

Thus far you've gathered all the estate information, read the will, determined which assets, if any, require probate, and chosen an attorney, if you need one. The total value of the assets requiring probate and the relationships of the surviving beneficiaries to your spouse or parent will determine which probate procedures to follow in your state. You, or whomever the court has approved as executor, must continue managing the estate while the settlement process is being completed.

APPOINTMENT AS PERSONAL REPRESENTATIVE

To make the text easier to follow, hereafter, assume that you have been named executor or executrix in the will and that you have agreed to serve in that role.

Your state may require you to petition the probate court for official appointment as the estate's personal representative. If so, you must apply within a certain period of time—30 days following death is typical—or the court will assume you have waived the right to act.

If you file a petition you may preclude the estate from using the simplified probate procedures that are available in many states. A quick review of the estate's assets can tell you which probate procedures may be best.

Often, you can get the answer by calling the county probate office; the staff will tell you which of the following three procedures to follow:

1. Small estate or affidavit procedure
2. Summary or abbreviated probate, also called miniprobate
3. Full, formal probate

As executor or administrator, you must be bonded for an amount equal to the value of all the estate's personal property, plus any annual income that will be generated by the estate. The bonding requirement may be waived by a provision in the decedent's will. If there is no provision for waiving bond, courts will often allow a reduced bond if the estate's representative is also the sole or principal beneficiary. However, even the reduced bond must be an amount large enough to protect potential creditors or tax authorities.

The court will determine the amount of the bond. Your insurance agent or attorney can help you through the procedure of being bonded. The premium for the bond, which is regulated by law in most states, can be an expense of the estate.

If there were motor vehicles owned solely in the decedent's name, check with the department of motor vehicles to learn whether your state's law allows vehicles of less than a certain value to be transferred directly to you or the beneficiaries. In effect, this procedure removes the property from the category of probate assets.

You will have to contact creditors and inform them of your spouse's or parent's death.

Note:

Do not feel compelled to pay creditors right away.

Creditors are given three or four months in which to file a claim. Once formal claims have been made, you can pay creditors and then make distributions to beneficiaries of the estate. Even if you think it's proper to pay creditors promptly don't make payments before you legally must. There may be downstream repercussions from prematurely disbursing the estate's funds.

Basic Responsibilities of the Personal Representative

- File an inventory with the court of all assets; i.e., money and property owned on the date of death.

- File reports with the court periodically indicating a description of property received and funds spent from the estate.
- Open a bank account in the deceased estate's name.
- Set up separate accounts for each minor child who is a beneficiary.
- Obtain the court's permission to spend the estate's funds.
- Obtain the court's permission to dispose of property of the estate.
- Obtain appraisals of estate property, if required.
- Notify and deal with creditors.
- Oversee the filing of income, estate, and inheritance tax returns.
- Be completely accountable for all assets collected and amounts paid from the estate.
- Distribute the estate assets.
- Provide a final accounting to the court.

Estate Management

As executor, you have a fiduciary position—a position of trust—to manage, for yourself and the benefit of others, all the assets and financial affairs of the estate. As a fiduciary you cannot favor the interests of one party over another, nor can you put your own interests before the interests of the estate and its beneficiaries. The estate must be managed and administered fairly and prudently.

While the estate settlement is proceeding, you may be required to keep records, revise inventories, provide detailed accounting, examine insurance contracts, collect rents, pay taxes, review investments or make investment decisions, and a host of additional, day-to-day management tasks.

Before you can pay any bills, you need to open an estate checking account. The bank you choose should be convenient to you and your attorney, and should be federally insured. Look for a checking account that requires a small minimum balance with low, or no, fees.

The estate account will be mainly a parking place for funds that will be distributed as the estate is settled. If it turns out that you have substantial funds in the account for a lengthy period of time, you might want to switch some money to a higher yield savings account or money market fund. Before moving funds into a new vehicle, you may be required by state law to obtain permission from the court. When you open the estate account, title it as follows:

Estate of (Your spouse's or parent's name), Deceased,
(Your name), Executor/ Executrix

Persons or businesses who are unaware of the death may send checks made out to your spouse or parent. As executor, you can endorse these checks made payable to your spouse or parent, and deposit them into the estate account. Any estate debts or bills should be paid from this account, not from your personal checking account. Again, you will be required to keep careful records of every item that goes into the account, as well as what is paid out of it.

Debts and Claims Against the Estate

As executor, you are responsible for determining the truthfulness of claims against the estate and for paying the debts of the estate. These may include funeral expenses, medical bills, phone bills, and mortgage and loan payments. If you have an attorney, he or she can do any or all of the tasks listed below:

- Pay bills
- Publish death notices to notify creditors of the death; such notices are usually printed in the local newspaper
- Retitle and reregister assets to your name as personal representative
- Keep track of estate expenses that may be deductible on various tax returns, such as legal and accounting expenses for work done to settle the estate

Before any bill is paid, you or your attorney need to establish whether it is:

- your debt,
- the decedent's debt, or
- a jointly held debt—such as:
  - charges on credit card accounts that you are authorized to use,
  - loans signed by both you and your spouse or parent,
  - property taxes, if both of you owned real estate, or
  - household expenses.

Remember, you are not required to pay your spouse's or parent's debts; the estate is responsible for these.

Filing Tax Returns and Paying Taxes

As the surviving spouse or adult child, you may have to file a profusion of tax forms, as well as pay taxes. First, there are the regular federal and state income taxes, if applicable; these are the same forms you would have filed if your spouse or parent had not died.

Then there may be estate income tax returns to file, as well as inheritance and fiduciary returns, all with accompanying taxes to be paid. If you have these tasks to face, an accountant or tax attorney can be extremely helpful.

The following is a list of the three types of tax returns involved in estate settlement and an explanation of what you or your professional advisors must do in each case:

1. *Form 1040, U.S. Individual Income Tax Return,* should be filed as usual. This form will show your income and deductions for the whole tax year, and the decedent's income and deductions until the date of death. When you file this form, be sure to include a notice to the IRS stating that this Form 1040 is the final income tax return.

   As a surviving spouse, you may file a joint return for the year in which your spouse died, and you may get special consideration for the two following years if you meet special IRS requirements for a qualifying widowed person. (See Chapter 8 for more information.)

2. *Form 1041, Fiduciary Income Tax Return,* if required. For tax purposes, you can consider your spouse's or parent's income in two parts. The first is income generated while your loved one was alive, which is reported on the Form 1040 discussed in paragraph 1. The second, income generated after your spouse's death, is considered income of the estate, and is reported on Form 1041.

3. *Form 706, U.S. Estate Tax Return,* is filed only when the gross estate is valued at more than $650,000 (for 1999). The return is due within nine months of death, unless you obtain an extension. The form must be accompanied by the following:
   - a copy of the will certified by the local probate court;
   - IRS Form 712, Life Insurance Statement for each life insurance policy;
   - a certified copy of the death certificate;
   - appraisals of real estate and personal property;

- certification by the state that death and inheritance taxes were paid;
- additional documents as needed to support any schedules accompanying Form 706.

The Unified Tax Credit: Only for the Rich

A federal law enacted in 1981 provides a unified tax credit for each person's estate. This tax device is called unified because it combines credits for estate and gift taxes, and gives you a credit on your federal estate tax bill.

Basically, the law allows the estate to take a credit against the taxable estate; the amount of the credit increases as shown:

Year	Unified Credit	Exception Equivalent
2000 & 2001	$220,550	$675,000
2002 & 2003	229,800	700,000
2004	287,300	850,000
2005	376,300	950,000
2006 & later	345,800	1,000,000

Consider this example: Let's say the taxable estate is valued at $1,000,000. The federal estate taxes on that amount are $345,800 less the credit of $211,300 in 1999. Thus, the amount the estate would pay is $134,500. If the taxable estate was valued at $500,000, the tax would be $155,800 less the unified credit of $211,300 which would equal zero.

If tax on the estate is less than $211,300, you don't get to reapply the unused tax credit elsewhere—the remaining amount cannot be applied against any other taxes.

Your spouse's estate may also qualify for the unlimited marital deduction which allows you, as a surviving spouse, to deduct up to 100 percent of the value of the gross estate depending on what portion of your spouse's estate is given outright to you by will or other devices. The marital deduction alone might eliminate any federal estate tax owed to the government.

Distributing the Estate

While distribution of assets is often considered to be one of the last steps in estate settlement, the process actually may have started soon after death. Nonprobate assets may have passed automatically to survivors and may already be in their possession.

Once claims and taxes have been paid and debts settled, you are ready to distribute the remaining probate estate. You or your attorney must follow the instructions in the will and any other procedures required by the probate court. If the estate is large, you may need professional help to distribute the assets.

Once the distribution is complete, the executor must file a final accounting with the court for all income, expenses, and administration of the estate. If you are involved in formal probate procedures, the actual termination of the estate may require a court-issued decree; for informal probate procedures, you may only have to prepare a signed closing statement that demonstrates that the estate has been fully administered.

Settling an estate can be complex, legally demanding, and time consuming. As executor, you will be called upon to make a multitude of decisions that can affect your life and the lives of others for years to come. Your actions in hiring competent professionals, directing the settlement, and understanding what the professionals are doing will give you the confidence to proceed.

Knowing that everything was done correctly, costs were minimized, and assets protected and preserved is not only personally satisfying, it's a major part of maximizing your inheritance.

Postmortem Estate Planning Techniques

Although your spouse or parent is no longer with you to plan the distribution of the estate, there are a number of techniques your attorney may suggest that are still available to you to facilitate the estate settlement.

Postmortem techniques may do some or all of the following:

- Provide a more equitable distribution of the estate
- Result in lower estate tax liability
- Provide lower amount of gift tax liability on lifetime gifts
- Result in lower income tax liability
- Facilitate the transfer of property from the decedent to intended beneficiaries
- Preserve and protect certain property from creditors of the estate
- Possibly lower probate costs and administrative expenses

There are over 25 different postmortem techniques that can be used by an estate in an effort to redistribute property and/or provide estate, gift, and income tax savings. The following is a brief description of six of the major techniques:

1. *Qualified disclaimer.* Used where the estate of your spouse has overqualified the estate for the marital deduction, thus avoiding wasting some of the unified credit.

2. *Homestead allowance.* This technique protects the homestead against the claims of creditors in recognition of the custom that the surviving spouse and children should not lose their principal place of living due to the spouse's or parent's death.

3. *Exempt property award.* Most states have laws which provide the survivors with the right to receive certain personal property free from the claims of creditors.

4. *Election against the will by the surviving spouse.* This is also known as the elective share statute, and ensures that the surviving spouse will be entitled to at least some minimal part of the estate in the event the deceased spouse leaves an amount of property by will that is less than that prescribed by the state statute.

5. *Family settlement agreements.* This is an informal means of redistributing the estate where shortly after the death all the family members and heirs gather to determine how the estate should be distributed.

6. *Use of alternate valuation date.* This allows assets to be valued six months after the date of death, rather than on the date of death, which is especially valuable if the assets have depreciated significantly since the date of death.

Here are some other postmortem planning techniques to consider:

- Section 303 stock redemption
- Use of the installment method of paying estate taxes
- Election to report administration sale expenses on either Form 706 or 1041
- Waiver of executor's commission and fees
- Election of the QTIP by executor
- Election by the surviving spouse to split gifts made by your spouse

The selection of appropriate postmortem planning techniques depends on many factors and requires expert legal assistance. While the techniques listed above are a few of the better known ones, your attorney may suggest others that will also provide benefits and tax reductions.

PART TWO

A Look at the Big Picture

CHAPTER 7

Retirement Planning
Making the Money Last

Retirement income planning is much like Aesop's fable of the goose and the golden egg. The fable relates the story of a poor farmer who discovers a beautiful glittering golden egg in the nest of his pet goose. At first he's suspicious, thinking it must be some kind of trick. He starts to throw the egg away but instead has it appraised.

He is delighted to learn it is pure gold. He can't believe his good fortune. His delight and wonderment grow the following day when the goose lays another golden egg. Each day the experience is repeated and the farmer becomes tremendously wealthy. But with wealth comes impatience and greed. The farmer is unable to wait for a golden egg to arrive each day. He decides to kill the goose and get all the eggs at once. When he does, he finds the goose is empty and he has no way to get anymore. The farmer destroyed the goose and thereby any future eggs.

A correlation can be made to your assets (the goose) and the income (golden eggs) produced by those assets. If you begin to spend the assets your income will be reduced, and if you exhaust your assets the income will stop altogether. Once you add the impact of inflation, increased longevity, and the increased probability of nursing home care solving your income/retirement planning needs seems overwhelming.

Think of income and retirement planning as a stool which is held up by these three legs:

1. Income from government benefits
2. Income from pensions (either survivor benefits and/or your own pension)
3. Income from personal investments

Income and retirement planning is an essential part of maximizing your inheritance. In this chapter, you learn how to determine how much income you'll need, how much you'll have available, and how to meet your needs.

THREE MAJOR FACTORS AFFECTING INCOME/RETIREMENT PLANNING

Inflation, Social Security and pensions, and long-term care needs will likely have a profound impact on you. Today, on average, everyone is living longer. You need to plan for more years of retirement than people in the past. A few years ago the average person retired at age 65 and died seven years later at 72.

Widows who reach age 65 today can expect to live to age 89; widowers to age 83. Also, people are retiring at an earlier age. An increasing number of people spend as many years or more in retirement as they did working. Your retirement money may need to last 25 to 30 years!

Let's take a quick look at inflation, Social Security and pensions, and long-term care in the context of your long-term income and retirement planning needs, and then explore their impact on retirement.

Inflation

Inflation seems likely to be always around, digging away at your carefully acquired and accumulated retirement dollars. Unless you invest to stay ahead of rising prices, your retirement funds will buy less each year.

Suppose you need $30,000 annually in income from your investments and you have $200,000 of investment assets that yield 6 percent while inflation is 4 percent (see Figure 7.1). During the first year, your investments (column C) generate $12,000 of income (column D). This is $18,000 (column E) short of the $30,000 needed (column B). The

FIGURE 7.1　Income/Retirement Analysis—Adjusted for Inflation

| Investment Income Required .. $ 30,000/yr | Investment Return ...... 6% |
| Investment Assets .... $200,000 | Inflation Rate .... 4% |

A Year	B Income Need Adjusted for Inflation	C Value of Investment Assets	D Investment Income	E Use of Investment Assets	F Investment Assets Value End of Year
1	$30,000	$200,000	$12,000	$18,000	$182,000
2	31,200	182,000	10,900	20,300	161,700
3	32,448	161,700	9,702	22,746	138,954
4	33,330	138,954	8,337	24,992	113,961
5	34,247	113,961	6,837	27,409	86,551
6	35,201	86,551	5,193	30,007	56,554
7	37,959	56,544	3,792	34,167	22,377
8	39,478	22,377	1,742	22,377	0
9	41,057	0	0	0	0
10	42,699	0	0	0	0

$18,000 comes out of the $200,000, leaving $182,000 at the end of the year. In the second year, the investments generate only $10,900; meanwhile, the income need has risen 4 percent (column B).

You spend more of your assets to meet current needs (the goose is being eaten alive!). Eventually the assets are completely spent and the income disappears by the eighth year.

Social Security and Pensions

Today the maximum Social Security benefit for an heir at age 65 is $19,440. This number is automatically raised each year to reflect rising prices. For someone needing $40,000 a year, Social Security will only go a short way towards meeting postretirement needs. What's more, Congress has begun taxing Social Security benefits (up to 85 percent of benefits are now taxable).

It is possible to start receiving Social Security benefits before you are age 65, but the benefits received at age 62 are reduced by 20 percent.

If employed, any company-sponsored pensions that may be forthcoming will also favorably impact your long-term cash flow.

Long-Term Care

One out of four Americans over 65 will spend time in a nursing home. Nursing homes cost between $30,000 and $80,000 each year and by the year 2020 costs may run as high as $160,000. Medicare health insurance pays only a tiny fraction of America's nursing home bills. An increasing number of insurance companies offer long-term care policies (see Chapter 12 Long-Term Care). The premiums depend on your age, the deductible, the amount of daily benefits, and how long you want to receive benefits.

Medicaid pays a big portion of nursing home expenses. However, Medicaid is a welfare program and to qualify you must be poor. Some financial advisers tell people to qualify for Medicaid by giving away their assets. Others warn of losing control of finances and becoming dependent on welfare.

Conclusion

With the prospects of a long postwork life, inflation, and the need for long-term care, you have every reason to wonder how you are going to pay for your retirement. Plan on a combination of Social Security, pension, and personal investments. If those aren't enough, you may have to continue working longer than you had hoped, or return to work at a later time.

RETIREMENT PLANNING ANALYSIS FOR INHERITORS

One of the most perplexing problems surviving spouses and heirs face is determining whether they will have enough income to survive over their lifetime.

While not perfect, a retirement analysis can give you a strong indication if you are headed for trouble or if you have a rosy future. Obviously the assumptions used in any retirement analysis cannot be carved in stone. For this reason, you should redo your retirement analysis on an annual basis using new assumptions for inflation and investment yield.

Step 1: Determining Your Average Rate of Return

A valuable number for you to know is the average rate of return of all your income-producing investments. This will give you a number to work with and a basis for improvement should you need to increase your income.

In the example in Figure 7.2, the rate of return is determined for each income producing asset, then the percentage of that asset versus the total assets is determined (i.e., the $5,000 savings account is 5 percent of the total $100,000).

Each rate of return is then multiplied by the percent of the total, resulting in the weighted rate of return for each asset. These weighted rates of return are then added providing a total average rate of return.

A worksheet is provided in Figure 7.3 for you to figure out your average rate of return.

Step 2: Determining Income Needs at Various Years

If you've already done a budget analysis, the initial work for determining your income need is already done. If not, you need to do a realistic appraisal of your expenses, both current and future. This requires making estimates of expected dollar outlays for each budget item. It is important to recognize that over the years some expense items will increase and some will decrease or even disappear.

FIGURE 7.2   How Average Rate of Return Is Calculated

Asset Category	Value	Rate of Return %		Percent of Total %	Weighted Avg ROR%
Savings Account	$ 5,000	4.0	×	5	0.200
CDs	25,000	5.5	×	25	1.375
Common Stocks	25,000	6.5	×	25	1.625
IRA	10,000	8.0	×	10	.800
Municipal Bonds	25,000	6.0	×	20	1.200
Credit Union	15,000	5.0	×	15	.750
	$100,000			100%	5.95%

FIGURE 7.3 Average Rate of Return Worksheet

Asset Name	Value	Rate of Return	Percent of Total	Weighted Rate of Return
Totals	**$**		**100%**	**%**

Here's an example: Martha, age 66, has examined her expenses, and determined them to be $2000/month. She read that inflation is currently 2.0 percent, but feels it will be higher over the years ahead. She decides that 4.0 percent for inflation is realistic. Also, using the life expectancy table in Figure 7.4 she sees that she has a 50 percent chance of living 18 years longer or more.

Using the Table of Inflation Factors in Figure 7.5, she quickly determines her future expense estimates as:

Age	Year	Current Expenses	×	Inflation Factor (4%)	Future Expenses
67	1	$2000	×	1.04	$2080
71	5	2000	×	1.22	2440
76	10	2000	×	1.48	2960
81	15	2000	×	1.80	3600
86	20	2000	×	2.19	4382

FIGURE 7.4   Life Expectancy Tables

Age	Male	Female	Age	Male	Female	Age	Male	Female
41	34.2	39.6	56	21.5	26.0	71	11.5	14.5
42	33.3	38.6	57	20.8	25.2	72	10.9	13.8
43	32.5	37.7	58	20.0	24.4	73	10.4	13.2
44	31.6	36.7	59	19.3	23.5	74	9.9	12.5
45	30.7	35.8	60	18.6	22.7	75	9.4	11.9
46	29.8	34.9	61	17.9	21.9	76	8.9	11.3
47	28.9	34.0	62	17.2	21.1	77	8.4	10.7
48	28.1	33.1	63	16.5	20.4	78	8.0	10.1
49		32.2	64	15.8	19.6	79	7.5	9.5
50	26.4	31.3	65	15.2	18.8	80	7.1	9.0
51	25.6	30.4	66	14.5	18.1	81	6.7	8.4
52	24.7	29.5	67	13.9	17.4	82	6.3	7.9
53	23.9	28.6	68	13.3	16.6	83	6.0	7.4
54	23.1	27.7	69	12.7	15.9	84	5.6	7.0
55	22.3	26.9	70	12.1	15.2	85	5.3	6.6

Tables are furnished by the Department of Health and Human Services and reflect life expectancies for all races in the year 1989.

Thus, Martha can see that her income needs will be increasing if she wishes to maintain her current standard of living. A worksheet is provided for your use in Figure 7.6. The guide to retirement expenses in Figure 7.7 will help you determine what expenses you will need to include when determining your future income needs.

Step 3: Determining Income

Now that you know your future expenses, you need to determine the income you can expect in your retirement years. Identifying your sources of income should be fairly straightforward, especially if you've already read the chapter on organization (Chapter 5). You need to develop a comprehensive sheet of all your income sources.

Figure 7.8 is a list of possible sources of income. Set up your own list and include the monthly income you expect from each source (or

FIGURE 7.5   Inflation Factors

Compound Sum of $1.00

Example: You invest $100 in a savings account that pays 7% a year, compounded annually. At the end of the tenth year you will have $196.70 in your account ($100 × 1.967).

Year	4%	5%	6%	7%	8%	9%	10%	11%	12%	13%	14%
1	1.040	1.050	1.060	1.070	1.080	1.090	1.100	1.110	1.120	1.130	1.140
2	1.082	1.103	1.124	1.145	1.166	1.188	1.210	1.232	1.254	1.277	1.300
3	1.125	1.158	1.191	1.225	1.260	1.295	1.331	1.368	1.405	1.443	1.482
4	1.170	1.216	1.262	1.311	1.360	1.412	1.464	1.518	1.574	1.630	1.689
5	1.217	1.276	1.338	1.403	1.469	1.539	1.611	1.685	1.762	1.842	1.925
6	1.265	1.340	1.419	1.501	1.587	1.677	1.772	1.870	1.974	2.082	2.195
7	1.316	1.407	1.504	1.606	1.714	1.828	1.949	2.076	2.211	2.353	2.502
8	1.369	1.477	1.594	1.718	1.851	1.993	2.144	2.305	2.476	2.658	2.853
9	1.423	1.551	1.689	1.838	1.999	2.172	2.358	2.558	2.773	3.004	3.252
10	1.480	1.629	1.791	1.967	2.159	2.367	2.594	2.839	3.106	3.395	3.707
11	1.539	1.710	1.898	2.105	2.332	2.580	2.853	3.152	3.479	3.836	4.226
12	1.601	1.796	2.012	2.252	2.518	2.813	3.138	3.498	3.896	4.335	4.818
13	1.665	1.886	2.133	2.410	2.720	3.066	3.452	3.883	4.363	4.898	5.492
14	1.732	1.980	2.261	2.579	2.937	3.342	3.797	4.310	4.887	5.535	6.261
15	1.801	2.079	2.397	2.759	3.172	3.642	4.177	4.785	5.474	6.254	7.138
16	1.873	2.183	2.540	2.952	3.426	3.970	4.595	5.311	6.130	7.067	8.137
17	1.948	2.292	2.693	3.159	3.700	4.328	5.054	5.895	6.866	7.986	9.276
18	2.206	2.407	2.854	3.380	3.996	4.717	5.560	6.544	7.690	9.024	10.575
19	2.107	2.527	3.026	3.617	4.316	5.142	6.116	7.263	8.613	10.197	12.056
20	2.191	2.653	3.207	3.870	4.661	5.604	6.727	8.062	9.646	11.523	13.743
25	2.666	3.386	4.292	5.427	6.848	8.623	10.835	13.585	17.000	21.231	26.462
30	3.243	4.322	5.743	7.612	10.063	13.268	17.449	22.892	29.960	39.116	50.950

FIGURE 7.6   Future Expense Worksheet

Age	Year	Current Expense	Inflation × Factor	Future Expense

FIGURE 7.7   A Guide to Some Future Retirement Expenses

Expenses That Usually Decrease:	Expenses That Usually Increase:
• Mortgage payments (eventually eliminated)	• Rent
• Food	• Property tax
• Clothing	• House upkeep (repairs)
• Taxes (income/Social Security)	• Utilities and telephone
• Debt repayment (eliminated)	• Auto, home, and liability insurance
• Life insurance (if any)	• Long-term care
• Household furnishings	• Vacation and travel
• Personal care	• Recreation and entertainment
• Medical insurance (often reduces at age 65, but may increase later)	• Contributions and gifts
• Savings and investments	• Medical costs (in later years)

annual income, if that's easier). If the income will not start until a specific date, note the date.

Employment Income

There are many questions to ask yourself in this area:

- If you are working now, will you continue at retirement age?
- If you continue, how long do you expect to work?
- Will you go from full time to part time?
- If you continue to work for the same employer, how will it affect any pension or 401(k) benefits?

Although it may not be financially necessary, it may be desirable for you to work during some part of your retirement years, especially if it is something you've always enjoyed doing.

FIGURE 7.8   Sources of Income During Retirement

• Wages	• IRA distributions
• Self-employment	• 401(k) distributions
• Monthly pension	• 403(b) distributions
• Social Security	• Real estate income
• Interest	• Trust income
• Dividends	

Social Security

Working during retirement can reduce your Social Security income. Under the existing rules you can only earn a limited amount (called earned income) before Social Security benefits are reduced.

In 1999, if you are under age sixty-five, you're allowed to earn $9,600 of working income and keep all of the Social Security benefit. Above $9,600, you lose one dollar for every two you earn. At age sixty-five through age sixty-nine the amount changes to $15,500. Above this amount you lose one dollar for every three you earn. At age 70, you can earn any amount of income you wish from employment without losing any Social Security retirement benefits.

It is important to remember that for Social Security retirement income purposes, earned income is income generated by you working at a job or being self-employed. It does not include pension income interest, dividends, capital gains, IRA distributions, or rental property.

Also keep in mind that a person's income plus one-half of their Social Security benefit can result in up to 85 percent of the Social Security benefit being included in their taxable income.

IRA Income

Withdrawals from IRAs (and most other retirement plans) must begin by age 70½ (except for the new Roth IRA). The rule is that you must withdraw the required amount from the total value of all your IRA accounts each year after you reach 70½.

To figure IRA withdrawal amount, add the values of all your IRAs together (excluding Roth IRAs) as of the year's end. Apply the proper life expectancy number (government tables are required for this calculation) to determine the minimum withdrawal amount. Then pick which IRA, or IRAs to pull the money from. You may be able to lower the required distribution by starting the IRA jointly with your child. Make sure to allow yourself enough time to withdraw the money. The IRA trustees have forms that you must complete before they will release the funds.

Interest and Dividends

Most interest and dividends are paid on a quarterly basis. Capital gain dividends from mutual fund holdings are usually paid once a year (typically in December). Municipal bonds may pay once a year, twice a year, or quarterly. Certificates of deposit pay at various times; some only after several years. If you do your retirement planning on a monthly basis you need to convert these figures to monthly income. Figure 7.9 provides a worksheet for your use. Figure 7.10 provides a worksheet you can use to determine your total income.

Step 4: Determining Future Income Projections

This step requires a little more work on your part, but it is worth it. You need to list the components of your income and factor in any cost-of-living (COLA) increase for each component. For example, if you feel Social Security will have an annual 3 percent cost-of-living increase then it must be factored in for future years.

This example may help you walk through these calculations. Jane has the following income sources:

- Social Security = $1200/month, COLA applies
- Pension benefit = $1500/month, COLA applies
- Investment income = $1000/month; growing at 2.5%/year
- Interest bearing savings account = $400/month
- IRA account with interest at 5% = $300/month

Jane feels that 3 percent for the cost-of-living increase is appropriate. Using the inflation factors in Figure 7.5, she is able to calculate the following:

FIGURE 7.9 Interest and Dividend Conversion Worksheet

1) Interest Bearing Accounts:	Current Rate	Annual Income	Monthly Income
a) _____	_____ %	$ _____	$ _____
b) _____	_____ %	_____	_____
c) _____	_____ %	_____	_____
d) _____	_____ %	_____	_____
e) _____	_____ %	_____	_____
Totals:			
2) Dividends and Capital Gains:			
a) _____		_____	_____
b) _____		_____	_____
c) _____		_____	_____
d) _____		_____	_____
e) _____		_____	_____
Totals:			
Total of 1 and 2:		$ _____	_____

	Now	1 yr.	5 yrs.	10 yrs.	15 yrs.	20 yrs.
Social Security	$1200	$1236	$1391	$1612	$1869	$2167
Pension benefit	1500	1545	1738	2015	2337	2709
Investment income	1000	1025	1131	1280	1448	1628
Interest	400	400	400	400	400	400
IRA account	300	300	300	300	300	300
Totals	$4400	$4506	$4960	$5607	$6254	$7204

If Jane's estimated expenses in 15 years are greater than $6254/ month, she will need to consider making some changes now to either decrease expenses or increase income. Otherwise, she may face the problem of diminishing assets.

Step 5: Putting the Long-Range Income and Expenses Together

Now you are ready to do the final number crunching in your retirement plan. A financial planner may be of value here if you don't

FIGURE 7.10 Master Monthly Income Worksheet

You may wish to list all the income you receive by the month you receive it.

Monthly Income Worksheet   Year _____

Income Source	Jan.	Feb.	Mar.	Apr.	May	Jun.	July	Aug.	Sept.	Oct.	Nov.	Dec.
Wages												
Self-employment												
Monthly pension												
Social Security												
Interest												
Dividends												
IRA distributions												
401(k) distributions												
403(b) distributions												
Real estate												
Trust												
Miscellaneous												
Total												

wish to do this step yourself. There are also software programs available to provide the spreadsheet information, but you can do it yourself with a calculator.

Here are the seven steps to follow when building your retirement-planning master worksheet:

1. Set up a long-range retirement plan worksheet using the form in Figure 7.11. Figure 7.12 is a sample worksheet for you to follow.
2. Using the Inflation Factors Table (in Figure 7.5), calculate your future income for each year for columns 4, 5, 6.
3. List in column 3 the future expenses determined in Figure 7.6.
4. List the actual investment income you expect for each year in column 8 (from Figure 7.10).
5. Subtract the total of columns 4, 5, 6 from column 3. This will provide you with the income required from investments, which is entered in column 7.
6. If the amount in column 7 is greater than that shown in column 8, determine that difference and list it in column 9 as a negative. If the amount in column 7 is less than column 8, list that difference in column 9 as a plus.
7. Add or subtract the amount in column 9 from your investment assets, listed in column 10.

TAKING A HARD LOOK AT YOUR RETIREMENT ANALYSIS

If your retirement plan doesn't work out the way you had hoped, here are a few suggestions to improve it.

- Work additional year(s) before retiring.
- Delay or advance Social Security payments.
- Delay or advance IRA, 401(k), or other pension benefits.
- Sell your personal residence and buy a less expensive home or rent.
- Consider working part time.
- Cut back expenses.
- Increase your investment yield.

FIGURE 7.11 Long-Range Retirement Planning Worksheet

(1) Year	(2) Age	(3) Required Income	(4) Social Security	(5) Pension	(6) Employment Income	(7) Investment Income Required	(8) Actual Investment Income	(9) Add or Subtract to Col. 10	(10) Investment Asset Balance
1									
2									
3									
4									
5									
6									
7									
8									
9									
10									
11									
12									
13									
14									
15									
16									
17									
18									
19									
20									
21									
22									
23									

FIGURE 7.12   Sample Long-Range Retirement Planning Worksheet

(1) Year	(2) Age	(3) Required Income	(4) Social Security	(5) Pension	(6) Employment Income	(7) Investment Income Required	(8) Actual Investment Income	(9) Add or Subtract to Col. 10	(10) Investment Asset Balance
1	66	$39,710	$11,053	$12,360	-0-	$16,297	$16,940	$ 643	$279,443
2	67	41,496	11,440	12,730		17,326	16,979	(347)	279,096
3	68	43,364	11,841	13,112		18,411	16,958	(1453)	277,643
4	69	45,315	12,255	13,506		19,554	16,869	(2684)	274,958
5	70	47,355	12,684	13,911		20,759	16,706	(4052)	270,905
6	71	49,406	13,030	14,328		22,128	16,400	(5668)	265,237
7	72	51,712	13,486	14,758		23,468	16,115	(7853)	257,884
8	73	54,041	13,958	15,201		24,881	15,669	(9212)	248,672
9	74	56,471	14,657	15,657		26,368	15,109	(11259)	237,413
10	75	59,013	14,952	16,126		27,935	14,425	(13510)	223,903
11	76	61,668	15,475	16,610		29,583	13,604	(15979)	207,924
12	77	64,443	16,010	17,109		31,324	12,633	(18691)	189,233
13	78	67,343	16,578	17,622		33,143	11,498	(21845)	167,588
14	79	70,374	17,158	18,151		35,067	10,182	(24885)	142,703
15	80	73,540	17,756	18,695		37,089	8,670	(28419)	114,284
16	81	76,850	18,519	19,256		39,075	6,944	(32131)	82,153
17	82	80,308	19,167	19,834		41,307	4,991	(36316)	45,837
18	83	83,922	19,837	20,429		43,656	2,785	(40871)	4,966
19	84	87,698	20,532	21,042		46,124	301	(45823)	0
20	85	91,645	21,251	21,673					

You may also wish to play what are called what-if scenarios with re-tirement factors that you can't control. These include:

- Higher or lower inflation rates than expected
- Cost-of-living adjustments being modified
- Increase/decrease in income taxes
- Higher or lower return on investments

SUMMARY

You may be one of the fortunate surviving spouses or heirs whose retirement income is sufficient to satisfy all your needs. Usually there are no easy answers for shortfalls that are often evident once the pre-ceding analysis is complete. However, by completing the process of examining your retirement picture, you should feel you have done the best job possible and know what is required to face the future.

CHAPTER 8

The Inheritor's Guide to Taxes

One way to help maximize your inheritance is to reduce the amount of taxes you pay. There is an old saying in financial circles: It is not what you earn, it is what you get to keep. This concept can help you to retain more money to invest or spend, depending on your personal financial situation.

This chapter is not intended to replace the services of your CPA or tax preparer—tax laws change often and the information given here is based on the latest information available from reliable sources.

The aim of recent tax reforms was to simplify the tax system but Congress was not successful in their endeavors. The system is still highly complex. Most taxpayers feel compelled to have even the most basic tax returns prepared by professionals. Also, there are many types of taxes including Social Security, state, excise, property, sales, and estate and inheritance taxes.

TAX PLANNING TIPS

Here are eleven things you can do to make the job of preparing your tax return easier:

1. If you are a younger widower or heir, obtain Social Security numbers for your children who will be one year old or older

by the end of the year. These numbers need to be listed on Form 1040. Call your nearest Social Security office and ask them to send you Form SS-5, the application for a Social Security number card.

2. Keep track of all tax-exempt income you receive. You need to report it on Form 1040 even though it is not taxable.

3. Obtain Form 8615 from the IRS if you have children under the age of 14 who have more than $1,300 in unearned income. Note that if your child's gross income is less than $5,000, you can choose to report it on your own tax return. If you do, use Form 8814.

4. Sort out your records of interest payments. The Tax Reform Act made big changes in this area. Talk with your tax preparer if you're unsure how to separate these payments.

5. Convert your consumer interest payments. Interest paid on consumer debt is nondeductible. However, interest paid as part of a home equity mortgage (up to $100,000 on your principal residence plus one other residence), remains 100 percent deductible, regardless of how the loan proceeds are used. I would suggest that you remortgage your home instead of using your credit card or taking out a consumer loan. By doing so you'll be able to fully deduct the interest payments. (See Chapter 10 for a rundown of mortgage interest rules.)

6. Set up a separate bank account for any money you borrow to make investments. Because you need to substantiate any deductions for investment interest expense, you need to be ready to prove that the money you borrowed was actually spent on investments rather than personal use.

7. Pay close attention to miscellaneous expenses such as job hunting costs and professional dues. Some miscellaneous expenses are fully deductible and others are deductible only if they total more than 2 percent of your adjusted gross income.

8. Keep accurate records of the income and expenses of any rental real estate. Keep separate records for units that you yourself actually manage and for those that you don't. The tax rules on deducting losses are different. For vacation homes that you rent for part of the year, keep a diary showing when you use it personally and when you rent it.

9. Fill out a sample tax return for the coming tax year as soon as possible. An estimate will help you project taxes for the next year. In addition, you will see where mistakes may be and have plenty of time to correct them for the coming year.

10. Notify the IRS when you move. Use federal Form 8822, Change of Address, when you need to change your address. This form helps eliminate the risk of not receiving an IRS notice in time to respond to it.

11. Medical payments paid by the estate within one year after death may be treated as deductible on the final return. A statement must be attached confirming that the same expenses were not deducted for federal estate tax purposes and that an estate tax deduction for them is waived.

Also, set up your record keeping. Once you have figured out your tax bill for the current year, it will probably be obvious where you lacked sufficient records to substantiate your deductions. Set up and improve your record-keeping system to accommodate your current needs.

FILING STATUS

It is important to file your status correctly because your tax rate is dependent on it. You can qualify as a surviving spouse for two tax years following the year in which your spouse died under any of the following three conditions:

1. You maintain a household for certain dependents;
2. You have not remarried; or
3. You filed or could have filed a joint return with your spouse for the year in which he/she died.

As a surviving spouse, you compute your tax using the same rates married couples use when filing joint returns. If your spouse died before filing a return for the current year, you or a personal representative will need to file and sign the return for your spouse.

If your spouse did not file a return, but had tax withheld, you or someone acting in your behalf will need to file a return to get a refund. The person who files the return needs to write "deceased" in capital letters, the deceased's name, and the date of death across the top of the tax return.

A joint return must show your spouse's income for the current year up to the date of death, and all of your income for the current year. Write "filing as surviving spouse" in the area where you sign the return.

If someone else is your spouse's personal representative, he or she will need to sign as well. The surviving spouse rate schedule initially allows more taxable income to be taxed at the 15 percent and 28 percent rate than the rate schedules for heads-of-household, or single individuals. Here's a simple comparison of taxes on $50,000 taxable income:

STATUS:	Tax	Widow(er) Tax Savings
Qualifying widow(er), joint return	$ 8,495	—
Head of household	$ 9,587	+$1,092
Single	$10,705	+$2,220

The surviving spouse tax status is a nice tax break, but is available to you for only two tax years after your spouse's death. If more than two years have passed, you will have to file as single, unless you are able to file as a head of household meeting all five of the following criteria:

1. You were not married at the end of the filing year.
2. You maintain a household for your children, dependent parent, or other dependent relative.
3. The household has to be your home and it must also be the main home for a qualifying dependent, as described in 2, for more than half of the filing year.
4. You provide more than 50 percent of the cost of maintaining the household.
5. You were a U.S. citizen or resident alien during the entire tax year.

UNDERSTANDING YOUR MARGINAL TAX BRACKET

It is not what you earn that really counts in the accumulation and preservation of wealth; it is what you keep. This statement leads to a fundamental principle for maximizing your inheritance. Rates of return before taxes are meaningless; after-tax rates of return are most important.

It is also important to realize that overall aggregate tax rates are not the same as marginal tax rates. For example, a person paying $25,000 in taxes with an income of $140,000 has an overall tax rate of 18 percent. However, their real tax rate is probably 31 percent. Every dollar above $124,500 will be taxed at 31 percent (the marginal tax rate).

It is equally important to realize that a low or nonexistent tax bracket may provide advantages unavailable to high tax bracket persons. For example, if you are in a zero tax bracket, you might wish to accelerate your IRA income, thus removing it from the confines of your IRA and perhaps moving to a Roth IRA.

Figure 8.1 is a tax measuring table to help you see what marginal tax bracket your income reaches (using 1998 income tax rates).

ESTIMATED TAXES

Most people pay their taxes to the Internal Revenue Service during the course of the year when withholding taxes are deducted from their salaries or pension payments. As a widowed person or heir, you may

FIGURE 8.1   How to Determine Your Marginal Tax Bracket

Joint Return		Single Return	
Taxable Income	**Marginal Tax Bracket**	**Taxable Income**	**Marginal Tax Bracket**
Above $278,450	39.6%	Above $278,450	39.6%
$278,450	36%	$278,450	36%
$155,950	31%	$128,100	31%
$102,300	28%	$61,400	28%
$42,350	15%	$25,350	15%
—0—		—0—	

have income which is not subject to regular withholding, such as interest, dividends, capital gains, certain pension income, self-employment wages, partnership income, and so forth. It is likely you will need to make estimated tax payments. The tax rules require that you pay this tax in quarterly installments during the year rather than in a lump sum on April 15.

How do you know if you must file an estimated return? You will need to pay estimated tax if:

- you expect to owe at least $500 in tax after subtracting any regular withholding and tax credits;
- you expect your withholding to be less than 90 percent of the tax shown on your tax return;
- you anticipate your withholding to be less than 100 percent of the tax shown on your prior year's tax return;
- your adjusted gross income is more than $75,000; or
- your current adjusted gross income exceeds the current year's adjusted gross income by more than $40,000.

Estimated taxes are due in four equal installments. For instance, if you owe $1,000 of estimated tax, you would pay $250 each on April 15, June 15, September 15 and January 15. Note that these dates are not spaced evenly. There are two months between the April and June filings and four months between September and January filings. If you work, you can also adjust your W-4 form so that enough money is withheld by the end of the year to equal your anticipated tax liability. This way, you can avoid estimated filings. Estimated payments are filed on vouchers (Form 1040-ES), which you can obtain from the IRS.

A nondeductible penalty established by the IRS is charged for failure to make estimated tax payments as required and must be paid at the time your tax return is filed. Although the computations are somewhat complicated, Form 2210 (Underpayments of Estimated Tax by Individuals) does provide directions. Taxpayers sometimes intentionally underpay the first payments for the estimated tax for the year and then make up the difference with a large final payment. The danger in this is that the penalty applies from the date of each underpayment. The IRS may not detect the ploy, but, if it does, the penalty will be imposed.

A Tracking Form for estimated payments is provided in Figure 8.2.

FIGURE 8.2   Keeping Track of Estimated Taxes

Internal Revenue Service Payment Record				
Qtr.	**Date Paid**	**Amount**	**Check Number**	**Due Date**
1				
2				
3				
4				

State of _____ Payment Record				
Qtr.	**Date Paid**	**Amount**	**Check Number**	**Due Date**
1				
2				
3				
4				

CLAIMING DEPENDENTS

Claiming an exemption for a dependent can be important in your tax computations. There are five tests that you need to apply in order to claim a dependent and obtain an exemption.

1. *A support test.* You need to provide over 50 percent of the dependent's total support, including food, lodging, clothing, education, medical expenses, recreation, transportation, and other necessities. If you share the support with other persons, it needs to be more than 50 percent of the total spent for the dependent. If less than 50 percent is provided, either by you alone or you with contributors, you will not be able to claim any exemptions.

2. *A gross income test.* Your dependent must have less than $2,150 in gross income, unless he or she is your child and is (a) under 19 years of age, or (b) a full-time student during five months of the year *and* is under the age of 24.

3. *A citizenship test.* Your dependent must be a U.S. citizen, resident or national, or a resident of Canada or Mexico.
4. *A joint return test.* Your dependent cannot file a joint return with anyone else.
5. *A relationship or member of household test.* Your dependent must live in your household for the entire year, or be related to you (i.e., child or grandchild).

Because each exemption for a qualified dependent in 1998 is worth $2,650 in deductions, obviously it is important to claim every exemption you can.

IRAS, TAXES, AND SURVIVING SPOUSES

If you are the beneficiary of an IRA account you will have to declare the IRA payments (unless you elect other options), whether lump sum or periodic, as ordinary income because they are received just as though you were the original owner of the IRA. The IRA distributions are considered income. If you take the IRA account as a lump sum distribution, be aware that you may have to pay income taxes and the estate may owe estate taxes on those proceeds.

If you are a surviving spouse and under age 59½ your deceased spouse's IRA can be taken by you without the 10 percent IRS penalty. (There is no penalty after age 59½).

As an IRA spousal beneficiary, you may elect to roll the funds over into your own IRA, avoiding current taxes. You can also make your own deductible IRA contributions to that IRA account if you qualify. You also have the option of leaving the funds in your spouse's name. Distributions from that IRA account do not have to begin until your spouse would have reached the age of 70½. If your deceased spouse was already receiving payments according to a schedule and you are the beneficiary, you must receive distributions at least as rapidly.

A rollover IRA means taking receipt of the assets for up to 60 days before reinvesting them into a new retirement IRA plan. A transfer means moving the assets from one IRA custodian to another IRA custodian. Rollovers are allowed once a year. Transfers can occur as often as you wish. Losses that are incurred in an IRA account are not deductible.

There are two types of rollovers for IRAs. One is an IRA-to-IRA rollover. In this case, all or a portion of the existing funds are withdrawn and checks come to you. The funds are not subject to current income taxes as long as they are deposited into another IRA within 60 days. Each IRA can be rolled over once every 12 months.

The other type of rollover is from a qualified retirement plan to an IRA. If your spouse was a participant in a company retirement plan, such as a pension or profit sharing plan, you may take the proceeds from that plan and roll them into an IRA. Again you may receive those proceeds yourself and then have 60 days in which to roll that money into an IRA. Also, be aware of the IRS ruling that requires 20 percent withholding on rollovers. Use a direct custodian-to-custodian transfer to avoid the 20 percent withholding.

If you are a beneficiary other than a surviving spouse, you are required to take the IRA distributions in a lump sum (which is taxable) unless your parents had set up a joint age distribution plan. If so, then you are taxed as the distributions are paid to you.

There are different tax treatments of regular IRA withdrawals depending upon your age:

- *Before age 59½:* Withdrawals are taxable as ordinary income plus a 10 percent penalty for early withdrawal. Withdrawals from the deceased spouse's IRA escape the 10 percent penalty.
- *Age 59½ to 70½:* Withdrawals are taxable as ordinary income and there is complete flexibility on amounts and timing of withdrawals.
- *Age 70½ and later:* Withdrawals are taxed as ordinary income. Minimum distributions must begin by age 70½ and are based on life expectancy. A 50 percent penalty is imposed if minimum distributions are not withdrawn. Distributions can exceed the minimum requirement.

TAXES AND LUMP SUM RETIREMENT PLAN DISTRIBUTIONS

As a surviving spouse, you normally have two choices when receiving a lump sum distribution from your deceased spouse's retirement program: (1) you can roll over part or all of it into an IRA or (2) you can take the money and pay tax on the distribution. If you elect to pay taxes, the lump sum distribution may qualify for five- or ten-year averaging. If your spouse made nondeductible contributions to a company pension or annuity plan, those parts of the distributions will be considered nontaxable.

If you wish to use the five-year averaging, all five of the following requirements must be met for a lump sum distribution:

1. The lump sum distribution must represent the entire account balance from the employer's plan.
2. Your spouse must have been age 50 or older on January 1, 1986. If so, you have the option of choosing either ten-year averaging using the 1986 tax table rates or five-year averaging using the current year's tax rates.
3. The plan must have been a qualified pension plan, profit sharing plan, or stock bonus plan.
4. Your spouse must have participated in the plan at least five years before the year of the distribution, or the distribution was to be paid to a named beneficiary when your spouse died.
5. One of the following conditions also needs to be true:
    • the distribution is paid to a beneficiary of the employee who died;
    • the employee quit, retired, was laid off, or was fired before receiving a distribution;
    • the person was self-employed or an owner-employee and became disabled; or
    • the employee was age 59½ or older at the time of distribution.

In addition to the above requirements, you can use averaging only once and you will need to use it for all qualifying lump sum distributions you received in that year.

The only requirement to use ten-year averaging is that your spouse needs to have been age 50 or older on January 1, 1986. Ten-year averaging allows you to use 1986 tax tables, while five-year averaging requires the use of current tax tables. Five-year averaging will no longer be available after December 31, 1999.

Rollover or Forward Averaging

Would it be best for you to roll the lump sum distribution from your spouse's retirement plan into an IRA or to elect five- or ten-year averaging? There are two things to consider when you are making the choice for five- or ten-year averaging:

1. The current tax rate may be lower than future tax rates. Also, if you pay the tax at this time, you have unrestricted after-tax use of the funds now and in the future. This eliminates uncertainty about the effect of future tax laws.
2. If you do pick the IRA rollover you will defer paying taxes until a future date. You will accumulate more wealth without taxation during that period. Higher taxes in the future may be offset by the investment values you accumulate within your IRA.

Note:

If your spouse or parent made nondeductible contributions to a company pension or annuity plan, those parts of the distributions received are considered nontaxable.

BEFORE FILING YOUR TAX RETURN

Before you mail your tax return, double check everything. Don't forget to:

*   Include your name, address, and Social Security number on the first page of the return. If you use the IRS preaddressed label, correct any incorrect information.
*   Write your name and Social Security number on every page you send to the IRS.
*   Attach Copy B of your W-2 form.
*   Sign and date the return.
*   Staple your check or money order to the return. Don't forget to sign the check and write your Social Security number on it.
*   Make a copy of the return for your own records.
*   Make certain every form and related schedule is included.
*   Recheck your arithmetic using a calculator.
*   Address the return to the IRS center in your state.
*   Mail the return on or before April 15th. The IRS won't accept an office postage meter as proof of the date of mailing if there is any doubt as to when the return was actually filed.

GIFTING

If you wish to give money and can afford it, consider setting up a gift-giving program (covered in detail in Chapter 13) for your children or grandchildren. You can still shift a certain amount of income to your family members in lower tax brackets. The best time to do this is early in the year.

Children under the age of 14 who have investment income below $1,300 in 1999 pay tax at their own lower tax bracket. Their investment income over that amount, regardless of its source, will be taxed at their parent's tax bracket. It may be better to have $1,300 taxed in the child's lower bracket. If you have children who are age 14 or over, consider shifting even more than $1,300 income to them. The entire amount may be taxed in their lower bracket.

Many times the surviving spouse will have two cars and wish to dispose of one of them. If it's an old car and you can't sell it, consider making a charitable contribution. Donate it to a high school or community college with an automotive trades or studies program.

HANDLING WORTHLESS SECURITIES

Joan found some old stock certificates of the Empty Hole Oil Well Company that her husband had acquired. He paid $10 per share for them. Joan called her financial planner and learned that the shares had been worthless since 1994. Since a taxpayer can go back seven years to claim deductions, she can file an amended return (Form 1040X) for the year 1994 to claim the deduction and receive a refund.

Securities are deductible only for the year in which they became worthless. The IRS keeps a list of companies whose stock has become worthless. If the company is not on the list, the IRS will not accept the deduction unless there is a real transaction or the worthlessness can be otherwise proven.

ARE SOCIAL SECURITY BENEFITS TAXABLE?

A portion of Social Security benefits may be included in your gross income if your modified adjusted gross income exceeds a base amount.

Modified adjusted gross income is your adjusted gross income plus tax-exempt interest, such as municipal bonds.

The base amount for a modified adjusted gross income is $25,000 for individuals. In your first and second years as a surviving spouse, you may be able to file a joint return for which the base is $32,000. The benefits, if they are taxable, are included in your gross income. For example, assume you file an individual return, have an adjusted gross income of $25,000, receive $9,000 of municipal bond interest, and also receive $12,000 of Social Security benefits during the taxable year. To figure the modified adjusted gross income add the adjusted gross income, tax-exempt interest, and one-half of the Social Security benefits. In this example:

$$\$25,000 + \$9,000 + \$6,000 = \$40,000$$

A modified adjusted gross income of $40,000 is $15,000 greater than the base amount of $25,000.

The amount of Social Security benefits that will be included in your gross income is $6,000 because it is the lesser of one-half of your Social Security benefits ($6,000) and one-half of the excess of your combined income over the base amount ($15,000 ÷ 2 = $7500).

The maximum amount that will be subject to tax is now up to 85 percent of the Social Security benefits you receive. This applies only to the extent that adjusted gross income exceeds $44,000 for joint returns or $34,000 for single and head-of-household returns. If your adjusted gross income falls between the old and new threshold amounts, only 50 percent will be subject to tax. Tax-exempt interest is only used to figure the amount of benefits that will be included in your gross income. It will remain free of taxation.

The form shown in Figure 8.3 can be used to compute your taxable Social Security income. It is important to note that as a qualifying widow(er) with dependent children you can file using joint return rates, allowing you to use the $25,000 base amount for the first and second years you are a widowed person.

ARE LIFE INSURANCE PROCEEDS TAXABLE?

Life insurance proceeds paid to a named beneficiary due to the death of your spouse or parent are not taxable income for federal or

FIGURE 8.3   Determining Taxes on Social Security Benefits

This worksheet will help you estimate taxes on your Social Security benefits.	
List your income to determine if you exceed either of the Social Security thresholds.	
1. List total income reported on Form 1040, excluding Social Security benefits.	
2. List 50% of your annual Social Security benefits.	
3. List all tax-exempt interest.	
4. Modified Adjusted Gross Income (add Lines 1 through 3).	
5. First threshold: subtract $32,000 from line 4 ($25,000, if single).	
If line 5 is zero, STOP. You owe no taxes on your Social Security benefits.	
6. Second threshold: subtract $44,000 from line 4 ($34,000, if single).	
This section will help you estimate how much of your Social Security benefits will be taxed.	
7. Multiply line 5 by 0.50 (50%).	
8. Multiply line 6 by 0.35 (35%).	
9. Add lines 7 and 8.	
10. Multiply annual Social Security benefits by .85 (85%).	
11. Multiply annual Social Security benefits by .50 (50%).	
12. Multiply line 6 by .85 (85%).	
13. Add lines 11 and 12.	
14. Enter whichever amount is smaller from line 9, 10 or 13.	
Line 14 is an estimate of how much of your Social Security benefits will be considered taxable income.	
15. Multiply line 14 by your estimated tax rate.	
Line 15 is an estimate of how much your taxes will be.	

state income tax purposes. If you take the proceeds of a life insurance policy in installment payments, each nontaxable installment equals the total amount payable at death divided by the number of installments to be paid. Anything paid over this amount in each installment is taxable income.

SETTLING WITH THE IRS

If you're unable to pay your federal income taxes, call 800-829-1040 well before April 15 and explain your situation. If the tax bill is under $10,000 you will be sent a one-page form (Form 9465, Installment Agreement Request) to attach to your regular return. The Internal Revenue Service promises to respond within 30 days. Those who owe more than $10,000 must complete a financial statement and provide additional documentation.

The IRS usually allows payments to extend for two or three years if the tax owed is less than $10,000, with the average agreement lasting one to one-and-a-half years. Interest and late penalties on the unpaid tax continue to accrue but they are less than the penalty for not filing a tax return at all. If back taxes are so high that it is likely they will never be repaid, taxpayers can file an offer-in-compromise. How much the IRS will settle for varies with each case.

CHAPTER 9

Insurance

Understanding the Great Mystery

The insurance industry is one of the largest industries in the world and distributes hundreds of millions of dollars each year in claims and benefits. Yet it remains a mystery to most people. An insurance policy is simply a contract between you (the insured) and an insurance company (the insurer) under which the insurance company promises to pay for your losses according to the specified terms of your contract.

You are transferring your risk of monetary loss to the insurance company for which you pay a premium. The insurance company accepts your risk because it hopes to make a profit by collecting premiums from the large number of the people it insures and investing the money. The insurer pays claims and operating expenses with the premiums collected and the earnings on that money. The insurer hopes its expenditures will be less than the total of collected premiums plus the invested earnings from those premiums.

The Concept of Risk

Whenever you have a financial interest in something—whether it be your life, your health, your possessions, or your job—you face risk. You face the possibility that your budget will be upset or your net worth reduced drastically. You must devise ways of dealing with risk to avoid losses that could affect your financial health. You have several options:

- You can ignore the risk.
- You can take action to lessen the risk.
- You can share the risk.
- You can assume the risk.

When you weigh the potential costs of ignoring or assuming the risk entirely, insurance often becomes a bargain.

LIFE INSURANCE

Why is it called life insurance? This is one of the great misnomers in our society because life insurance proceeds are paid upon the death of the insured to provide funds for costs which may befall its benefactors. As a widowed person or heir, you are probably more aware of this than other people. If your spouse or parent owned life insurance policies, you know the benefits of this coverage.

Life insurance is an intangible, and even if you own it, you can't see it, touch it, smell it, or taste it. The only thing that makes it ultimately real is the event that causes the payout of the benefit. Deciding if you need life insurance is an important issue. Here are four situations in which to consider owning life insurance:

1. If you have anyone dependent on you for an income or if your death would affect the income flow of your beneficiaries
2. If you feel that your debts would be a burden to your heirs
3. If your estate is fairly large and will be subject to high estate taxes
4. If you want to leave an inheritance or a charitable bequest

The Right Amount

You want to have enough coverage to bridge the gap between what your dependents will need and the resources available after your death. Figure the costs your dependents will face: mortgage payments and other loans, college expenses, health costs, and everyday living expenses. Also, consider your present resources: employer-provided life insurance (if available), your liquid assets, potential pension benefits, and Social Security survivor benefits.

Then use the form in Figure 9.1 as a guide to determine the right dollar amount for your insurance.

1. Estimate how much money your survivors will need.
2. Determine how much debt payment you will have to make, how much emergency reserve money your survivors will need, and any estate settlement costs.
3. Add all these items together to determine your total capital needs.
4. Determine your total capital available by adding your existing insurance, any current assets that can produce income, and any other lump-sum distributions available to your heirs at your death.
5. Take the total capital available and subtract it from the total capital needs to determine how much net capital is needed.

In the example provided in Figure 9.1, the total capital need is $558,943, and the total capital available is $490,700. The net capital

FIGURE 9.1   Inheritor's Capital Needs Worksheet

	Yours	Example
A. Family Income Needs (yearly):		
1) After-tax income needs	_____	$ 43,500
2) Less: Estimated Social Security Benefits	_____	−12,000
3) Less: Pension Survivor Benefit Income	_____	−3,600
4) Equals: Income Needed from Investment Capital	_____	26,400
5) Capital needed assuming 7% after-tax return (Divide A4 by 7%)	_____	$377,143
B. Debt Repayment Needs:		
1) Home Mortgage(s)	_____	$ 47,000
2) Charge and Credit Cards	_____	1,500
3) Bank loans (cars, etc.)	_____	4,800
4) Other	_____	0
5) Total	_____	$ 53,300

FIGURE 9.1 (Continued)

C. Other Funding Needs:
   1) Emergency Reserves (6 months)   _____ $ 21,000
   2) College Education (See Chapter 12)   _____   100,000
   3) Other   _____   0
   4) Total   _____ $121,000

D. Estate Settlement Costs:
   1) Funeral Expenses   _____ $ 5,000
   2) Administration/Probate Fees   _____   1,500
   3) Federal Estate Tax (See Chapters 6, 15)   _____   0
   4) State Death Tax (See Chapters 6, 15)   _____   0
   5) Uninsured Medical Costs   _____   1,000
   6) Other   _____   0
   7) Total   _____ $ 7,500

E. Summary of Total Capital Needs:
   A. Family Income Needs   _____ $377,143
   B. Debt Repayment Needs   _____   53,300
   C. Other Funding Needs   _____   121,000
   D. Estate Settlement Costs   _____   7,500
   E. Total   _____ $558,943

F. Assets Available to Produce Income:
   1) Investments and Cash Reserves   _____ $400,000
   2) Pension   _____   0
   3) Profit-Sharing and 401(k)   _____   21,700
   4) IRA, Keogh (HR-10)   _____   19,000
   5) Life Insurance on your life   _____   50,000
   6) Total Assets Available   _____ $490,700

G. Capital Needs/Assets Summary:
   1) Total Capital Needed (E)   _____ $558,943
   2) Total Assets Available (F6)   _____   490,700
   3) Net Capital Needed   _____ $ 68,243

needed in this case is $68,243. Notice that in the first line-item listing, after-tax income needs, you need to include mortgage or rent payments, utilities, food, clothing, installment payments, medical/dental payments, educational payments, entertainment, child care, home/auto maintenance, and any other needs.

Once you determine the amount of insurance coverage needed, it is important to pick the right kind of policy for your situation. Basically, there are four types of life insurance available today:

1. Term
2. Whole life
3. Universal life
4. Variable life

Term Insurance

Term insurance is pure protection against financial loss resulting from death occurring during a specified period of time. Term insurance offers the most coverage for the least amount of initial premium. It is not designed to meet a permanent lifetime need.

There are three types of term insurance:

1. Annual renewable term
2. Level term
3. Decreasing term or mortgage insurance

Annual Renewable Term Insurance

Also called yearly renewable term, this is the simplest form of life insurance available. It requires an annual premium which provides you with a specific death benefit for the following year. There are no cash values or side funds available.

Quality contracts provide you with both a renewable and a convertible clause. This means you may renew the contract each year by paying the premium without taking any medical exam. You may convert the contract to any cash value or universal life contract by completing a form provided by the insurance carrier. Because term policies have no cash values, premiums are determined mainly by mortality costs. This means that your premium increases annually as the probability of your death increases. As you become older, this type of coverage eventually can become very expensive and usually is renewable only until age 75, making it unsuitable for estate or postretirement planning.

Level Term Insurance

With level term insurance, premiums and coverage remain level for a certain period of time. This period can be 5, 10, 15, 20, and even 30 years. After the level premium period ends, renewal may be available for the next period, at which time a medical exam is often required.

Level term is best if you need ten years or more of coverage. Over an extended period of time, level term plans are generally more cost effective than annual renewable term policies.

Decreasing Term or Mortgage Insurance

This coverage usually decreases annually by a specified percentage over a predetermined period during which the premiums remain level. This is the most expensive type of term policy you can buy. Your coverage ends when the policy face amount reduces to zero or the term expires. This type of coverage is often sold in conjunction with mortgages through mortgage placement firms or banking institutions.

Because term insurance offers the most economic way to purchase a large amount of life insurance protection for a specific period of time it is particularly advantageous for younger widowed persons who have elderly parents or children under 18. Let's say that you are a widowed person or inheritor with an elderly parent who is dependent on you for support and whose life expectancy is only another four or five years. If you should die, there might be financial problems for your dependent. You can buy a ten-year term policy in this case to put some cushion on the time frame.

You can also use life insurance if you have college-bound children dependent on your income to pay for their education. You might want to buy some inexpensive term insurance to cover their college costs.

Shopping for Term Insurance

One way for you to shop for term insurance without an insurance agent is to call one of the insurance quote firms that provide computerized analyses. It will list four or five of the lowest cost policies in its database to fit your particular situation. Such firms usually deal with insurance companies that have quality ratings in the insurance industry. Here are four resources:

1. Insurance Information, 23 Route 134, South Dennis, MA 02667. Telephone: 800-472-5800. E-mail: www.iii@cape.com. It provides comparisons of policies, but does not sell insurance.
2. Insurance Quote, 3200 North Dobson Road, Building C, Chandler, AZ 85224. Telephone: 800-972-1104. Web site: www.Iquote.com.
3. Select Quote, 595 Market Street, 6th Floor, San Francisco, CA 94105. Telephone: 800-343-1985.
4. Term Quote, 6768 Loop Road, Centreville, OH 45409. Telephone: 800-444-8376. Web site: www.term-quote.com.

Group Term Insurance

Group term life insurance is life insurance that your employer buys on your behalf. As long as your coverage does not exceed $50,000 you are not taxed on the premiums the employer pays. If your coverage is more than $50,000, you are taxed on the premiums paid for the excess based on an IRS table. You pay some tax for the extra coverage, but the tax cost is far less than the cost of similar coverage outside the company.

Whole Life Insurance

Some people continuously need some type of life insurance. Whole life insurance, as its name suggests, is designed to offer financial protection for your whole life. In addition to death protection, whole life insurance has a savings feature called cash value. You can borrow against this cash value, often at low interest rates. You can also set your own repayment schedule for any loan.

Because the policy offers permanent insurance coverage, premiums will be higher than for term insurance in the early years but lower over a long period of time. Whole life policies are most appropriate for those who want lifetime coverage, need the discipline of forced savings, and will not need to cash in the policy for at least 15 years.

After 15 years, the cash value is usually greater than the premiums paid into the policy. Another important feature of whole life insurance policies is that the cash value of the policies accumulates on a tax-deferred basis.

Universal Life

Universal life is a life insurance policy with an adjustable death benefit and flexible premiums. The pricing usually is based on current mortality and interest assumptions. A minimum premium is required in the first year, but afterwards the amount and frequency of your premiums are flexible.

Variable Life Insurance

Variable life insurance combines the traditional tax-deferred savings features of life insurance with the potential growth of equity-type investments. Similar to traditional whole life insurance, variable policies have fixed premiums and usually a guaranteed minimum death benefit.

The variable life policy is an investment vehicle that lets you decide how the money in the savings part of the policy should be invested—stocks, bonds, money market accounts, or a combination. However, as the name implies, the amount of insurance coverage provided may vary with the investment profits (or losses) generated in the investment part of the policy.

Variable life is best for those persons who need a tax shelter, have investment experience, and can tolerate the risk involved. It is not a product suitable for most widowed persons.

Compare Before Buying

It pays to shop for insurance. For example, a $100,000 universal life policy may cost a healthy 35-year-old $650 in annual premiums with one company and more than $900 with another. After you pick the policy type that seems best suited to your needs, you need to compare the rates and policy features. If you are buying whole life or universal life, compare the death benefits and the annual premium payments.

Other features you need to compare include the total death benefit and the annual premium payments. Look at the guaranteed cash value growth or projected investment yields after one year, three years, five years, seven years, and ten years. Check these yields for the number of years between your present age and 65.

Don't look only at the long-term gain even if you intend to keep this policy for 20 years or more. Compare the guaranteed rates to the projected rates. Also consider the loan rates in the policy. Check to see how the annual dividends, if any, are paid, and how they may be used to offset your premium costs.

When examining policies consider that Section 1035 of the Internal Revenue Code states that certain insurance policies may be exchanged for other insurance policies without any taxable gain or loss. In general, the following three types of exchanges are nontaxable:

1. Exchanging one life insurance contract for another, for an endowment, or for an annuity contract
2. Exchanging an endowment contract for another endowment contract or an annuity contract
3. Exchanging an annuity contract for another annuity contract

If you wish to exchange a life insurance policy, an endowment contract, or a fixed annuity contract for a variable annuity contract with either the same company or a different one, this will also qualify as a nontaxable exchange. In order to exchange life insurance policies, each policy will have to be on the life of the same person. If you would like to exchange an annuity for another annuity, the contract will need to be payable to the same person or persons.

In light of this feature, you should review any existing life insurance or annuity policies. If the return (i.e., yield) is low compared to other policies, consider a Section 1035 exchange. A competent insurance agent can be of value in these situations.

Who Should Own Your Insurance Policy?

If you own a policy yourself, or if you retain any ownership rights to a policy at your death, the proceeds at death will be included in your estate and may be subject to estate tax. If your estate will be less than the federal estate tax threshold including the proceeds from your insurance policy, then estate taxes will not apply. If your estate will be over the estate tax threshold, however, you may wish to set up a trust for your beneficiaries and let the trust own the policy. You can make annual gifts to the trust to pay the premiums. The trustee then pays the insurance premiums from the trust.

Upon your death, the insurance proceeds go into the trust tax free. The trust can then buy assets from your estate. In exchange for these assets, your estate receives cash. This cash can then be used to pay the estate taxes. The proceeds of the insurance policy that go into the trust are not included in your estate.

If your assets are concentrated in real estate or a business, the availability of these invested dollars is limited. Depending on your estate tax bracket, these assets may be subject to significant taxation upon your death. If your heirs do not have sufficient funds to cover your settlement costs and outstanding debts, they may be forced into a liquidation sale, sacrificing inherited belongings to raise quick cash. Proper insurance coverage can provide your heirs with immediate funds to meet such expenses.

Caution:

If you transfer a life insurance policy to a trust within three years of your death, the proceeds may be included in your estate if you die within that three-year period.

Accelerated Death Benefits

Even if your policy doesn't contain a cash value provision it may contain a living or accelerated benefit. This feature permits an advance of part of the death benefit while the insured is alive, provided a specified triggering event occurs. Triggering events differ depending on the policy and the insurance company, but they can include:

- Diagnosis of specified illnesses
- A life expectancy of a specified period, such as 12 months or less
- A need for long-term care based on an inability to perform the normal activities of daily living
- A debilitating illness or permanent confinement to a nursing home

Some companies have automatically added these provisions to their policies for free—even for policies already in existence. For others, the provision is optional and the company specifies what must be done by the insured to add the provision.

The terms of an accelerated benefit vary from company to company.

- Eligibility is usually limited to insureds with a life expectancy of 12 months or less (sometimes even 6 or 9 months).
- The advance amounts, and charges, vary from company to company. Advances range from 25 percent to 95 percent of the death benefit and many insurance companies place a dollar limit on the amount they will advance. If less than the entire death benefit is accelerated, the remainder (perhaps minus a small fee) is paid to the named beneficiary upon the death of the insured.
- Some insurance companies place a minimum on the death benefit to which the provision applies; others place a maximum.
- Some companies limit the manner in which distributed money may be spent (i.e., to reimburse medical expenses).

Accelerated benefits for people with a life expectancy of 24 months or less are free of federal income tax and are specifically exempt from state income tax in several states, including California and New York. There is also no state income tax due for residents of states that have no state income tax or for those that follow the federal lead in determining taxable income.

VIATICAL SETTLEMENTS

A *viatical settlement* is a sale of a life insurance policy in which you, the owner, transfer all rights and obligations under the policy including the right to choose the beneficiary and the obligation to pay premiums. In return, you receive an amount of money equal to a percentage of the full death benefit. Generally, the transaction carries no restrictions on how you (the seller) can spend the proceeds of the sale.

Anyone who has been medically diagnosed with a shortened life expectancy may qualify for a viatical settlement. A combination of unrelated conditions may combine to create a shortened life expectancy. While some companies will purchase policies from people with a life expectancy of five years or more, the bulk of the viatical settlement companies only purchase policies from people with a life expectancy of 24 months or less.

Providing Life Insurance on Children

Most insurance advisors advocate insuring the parent, not the child. A parent normally needs insurance on his or her life and not on the child's. If the parent dies, the child will receive the funds for such things as college education. Because a child's premium is fairly low, an insurance agent may suggest that an insurance policy will protect the insurability of the child in case he or she becomes chronically ill in the future. While this is true, the fact is that only 1.5 percent of applicants of all ages are denied insurance coverage for ill health. Consider buying your children life insurance only once your life is insured and your other needs are already met.

Life Insurance: Naming a Minor as a Beneficiary

Recently an agent had a client who unexpectedly died. There were two policies involved and the agent had the opportunity to work with the surviving spouse to help her invest the proceeds. During the discussions it was determined that a minor child was named as a primary beneficiary for part of the proceeds in one of the policies (not sold by this agent).

The mother of the minor child was under the impression she would receive the monies outright on behalf of the child. In this case or in any situation where a minor is named as a primary beneficiary, the insurance company will not pay a death benefit directly to a minor because of the risk of double liability. Before the proceeds can be paid, a probate court must appoint a guardian of the minor's property before the insurance company will pay the death benefit.

A living parent is not a guardian of the child's property without court appointment. To avoid any delays in having life insurance proceeds paid to a minor child who is named as a primary beneficiary, the beneficiary designation should name a custodian on behalf of the minor child in accordance with the resident state's Uniform Gift to Minors Act or Uniform Transfers to Minors Act. For example state: Mary Jane, custodian under the Maryland UTMA for Baby Jane.

Another solution is to set up a trust and name the trust as the recipient of the life insurance proceeds. A great deal of flexibility can be built into the trust and you can sidestep a number of legal restrictions imposed on outright distributions to minors. This is a safer and surer way to provide financial security for those who can't or don't want to handle large sums of money or other assets.

Choosing a Life Insurance Company

There are important criteria to consider when choosing a company for your insurance or annuity needs. You want a strong and secure company to meet your long time financial goals. You also want a company with significant experience, a good reputation, strong ratings, and a high quality investment portfolio. The three key factors to look at are:

1. Experience and reputation
2. Independent rating services evaluation
3. High quality investment portfolio (and philosophy!)

Your relationship with a life insurance company will likely last many years. Therefore you want to make sure that the company will be there when you have a claim or are ready to retire. Consider how long the company has been in business and how the company has fared in difficult economic times. Look for a company known for its integrity, financial stability, and timeliness in claims payment and service.

Several major rating services evaluate the claims paying ability and financial strength of insurance companies. The following companies are experts in analyzing insurance companies and are familiar with the various companies' strategies and management.

A.M. Best Company

A.M. Best profiles hundreds of life insurance and annuity companies, rates their financial condition, and lists the states in which they are licensed to do business. Because A.M. Best rates 3,800 insurance companies, it can provide an effective measure of a company's standing among its peers. A. M. Best Co., Inc., A.M. Best Road, Holdwick, NJ 08858. Telephone: 908-439-2200. Web site: www.ambest.com.

Standard & Poor Corporation

S & P has rated the claims paying ability of insurance companies since 1971. Their ratings show how a company can meet its obligations both now and in the future. The ratings range from AAA to C. Standard & Poor Corporation, 25 Broadway, New York, NY 10004. Telephone: 212-208-8000. Web site: www.standardandpoors.com/ratings.

Duff and Phelps Credit Rating Company

Duff and Phelps combines quantitative and qualitative analysis. The key factors it examines include the amount of surplus, profitability, and asset quality. This service also considers meetings with company managers highly important. These sessions measure top managers' experience and goals as well as their ability to match investments with obligations. Duff and Phelps Credit Rating Company, 55 East Monroe Street, Chicago, IL 60603. Telephone: 312-368-3131. Web site: www.dcrco.com.

Moody's Investor Service, Inc.

Moody's rates an insurer's credit quality. As such, the ratings are Moody's opinion of the ability of an insurance company to repay policyholder obligations and claims punctually. This service makes an effort to consider future worse case scenarios in assigning ratings. Moody's also includes quantitative as well as qualitative factors in its ratings. Moody's Investor Service Inc., 99 Church Street, New York, NY 10007. Telephone: 212-553-0300. Web site: www.moodys.com.

Weiss Research, Inc.

Weiss has evaluated insurance companies since 1989. To arrive at its ratings, Weiss uses numbers available through state insurance regulatory departments. It does not evaluate the management strength of a company. This service only considers the numbers as indicators of the company's ability to weather a deep recession. Weiss Research, Inc., 4176 Burns Road, Palm Beach Gardens, FL 33410. Telephone: 800-289-9222.

If you have difficulty finding the ratings for various insurance companies, a publication called *The Best's Agent Guide to Life Insurance Companies* is available in most libraries. This publication lists the phone numbers, many of them 800 numbers, for almost every company doing business in the United States. Most companies will provide their ratings information when you call them. They will even send you literature about the rating services and how their company stacks up in the overall rating from each particular service.

Other sources for additional information include these industry organizations:

- The American Council of Life Insurance, 1001 Pennsylvania Avenue NW, Washington, DC 20004. Telephone: 202-624-2000. Web site: www.acli.com.
- The National Association of Insurance Commissioners, Suite 1100, 120 West 12th Street, Kansas City, MO 64105. Telephone: 816-842-3600.
- The National Association of Life Underwriters, 1922 F Street NW, Washington, D.C. 20006. Telephone: 202-331-6000. Web site: www.agentsonline.com.

Your state's insurance department is also a good source of information.

The Medical Information Bureau

The Medical Information Bureau (MIB) is a nonprofit association that was created by and for insurance companies to protect against fraud by sharing information among member companies. When you apply for life, health, or disability insurance, you are usually asked to sign an authorization granting the insurance company broad access to medical information about you including information from your doctor or hospital. This information, together with the results of the company's investigations such as the results of a physical exam, are submitted to the MIB. The MIB has records on approximately 13 million people.

The insurance company compares the information provided by you with the information in the MIB. If the two are not consistent, the insurer will seek clarification from you or other sources. Thus, it is in your interest to ensure that MIB information concerning you is accurate. If you have not applied for health, life, or disability insurance in the last seven years, MIB should no longer have any information concerning you because information is only kept for seven years. The MIB maintains an Insurance Activity Index which is a report by each member company of all applications for the purchase of life insurance. The file is kept for two years so a company can check to see if you have applied for other life insurance during that period. If you apply for several policies within a short time, the activity may cause a company to question why you need so much insurance and/or question your health.

If you want to obtain a copy of your record, contact MIB at 617-426-3660 and ask for the proper form. You can also mail a request for the form to MIB, P.O. Box 105, Essex Station, Boston, MA 02112. If you find incorrect information in your record, you can request a reinvestigation by the insurer that provided the wrong information. You should also send a statement from your physician setting forth the correct information. If the MIB agrees, the information will be corrected. If they continue to list the inaccurate information, you have the right to have a statement included in your file.

DISABILITY INCOME INSURANCE

Most widowed persons and heirs don't give much thought to what they'd do if a disabling illness or accident were to stop them from earning a living. If you work and you become permanently disabled, your income would be substantially reduced. Your cost of living, however, would remain the same and might even increase.

For the younger widow or heir of about age 35, the chances of becoming disabled for three months or more is nearly three times as great as the chance of dying. At age 50, the odds are nearly four times as great. The greatest financial asset you have is your ability to generate an income. One of the most frightening situations is the loss of your ability to work for an extended period of time. Consequently, it is important to consider the financial consequences if your income is shut off as a result of a disability.

Note:

Unless you have enough income producing assets, disability insurance is a definite necessity for financial security. Income is required for basic needs—food, clothing, shelter, and the medical expenses connected with a disability.

In choosing a disability policy look for these seven features:

1. Noncancelable and guaranteed renewability
2. Monthly benefits that will replace 60 to 70 percent of your income until age 65
3. A cost-of-living adjustment rider which will protect the benefits from inflation
4. A future insurability option to increase insurance as your income rises, regardless of your health
5. A policy that eliminates premium payments while you are disabled, called a waiver of premium feature
6. A residual benefits clause which allows partial payouts for partial disabilities
7. A waiting period that will match your ability to pay for the policy along with your income needs (i.e., how long you can last before disability payments need to begin)

Group Disability Insurance

Your employer may provide protection for short-term illnesses or accidents. This type of coverage normally commences on the first or fourteenth day of your recovery and continues for 13 or 26 weeks. Employers may also provide long-term coverage with benefits to age 65. Both of these plans may have rigid definitions of disability and may be more difficult for you to collect on than private policies.

Group plans typically cover no more than 60 percent of your salary. If the employer pays the premiums, you can be taxed on the benefits. Disability insurance benefits are not taxable, though, if you pay the premiums.

HEALTH CARE INSURANCE COVERAGE

Health care insurance coverage is an essential element in maximizing your inheritance. Without adequate health care insurance, all of your financial accomplishments and goals could easily be wiped out. Health care insurance coverage is a necessary part of financial planning. Not only is it a way to meet the cost of illness and injury, but coverage is a vehicle to protect your existing assets and financial plans.

Types of Health Care Coverage

There are a wide variety of health care insurance products from which to choose including hospital, surgery expense, physician expense, major medical, comprehensive major medical, and dental policies. Understanding the basics of the various types of policies will make your choices easier. Following is a brief description of the types of health care coverage as well as terms used with medical insurance plans.

Hospital Insurance

Hospital insurance policies provide you with reimbursement covering the cost of hospital room and board and other expenses incidental to hospitalization. Basically, hospital insurance pays for a portion of the per day semiprivate hospital room and board charges which typically include floor nursing and other routine services. Additional expenses such as operating room, laboratory tests, X-rays, and medications you need while in the hospital are also covered.

Many hospital plans also offer reimbursement for some outpatient and out-of-hospital services. In most policies, hospital insurance is written to provide daily semiprivate room and board charges up to a specified number of days such as 90, 120, or 360. The maximum reimbursement for the added expenses, however, may be a stated dollar amount or a multiple of the daily room rate.

Surgical Expense Insurance

Surgical expense insurance provides insurance for the cost of surgery in or out of the hospital. Typically, a list of scheduled benefits is provided which states the dollar amount the insurer is required to pay for each surgical procedure.

Second Surgical Opinion

Most surgical expense plans fully cover the cost of a second surgical opinion. Some group health plans even require second opinions on specific procedures. Without second opinions, these health plans may reduce the surgical benefit they pay to you.

Physician Expense Insurance

Physician expense insurance, also called regular medical expense insurance, covers physician fees for nonsurgical care in a hospital, including consultations with specialists. Also covered are X-rays and laboratory tests performed outside of the hospital. These plans usually provide the maximum amount payable as listed on a scheduled list.

Major Medical Insurance

Major medical plans provide benefits for nearly all types of medical expenses resulting from either illness or accident. The amounts that you can collect under these policies are relatively large. Lifetime benefits of $100,000 to $1 million are common. Some policies have no limits at all.

Deductibles

Because major medical plans are designed to supplement basic hospital, surgical, and physicians expense policies they frequently include deductibles of $500 to $1000. Many plans currently offer an all-inclusive deductible for the calendar year. This allows a person to accumulate the deductible for more than one incident. In some plans, the deductible is on a per accident or per illness basis.

Coinsurance

This provision stipulates that the company will pay some portion, say, 70, 80, or 90 percent, of the covered amount of loss over the deductible rather than paying the entire amount. Because major medical limits now go up to $1 million or more, many plans have a stop-loss provision which places a cap on the amount of participation required. Without this feature a $1 million medical bill could still leave the insured with a large coinsurance cost.

Internal Limits

Most major medical plans are written with internal limits. Internal limits place boundaries on the amounts that are paid for certain expenses even if the overall policy limits are not exceeded by a particular claim.

Comprehensive Major Medical Insurance

A comprehensive major medical insurance policy combines basic hospital, surgical, and physicians expense policies with major medical protection in a single policy. The deductibles under a comprehensive major medical plan are usually low, often $100 or less. Most of these plans have a more favorable coinsurance clause than major medical policies and they may require no coinsurance on basic hospital expense claims.

Dental Insurance

Some employers offer dental insurance through group policies. Dental insurance usually covers necessary dental health care as well as some dental injuries sustained through accidents. Dental work is covered under most policies, but policies vary greatly. Some dental plans contain deductible and coinsurance provisions. Others have first dollar protection and pay for all claims. Premiums are often large in light of the dollar amount of coverages paid.

MediGap Policies

In 1990, Congress passed a new law which requires all states to comply with certain standards for MediGap insurance with supplements to Medicare coverage. The new law protects consumers by restricting certain sales practices of insurance agencies and companies. It also simplifies policies by limiting the types of plans that can be sold and specifying exactly what benefits each plan must contain. A detailed list of coverages is available from your local Medicare office.

AUTOMOBILE INSURANCE

If you own an automobile, you need auto insurance. In most states you can't drive without it. The following are the seven types of coverage which all auto insurers offer. You need to understand them before you make any decisions on buying automobile insurance or changing your existing policy.

1. *Bodily injury/liability injury.* If you are involved in an accident which kills or hurts other people, this part of your auto insurance covers legal costs and legal liability. You need to have this coverage. If you live in a no-fault state, you need less liability coverage because each insurance company pays for an accident regardless of fault. If you can afford it, you should carry a minimum of $100,000. If you have substantial assets, carry a minimum of $300,000. Supplement this policy with an umbrella policy. An umbrella liability policy adds coverage over the existing liability coverage you have with your automobile policy. This normally can be added very cheaply. (See Liability Insurance.)

2. *Collision coverage.* This coverage pays for the cost of repairing your car. Collision insurance is usually the largest part of your automobile insurance premium. However, the higher your deductible, the lower your cost. Please remember that insurance companies will pay only market or book value for your car. As your car ages less will be paid to fix it. Also, if you *total* the car, i.e., it is a complete loss, you may not receive enough cash back to buy a comparable car to replace it.

3. *Comprehensive coverage.* This includes theft, broken glass, vandalism, fire, flood, or other acts of God.

4. *Medical payments coverage.* This pays for doctor and hospital bills that result from an accident. Both you and your passengers are covered.

5. *Property damage liability.* This part of your policy pays for property damage caused by you while driving your car. For example, if you run into somebody's store, you are protected. You need to have at least $50,000 of property damage coverage.

6. *Uninsured motorists coverage.* Although it is against the law in most states to drive without automobile insurance, some people do. This insurance will protect you and your passengers if the other driver is uninsured or if you are the victim of a hit and run accident. It covers medical expenses, loss of wages, and pain and suffering.

7. *Underinsured motorists coverage.* If you are in an accident which is somebody else's fault and that person is underinsured, this part of your policy will cover the difference for liability claims.

Some cars are expensive to insure and insurance companies know which cars have a high vulnerability to theft or mechanical breakdowns or are expensive to repair. Before buying any car, check out the cost of a policy on it.

Premium discounts are often available for factors such as good driving record, multicar coverage, mature driver, antitheft devices, defensive driving courses passed, restrictive mileage usage, nonsmoker, and certain rural locations. Also included are discounts for seat belts or air bags. These discounts can add up to substantial savings, so be sure to ask your agent about them. Note, also, that if someone else is driving your car with your permission, your insurance coverage will normally cover everything as if you were driving.

HOMEOWNERS INSURANCE

Whether you are a renter or a homeowner, you need to understand what homeowners insurance can provide for you. Homeowners insurance usually covers much more than fire damage. Other coverage includes:

- Damage to your home or additional structures
- Liability for which you or your family are responsible, usually anywhere in the world
- Damage and theft to any of your property except, perhaps, your car
- Living expenses while your house is being repaired due to fire or some other catastrophe
- Injury to someone on your property

In covering your home, make certain that you insure for the replacement value of your home, not the fair market value. This is important even for a partial loss. Often your home needs to be insured for at least 80 percent of its replacement value for you to recover the full amount of a partial loss by fire or other casualty.

If your home is insured for less than 80 percent of the replacement value, you effectively become a coinsurer. Consider this example of Linda Smith who had a major fire in one of her bedrooms.

Replacement value of home	$250,000
Fire policy limit of current policy	150,000
Damages resulting from bedroom fire	40,000
Insurance company pays	24,000
Linda pays	16,000

Because Linda was covered for only 60 percent of the replacement value of her home ($150,000) rather than 80 percent ($200,000) she became the coinsurer for 40 percent of the loss. Therefore, she was responsible for $16,000 in damages. Had she insured for 80 percent of the replacement value, her insurance would have covered the full $40,000 less any deductible.

Protection of Personal Items

One of the quickest ways to ensure that your personal and valuable items will be protected is to take color snap shots of each room and its contents. Be sure to take close-ups of valuables including art, china, silver, and glassware. You will want to have a written and photographic inventory to keep in your safe-deposit box.

Using a videotape is a good idea if you can sequence the date. For example, hold up a newspaper and make sure the date on the newspaper is legible. Also check with your insurer to see if discounts are available for smoke alarms, senior citizens, burglar alarms, nonsmokers, or sprinkler systems.

If you have items of value that you would like to have appraised but can't find an appraiser, contact the American Society of Appraisers, P.O. Box 17265, Washington, D.C. 20041. Telephone: 703-478-2228. Ask for a free directory of Certified Professional Personal Property Advisors and include a self-addressed stamped envelope.

LIABILITY UMBRELLA INSURANCE

The diversity of activities in which people now engage sometimes exceeds the limits of coverage for the policies discussed so far. Hence, the insurance industry has developed an umbrella policy that provides a broader scope of coverage with higher limits of liability than normally encountered. The purpose of a liability umbrella policy is to provide excess liability coverage over and above what are referred to as the underlying limits.

The liability umbrella policy has two deductibles. The first deductible constitutes the limits of the underlying auto and personal liability policies. The second deductible, usually $250, covers any liability exposures beyond the scope of the underlying policies.

How much liability coverage is enough? Most insurance advisors agree that insurance is a very personal question. Look at what you can afford to pay and what assets you want to protect. You need to carry at least enough coverage to protect your total net worth.

It's an unfortunate aspect of our society today that if you are particularly successful or visible in your community, you are more likely to be sued and have to pay higher damage awards. Financial visibility greatly increases your risk. Therefore, you may want to increase coverage to protect the value of major assets such as your home or investment portfolio.

Liability rates vary from state to state. It may be cheaper for you to increase coverage with a $1 million dollar umbrella policy than to significantly increase the limits on your existing homeowners and auto policies. In most states, you can expect to pay at least $200 a year for a $1 million umbrella policy.

While the insurance industry may change dramatically in the years ahead, your need for insurance protection remains. Deal only with the most stable companies that are highly rated and easily accessible by phone and mail. Ignore the rest.

PART THREE

Ensuing Concerns

CHAPTER 10

You and
Your Home

Home ownership is part of the American dream. However, as a widowed person or inheritor the American dream may not look so wonderful to you at this point in your life because of pressures from family and friends. You may feel a lot of anxiety about home ownership. You may be wondering if you can take care of the property, if you should sell and buy a smaller home. You may be wondering if this is the right place for you to live if you have smaller children.

This chapter will help you decide whether to sell your property, buy another one, or just stay where you are. Also, it will enable you to take a look at refinancing and trade-offs between being a renter and an owner of real estate. It will also cover your home's stepped-up capital gains tax basis, housing alternatives, reverse mortgages, home repairs, and if you should rent or sell your property to your children.

TAX ADVANTAGES OF OWNING YOUR OWN HOME

There are many reasons to own your home, the best being tax advantages. Here are six tax-related reasons for home ownership:

1. The interest you pay on the mortgage for your home is tax deductible. Today you can carry up to $1 million in debt on your primary residence and as much as $100,000 on a second home.

2. A new law repeals the rule that allowed you to shelter profits from the sale of your home by rolling them into a more expensive home. Also gone is the $125,000 capital gain exclusion. In its place is a new provision that allows a couple of any age to pocket as much as $500,000 in profit tax free from the sale of a primary residence as often as every two years (if they lived in the house for at least two of the last five years). Single taxpayers can pocket up to $250,000.

3. Paying the mortgage helps you build equity. Each month a portion of your mortgage payment goes toward paying off the principal of your loan.

4. If you are an older person who might be faced with unfunded long-term-care needs, you will be happy to know that in many states your home is exempt when trying to qualify for Medicaid benefits.

5. Depending on the state you live in, your home will provide varying degrees of protection from creditors.

6. In the event of your death, all unpaid taxes on the appreciation of your home are forgiven, as is the portion of the house that was owned by your spouse.

As you can see, there are many advantages of home ownership. Your decision to buy, sell, rent, or keep your home should be made only after careful consideration. If you stay in your house, the following sections cover some areas to consider.

SHOULD I REFINANCE?

Before you decide to refinance you need to take a close look at your current financial picture. Don't refinance because everyone else is doing it or because friends and relatives say you should. Seriously consider refinancing your home to consolidate expensive debt (getting rid of mounting credit card charges, for example) and/or to improve your cash flow. If you plan to move in a few years, it won't pay to refinance or get a home equity loan because of the closing costs you will incur.

Is refinancing a good move for you? It depends on various factors including:

- upfront costs;
- how long you anticipate remaining in your home;
- the amount you plan to refinance; and
- the difference in interest rates between your existing mortgage and a new mortgage.

A good measure of whether or not refinancing is advantageous for you is to determine how long it will take you to recoup the costs. Refinancing a mortgage involves paying closing costs, which include appraisal fees, legal fees, and in most instances, a loan origination fee.

The origination fee, commonly referred to as *points*, is based on a percentage of the amount you refinance and can represent a substantial expense. For example, refinancing a $100,000 mortgage at three points will cost you $3,000 in points alone.

Another cost to consider is the possible payment of a penalty if you pay off a loan early. Also, opportunity costs need to be recognized. These costs equal the forfeited investment income on monies used to pay for the refinancing. In other words, if you pay $4,000 in refinancing costs, you have to realize the $4,000 could have been invested, earning income for you. Therefore, analyze the potential monthly savings very carefully.

Rules for Deducting Mortgage Interest

Interest on mortgage loans (including home equity loans) that are secured by your main or second home is generally deductible in any of the following situations:

- Loans (regardless of amount) incurred on or before October 13, 1987, that have not been increased since that date.
- Loans of $500,000 or less (for a single person) where the loan proceeds were used to buy, build, or substantially improve your home.
- The proceeds of the loans were not used as listed directly above, but are equal to or less than $50,000 (for a single person).

Mortgage Refinancing Analysis

In Figure 10.1, you can see that Alice can replace her current mortgage balance of $113,900 (at 10 percent for 30 years) with a new

FIGURE 10.1

Item	Description	Alice	You
1	Current monthly payment (principal and interest)	$ 1000	_____
2	Anticipated additional years in house	10	_____
3	Additional months in house (item 2 × 12)	120	_____
4	Total payment (item 1 × item 3)	120,000	_____
5	New mortgage payment	804	_____
6	New total payment (item 3 × item 5)	96,400	_____
7	Potential savings (item 4 − item 6)	23,520	_____
8	Prepayment penalty on current mortgage	0	_____
9	Closings costs on new mortgage	4,000	_____
10	Refinancing cost (item 8 + item 9)	4,000	_____
11	Total savings (item 7 − item 10)	19,520	_____
12	Monthly savings (item 1 − item 5)	162	_____
13	Months to break even (item 10 ÷ item 12)	24.6	_____

7.5 percent, 30-year loan. The breakeven point is 24.6 months. You can use the extra column in Figure 10.1 to analyze refinancing your own mortgage.

Refinancing an existing mortgage can significantly alter your cash flow, lower your taxes, and save you thousands of dollars in the long run. Tradition follows that the interest rate on a new mortgage should be 2 percent lower than the interest rate on the existing mortgage for refinancing to be favorable. However, do not take 2 percent as the ultimate rule as a basis for a final decision. If your new mortgage payments are lower, you must keep the house long enough to recover closing costs in order to break even.

Choosing a Mortgage Broker

Whether you are shopping for a new mortgage or refinancing your current one, a good mortgage broker can ease the hassle of shopping for a mortgage. The quality of mortgage brokers varies widely. Picking the wrong one can be an exercise in futility. Here are five questions to ask when selecting a mortgage broker:

1. *How many lenders does the broker represent?* Good mortgage brokers generally represent at least ten lenders from different areas of the country so they can shop nationwide to help you get the best deal. However, local lenders know your area best and you may get the better deal through them.

2. *What percentage of loans are actually funded?* For a typical mortgage company, 70 percent or more of the applications submitted to lenders should lead to closing.

3. *What references do you have from real estate agencies and banks?* Find out if the broker has been in business for at least two years.

4. *If your state requires that mortgage brokers be licensed, is the broker licensed?* Also, check with the licensing authorities to see if any complaints about the broker have been made.

5. *Can you get a written estimate of closing costs?* Most brokers will give you a written closing cost estimate, justifying every expense. Keep in mind these brokers typically get paid by the lender for originating the loan. About 80 percent of their income comes from origination fees and other commissions paid by the lender. In many areas, borrowers pay up front application fees that range from $300 to $500 and at closing they pay processing and document preparation fees to the lender.

REVERSE MORTGAGES

Reverse mortgages literally are mortgage loans that work backwards. They also go against most of the traditional principles of lending practice. Under a reverse mortgage, instead of sending a check to the lender every month to pay interest and reduce debt, you receive a check every month from the lender and the debt increases. Reverse mortgages vary from lender to lender but most have several characteristics in common. First, they are generally available only to senior citizens including widowed persons. Depending on the lender, a senior may be between 62 to 70 years of age and own his or her own home with little or no debt. This type of loan is either a term loan (based on the life expectancy of the homeowner or a certain period) or a line of credit.

The amount of the monthly payout you'll receive depends on the term of the loan, interest rates, the value of the home, and the percentage of current equity eligible to be loaned out. With a line of credit arrangement there is no monthly check; you simply tap the line of credit for cash whenever needed. Generally, the loan is not repaid until the house is sold or the borrower dies. The risks to the lender are obvious. With a loan based on life expectancy, the loan could eventually amount to more than is recoverable on the sale of your house. Also, there is no current cash inflow to the lender. Given these and other disadvantages, it's no wonder that lenders have not been flocking to offer reverse mortgages.

The risk to you, the homeowner, is also clear. The loan will eat away the value of your home and could wipe it out entirely. Deciding on a reverse mortgage is a serious step and often requires expert assistance. The advantages and disadvantages need to be carefully weighed before a lifetime commitment is made.

Two excellent resources are:

1. AARP's free Home Equity Conversion Information Kit. It includes a state-by-state reverse mortgage lenders list (excluding Alaska, South Dakota, and Texas) that lists more than 125 lenders, an overview of home equity conversion and reverse mortgages, and a guide to risks and benefits. Address a postcard to Home Equity Conversion Kit (D15601), AARP Home Equity Information Center EE0756, 601 E Street NW, Washington, DC 20049.

2. *Your New Retirement Nest Egg: A Consumer Guide to the New Reverse Mortgages* by Ken Scholen (National Center for Home Equity Conversion, 1995). Compares reverse mortgages including cash benefits, total loan costs, and leftover equity. NCHEC, 7373 147th Street W, Apple Valley, MN 55124.

IF YOU DECIDE TO SELL

Where to Live After the Sale

The first step in selling your house is deciding where to live once it's sold. Everyone's housing needs differ. Some people prefer quiet and privacy, while others like the hustle and bustle of big city life. Many want to live within walking distance of work, shopping, and restaurants. Others don't mind 45-minute drives. Most everyone wants to be near their friends. Because you have your own unique set of likes and dislikes, the best way to start your search is to list your needs. Classify them according to whether they are essential, desirable, or merely a plus. Such a classification is important for three reasons:

1. This procedure screens out housing that will not meet your minimum requirements.
2. It helps you recognize that you may have to make trade-offs because you will seldom find the perfect property that will meet all of your needs.
3. It can help you focus on those needs that you are willing and able to pay for.

In addition to single-family homes, townhouses, and patio homes, you might wish to consider manufactured homes. These are factory-produced housing units that are transported to a desired location. You can place them on either a permanent or temporary foundation, connect them to utilities, and use them as a residence. Because these homes were once more mobile than they are today, they used to be called mobile homes. Depending on size and features, their costs can range anywhere from $10,000 to $70,000.

You may also wish to consider condominiums. With a condominium, you own your own unit, arrange the financing, pay taxes, and pay for maintenance and building services. Typically you are assessed a monthly amount sufficient to cover your proportionate share of the costs of maintaining the common facilities. The cost of condominiums is generally lower than single-family detached houses. They tend to be built with more efficient land use and lower construction costs. Also, many existing apartment projects have gone through condo conversions. In effect, the apartments have been converted from rental to occupant-owned units.

Before You Buy a Condo

In the long run it pays to carefully check out the various operating and occupancy features of a condo before you buy. You should:

- Thoroughly investigate the reputation of the developer through local real estate brokers, banks, or the better business bureau, whether the building is brand new, under construction, or being converted.

- Read the rules of the organization.
- Investigate the condo government association, the restrictions on condo owners, and the quality of the property management.
- Check the construction of the building and its physical condition. If the building is being converted to condos, ask to see an independent inspection firm's report on the building's condition.
- Insist that any future changes in the building be put in writing.
- Ask occupants if they are satisfied with the living conditions.
- Determine how many units are rented; generally, owner-occupied units are better maintained.
- Determine if there is sufficient parking space.
- Watch for unusually low maintenance fees that will probably be increased soon.
- Consider the resale value. This was especially important in the mid-1980s when many condo units were impossible to sell without sharp price reductions.
- Compare the projected monthly assessment fees with those on similar buildings already in operation.

Another housing option to consider is cooperative apartments. These are apartment buildings in which each tenant owns a share of the corporation that owns the building and is known as a cooperative apartment, or co-op. You lease your unit from the corporation and are assessed monthly amounts in proportion to your ownership share. This proportion is based on the amount of space you occupy in the building.

Assessments cover the cost of service, maintenance, taxes, and mortgages on the entire building. Notice, though, that they are subject to change depending on the actual building operation costs and the corporation's policies. Most policies are determined by the board of directors. Because cooperative apartments are not profit motivated, monthly assessments are likely to be lower than rent on similar accommodations. Also, you, as a cooperative owner, receive tax benefits resulting from property taxes attributable to your proportion of ownership interest.

Tax Consequences

The second step in selling your home is to know the tax consequences. The sale of your home, like the sale of any other asset, creates taxable gain to the extent the net sales price exceeds your tax basis in the home (generally the cost of the home plus the cost of improvements you made to it).

Under the old laws, a home sale was eligible for two different tax breaks if it was your principal residence. First, tax on the gain was postponed indefinitely if you spent the proceeds on a new principal residence within two years before or after the sale. Second, if you were at least 55 years of age, you had a one time opportunity to exclude up to $125,000 of the gain on the sale of a home you had used as your principal residence for at least three of the five years before the sale.

A new law replaces these and allows you a tax-free gain of up to $250,000 ($500,000 for married couples) on the sale of your home. To qualify, you must have owned the home and used it as your principal residence at various times totaling at least two years out of the five years before the sale. If you used a prior two-year rollover when you bought your current home to defer any gain on the sale of your prior home, your ownership and use periods for the current home include those of the prior home, as well as those for all other homes for which you also used the two-year rollover. This means that you may be eligible to use the new rule right now. This exclusion can be used as often as you qualify for it, up to a maximum frequency of once every two years. Sales before May 7, 1997, are not counted in determining whether you have sold a home in the prior two years. If you can't meet the two-year residency rule because of unforeseen events such as a job change or a health problem, you can still exclude from your income the part of your gain that corresponds to the time you did spend residing in the home. For example, if for these reasons you resided in the home for only 18 months and sold it for a profit of $200,000, you would have to pay tax on only $50,000 of the $200,000 [$(18 \div 24) \times \$200,000 = \$150,000$ exclusion].

If a spouse is deceased on the sale date of the marital home, the surviving spouse may count toward ownership any period that the deceased spouse owned and used the home in his name only. This new law repeals the two-year rollover and age exclusions.

Other features of this new tax law include:

- It applies to co-ops as well as real estate you own outright, such as houses and condominiums.
- You can elect not to use the exclusion and pay tax on the gain. This could be advantageous if, for example, your overall tax bill

is low despite the gain, and you want to increase the tax basis of your new home.

- If your home is subjected to an involuntary conversion, that is, it is destroyed by fire or other disaster, or bought by the state against your will, the home is considered sold. You can still use the tax breaks available for involuntary conversions to the extent all of the gain is not covered by this provision, and your periods of ownership and use of the prior home before the involuntary conversion are counted toward your ownership and use of the home you replace it with.

- If you become incapacitated and require inpatient care at a licensed facility, including a nursing home, your use of the home as a principal residence during the five years before the sale need total only one year.

HAVING YOUR CAKE AND EATING IT TOO: THE LIFE ESTATE

Many times surviving spouses are advised by well-meaning relatives, lawyers, CPAs, or friends to give their house away to a child or children to protect their assets. However, there is a catch. If you give your home to your children, or anyone, their cost basis for tax purposes is what you originally paid for the house plus the stepped-up basis of your spouses' share at his or her death.

Let's say the house is worth $150,000 on the date you make the gift, but you originally only paid $50,000 for your house. When they sell the house your children would owe taxes on the value that is over $50,000. If they sell the house for $200,000, they will pay taxes on $150,000. A better option, especially if your total estate is less than $650,000, is a life estate. Using a life estate you can gift your house to your children (or anyone), live in it for the rest of your life, and provide the recipient with a big tax break. And it costs very little to do.

A life estate lets you continue to live in your home for the rest of your life. How? You set up what is called a lifetime tenancy which expires at your death. At that time, the house will belong to your heirs and they will have the tax advantage.

For example, Martha, a 63-year-old widow, has two adult children, Beth and Allan. Martha's $300,000 assets include her $150,000 home and other investments and personal items worth $150,000. She wants her children to receive the assets when she dies but is concerned that the home might have to be sold to pay nursing home costs in the future.

Instead of gifting the house now and creating a future tax problem for Beth and Allan, she can give them the *remainder interest* in her house (they will receive the house at her death) while Martha keeps a life estate. The overall benefits are many:

- There is no probate of the house at Martha's death.
- The life estate is easy and fairly inexpensive to set up. An attorney prepares a deed that transfers the remainder interest to the children while Martha retains a life estate.
- Martha can live in the house the rest of her life, even if her children sell their remainder interest before she dies.
- Thirty-six months following the date that Martha makes the life estate, the value of her house is no longer counted as her asset for Medicaid purposes.
- At Martha's death the children's cost basis is stepped up to its value on the date of Martha's death.

There are also tax ramifications of a life estate:

- The gift of the house to the children will immediately reduce Martha's lifetime estate and gift exclusion by $130,000 (the $150,000 fair market value of the home less the $10,000 annual gift she is permitted to give each child).
- The value of Martha's home at her death will be included in her gross estate for estate tax purposes.

Note:

Because of the way a life estate is taxed (i.e., the entire value of your house is included in your taxable estate and therefore subject to estate tax) this strategy works best if your estate is less than $650,000 (for 1999).

IF YOU DECIDE TO BUY

Let's reverse gears now and look at what you need to know if you're thinking of buying a home.

Buying a home usually requires a good deal of time and effort. Learning about available properties and their prices requires a systematic search and careful property analysis. Most people who shop the housing market rely on real estate agents for information, access to properties, and advice. Other sources of information, such as newspaper ads, are also used extensively to identify available properties. If you need a particular specialized type of property or know exactly what you want, you may wish to advertise your needs and wait for the sellers to contact you.

Most buyers rely on real estate agents because of their daily contact with the housing market. When using an agent, describe your needs explicitly so your agent can begin a search for the appropriate property. Agents will also help you negotiate with the seller and obtain satisfactory financing. Though not empowered to give legal advice, they may still help you prepare your real estate sales contract.

Most real estate firms belong to a local multiple listing service (MLS). An MLS compiles a list of properties for sale from information provided by the member firms in a given community or area. Brief descriptions of each property and its asking price are included. The list is updated weekly. As a rule, it is best to deal with a real estate agent who works for MLS member firms; otherwise you might lack access to a large part of the market.

You, as a buyer, need to remember that agents are typically employed by sellers. Unless you are using a buyer's agent, the agent's primary responsibility is to sell listed properties at the best possible prices. Also, because agents are paid only if they make a sale, some might pressure you to sign right away or miss the chance of a lifetime. Avoid that type of agent!

Select an agent who will work hard to match you with the property you want. Good agents recognize that their best interests are served when all parties to the transaction are satisfied. It needs to be a win-win situation.

Real estate commissions usually range from 5 to 7 percent. Such commissions are normally paid by the seller but are entirely negotiable.

Obtaining a Mortgage

If you have made the decision to buy a home, you may need to look at different types of mortgage loans. A fixed-rate mortgage is still the most popular and accounts for a major percentage of all home mortgages. With a fixed-rate mortgage, both the rate of interest and the monthly mortgage payment are fixed over the full term of the loan. The most common is the 30-year fixed-rate loan. Yet, because of the lender's assumed risk, it is usually the most expensive form of home financing.

A variation of this standard fixed-rate loan rapidly gaining popularity is the 15-year fixed-rate mortgage. Its chief appeal is that it is paid twice as fast, 15 years versus 30, yet the monthly payments are not significantly larger. The monthly payment on a 15-year loan is generally only about 10 to 20 percent larger than the payment on a 30-year loan. This brings you substantial savings on the mortgage.

For example, let's assume that you have a $100,000 loan with an 8 percent fixed rate of interest. For the 30-year loan, the regular payment would be $733 per month. The payments over the life of the loan would total $264,155. With a 15-year fixed-rate loan, the monthly payment is $955, which results in the total payment over the life of the loan of $172,117. This is a savings of $92,137.

Adjustable-Rate Mortgage

Another popular form of home loan is the adjustable rate mortgage, referred to as an ARM. Unlike the fixed-rate mortgage, the rate of interest, and therefore the size of the monthly payment, is adjusted in line with movements of market interest rates. The rate of interest on the mortgage is linked to a specific interest rate index and is adjusted at specific intervals (usually once a year) as the index changes.

When the index moves up, so does the rate of interest on the mortgage and in turn the size of the monthly mortgage payment. The new interest rate and the monthly mortgage payment will then remain fixed until the next adjustment date when the adjustment process is repeated.

There are many features of an ARM to consider. One is called the adjustment period—the time between one rate payment change and the next. Another feature is the index rate, which is used to measure the movement in interest rates. Many indices use an interest rate that is based on the behavior of one-year U.S. Treasury securities, but there are many other indices. Check which index your particular loan company uses.

Watch the interest rate ceilings (or caps). They place a limit on the amount the interest rate can be increased over a given period. Usually two kinds of interest rate caps apply: (1) a periodic cap that limits the interest rate from one adjustment period to the next; and (2) an overall cap that limits the interest rate increase over the life of the loan. Many ARMs have both a periodic and an overall interest rate cap.

If you do use an ARM, be aware of negative amortization. This is an increase in the principal balance because the monthly loan payments are lower than the amount of monthly interest being charged. In other words, you can wind up with a mortgage balance on the next loan anniversary larger than the last.

Another form of loan is called a convertible ARM. This is a loan that allows borrowers to convert from an adjustable rate to a fixed rate loan, usually at some time between the 13th and 60th month. A fee is usually charged to make the conversion to a fixed rate loan.

THE OPTION OF RENTING

After seriously considering buying a new home or maintaining an existing home, many widowed persons or inheritors find that they do not want the additional responsibilities associated with home ownership. Take Mary Beth for example. Almost all of her money comes from tax-free bonds. Her exemptions provide her with a total of $6,350 in deductions per year so she pays very little in taxes. A mortgage interest deduction would not help her much, if at all. She became tired of the responsibilities of ownership and decided to rent an apartment. Several of her friends live in the building or nearby so renting made sense for her. While she can't control the rent increases, so far they have been reasonable.

Remember that monthly rent payments only pay for the use of the property; they are in no way tax deductible. If you choose to rent, you should be familiar with rental contracts and know how to compare the cost of renting versus purchasing.

Understanding Rental Contracts

When you rent an apartment, duplex, house, condo, or any other similar unit you will normally be required to sign a rental contract, also called a lease agreement. Because a rental contract binds you (the lessee) you should make certain you fully understand the terms before signing it. As a rule, the contract specifies the amount of the monthly payment, the payment due date, penalties for late payment, the length of the lease agreement, security deposit requirements, the distributions of expenses, renewal options, and any restrictions which might include children, pets, or use of the facilities.

Most leases have a minimum term of either six months or one year and require payments at the beginning of each month. Most require a deposit or the last month's payment in advance as security against damages and infringement of the lease agreement. In the absence of any serious damage, the deposit usually is refunded to the lessee shortly after the lease expires. A portion of the deposit may be retained to cover the cost of cleaning and minor repairs.

Because the landlord has the control over your deposit, you will want to have a written statement describing any damage and evidence prior to your occupancy of the unit. This can help you avoid losing the entire deposit when you leave. You also need to clarify who pays expenses such as utilities, trash collection, and other maintenance items. It is a good idea for you to check the various landlord laws in your state or community. This will help you fully understand what your rights and responsibilities may be.

Can't Decide?

Many people rent because they won't have to submit a down payment or closing costs. Others rent because they'll have more mobility and won't have to worry about maintenance and upkeep. If you are undecided about whether to rent or own, you can at least get a clear financial comparison of the two options by filling in the numbers on the form in Figure 10.2.

HIRING HOME IMPROVEMENT CONTRACTORS

To close this chapter, let's focus briefly on something that all homeowners eventually face: hiring a contractor to do work on your home. There are often pitfalls, most frequently cost overruns, missed deadlines, and shoddy workmanship. Worse, there are fly-by-night contrac-

FIGURE 10.2   Rent or Buy Comparison

A. Cost of Renting

   1) Annual rental cost (12 × monthly rent) $_____

   2) Renters insurance   _____

Total rental cost   _____

B. Cost of Purchasing

   1) Annual mortgage payments (12 × monthly mortgage
       payment)   _____

   2) Property taxes (obtain from real estate agent)   _____

   3) Homeowners insurance (obtain from insurance agent)   _____

   4) Maintenance (your best estimate for the year)   _____

   5) After tax cost of interest lost on down payment and closing
       costs ($_____ ×_____% after tax return on funds)   _____

Total purchasing costs   _____

Less: (subtract)

   1) Average principal reduction in loan balance (obtain from
       real estate agent)   _____

   2) Interest portion of mortgage payment multiplied by your
       combined federal and state tax rate = tax savings   _____

   3) Savings due to property tax deduction (property taxes from
       above multiplied by combined federal and state tax rate)   _____

   4) Total value of deductions   _____

Now subtract the total value of deductions from the total
purchasing cost and compare with the total rental costs.   _____

tors who take deposits or payments for home improvements and then
disappear before finishing or even starting the work. (See Chapter 17
for more information on frauds and scams.)

    If you need something done to your home, choose a contractor
carefully. Be wary of door-to-door salespeople or telephone solicitors

promising monthly specials or bargains. Here are seven tips for hiring contractors:

1. Use a local well-established contractor. Get some recommendations from a friend or neighbor. Ask the contractor for references and check with those homeowners to find out if the work was done properly, on time, and within the contract price.
2. Check with your state or local consumer affairs office or the better business bureau.
3. Obtain more than one estimate, especially on larger jobs. Get all promises and plans in writing.
4. Check with your local consumer protection office for specific laws designed to protect you. Some states require licensing, cooling off periods, payment schedules keyed to completion progress, and other consumer protections.
5. Study the financing of the job. Be sure that you can comfortably meet the total monthly payment. Also, check with your bank and shop around for the best way to finance your home improvement. Often a home equity loan may be the best answer.
6. Make sure your contractor has liability insurance. Ask to see a copy of his worker's compensation policy. You may be liable if a worker is injured on your property during the job. Check with your insurance agent to find out if your homeowners insurance will cover you and to what extent.
7. Insist that your contractor follow state and local building codes and obtain the necessary building permits. Find out from your local building inspector what legal obligations are required in regard to building permits.

Here are five tipoffs to help you spot unscrupulous, fly-by-night home improvement outfits:

1. They arrive in an unmarked truck or van.
2. They come to your door claiming to have just done a job nearby and say they have material left over and can do the job for half price.
3. They promise to use your home as a demonstration model at a reduced price.
4. They use high-pressure sales tactics.
5. They refuse to give you a written estimate or contract.

Never pay a contractor the entire cost of a job before he does any work. Usually a down payment of 10 to 20 percent of the total is reasonable with additional payments scheduled when the job is half done. Never release the final payment until the project is completed to your satisfaction and you have proof that subcontractors and/or employees have been paid. If a completion date is critical (for example, a swimming pool for summer use), link the final payment to on-time performance and completion of the job.

Even if you follow all of these guidelines, problems still may arise. Frequently, effective communication between you and the contractor will resolve difficulties. Take time to talk with your contractor and try to work out any disagreements.

If the problems persist, document your dispute. Put everything that needs to be resolved in writing. Send a copy to the contractor and keep a copy for your file. State and local consumer agencies may help you with home improvement problems. Check your telephone directory for local government listings or call your state's consumer affairs office or the office of the attorney general.

CHAPTER 11

Funding College Education

One of the largest expenses for any parent is paying for a child's higher education. Most people, even those in two-parent families, are simply not prepared for the economic impact college costs will have on four or more years of their lives. If you fit into one of the following four groups, this chapter is for you. If not, you may find it interesting, but feel free to move on.

1. You're a young widowed person with small children and some time to prepare for the expense of college.
2. You're a widowed individual in your middle years with children ready for college or already in college.
3. You're an older widowed person with grandchildren whom you'd like to help with future costs.
4. You're an heir with children or other relatives you would like to advise and help attend college.

WHY COLLEGE?

Many people ask, "Is college worth it?" Actually, a college education gives a child an important edge in our competitive world. College graduates are predicted to earn $600,000 or more than noncollege graduates during 40 years of working life.

Your child can probably achieve wealth and happiness without college preparation but the road may be easier with a bachelor's degree. In addition, there are many educational opportunities available today to college-age children that open previously unknown frontiers for learning and future careers. Without a college education many doors are likely to remain closed.

Over the last ten years college costs have more than doubled. Some analysts place the annual rate of increase at 6 to 7 percent per year. The Independent College 500 Index for private colleges cites an escalation of 7.6 percent for 1992 and the National Center for Education Statistics' *Digest of Education Statistics* places the average jump in private college tuition and fees at 9.7 percent over the last 17 years. *The College Costs Book,* available in most libraries, contains the average annual cost of every institution in the United States. This information is also available on CD-ROM.

How much you will actually spend on college depends on the following:

- Where the college is located.
- Whether the student attends a community college or a state or private university.
- Whether the student qualifies for in-state or out-of-state tuition at a state university.

For 1998, the average annual college costs for a school in the middle United States were:

- Community college: $3,337
- State university: $11,481
- Private university: $24,384

Except for community college, these figures include tuition, fees, room and board, books, supplies, and miscellaneous costs such as transportation. Community college costs do not include room and board because most attendees live at home. At current rates, by 2005 the cost of four years of college could reach $68,000 at a public university and $200,000 at a private institution.

Basically, there are only four ways to pay for college: (1) save for it, (2) pay out of current income, (3) cash in assets, or (4) have others pay for it. You may have to look at many aspects of your financial situation to choose the right combination of these.

CAN YOU AFFORD A COLLEGE EDUCATION FOR YOUR CHILDREN?

Many widowed people and heirs feel obligated to provide money for college at the expense of their own well-being and financial security. For example, Norma regularly dipped into her $100,000 of savings to fund her son's college education. Not only did she deplete this asset but she also lost the earning power of that money forever. She didn't realize that there were other sources to help fund a college education until it was too late. If you have young children, the easiest way to give your child the best educational experience is to start planning as early as possible. As such, you need to become educated about the following subjects:

- Financial aid;
- Saving money;
- Positioning assets for growth now and income later; and
- Strategies to minimize the tax impact of your college investment dollars.

If your planning choices are limited by too few assets and all your income goes toward survival needs, there is still hope. Financial aid, student loans, sports scholarships, and work-study programs are available but to get them for your child you must pursue them with vigor.

The worksheet in Figure 11.1 will help you calculate a realistic estimate of how much money you will need when your child is ready for college.

Laura, a 32-year-old widow, has two children, Jody and Sam, ages seven and nine. Her research suggests that college costs will accelerate at six percent annually and that a state university is all she can afford. Using the college cost worksheet she came up with the following figures:

FIGURE 11.1   Estimating College Costs for Your Child

1. Determine the years each child will attend college in the first column. The second column lists how many years that is from now.
2. Start with a base number of $3,300 for community college, $11,400 for state university, and $22,000 for private college.
3. Using the cost factor multiplier table in Figure 11.2, multiply the base number by the factor for either 6 or 7 percent inflation.
4. Enter this number on the appropriate line in each child's column. Repeat this for each year for every child.
5. Add the dollar amounts across each line to determine the total cost per year.
6. Add the dollar amounts down each column to determine the total cost for each child.

COLLEGE COST WORKSHEET

Years of College Attendance	Number of Years from Now	Child 1	Child 2	Child 3	Total Cost per Year
2000	1				
2001	2				
2002	3				
2003	4				
2004	5				
2005	6				
2006	7				
2007	8				
2008	9				
2009	10				
2010	11				
2011	12				
2012	13				
2013	14				
2014	15				
2015	16				
2016	17				
2017	18				
2018	19				
2019	20				
Total Cost per Child		$	$	$	

FIGURE 11.2   Cost Factor Multiplier Table

No. of Years from Now	at 6%	at 7%
1	1.06	1.07
2	1.12	1.14
3	1.19	1.22
4	1.26	1.31
5	1.34	1.40
6	1.42	1.50
7	1.50	1.60
8	1.59	1.72
9	1.69	1.84
10	1.79	1.96
11	1.90	2.10
12	2.01	2.25
13	2.13	2.41
14	2.26	2.58
15	2.39	2.76
16	2.54	2.95
17	2.69	3.16
18	2.85	3.38

Years of College Attendance	Number of Years from Now	Jody	Sam	Total Cost per Year
2007	9	$19,266		$ 19,266
2008	10	$20,406		$ 20,406
2009	11	$21,660	$21,660	$ 43,320
2010	12	$22,914	$22,914	$ 45,828
2011	13		$24,282	$ 24,282
2012	14		$25,764	$ 25,764
2013	15			
Total Cost per Child		$84,246	$94,620	$178,866

Using the annual savings chart in Figure 11.3, Laura finds that she needs to save $5,392 ($84,246 × .064) per year until Jody starts college and $4,636 ($94,620 × .049) per year until Sam starts college to have the lump sums required to fund college costs.

FIGURE 11.3   Annual Savings Chart

The factors below assume a return of 8 percent on an investment and do not account for any taxes due.

Child's Current Age	Factor	Child's Current Age	Factor
1	.025	10	.074
2	.027	11	.087
3	.031	12	.104
4	.034	13	.126
5	.038	14	.158
6	.043	15	.205
7	.049	16	.285
8	.056	17	.445
9	.064	18	.926

Now, Laura knows what she must do. She has $289,000 in insurance proceeds and she works full time earning $34,500 a year. Social Security provides $998 per month. Her plan may require investing some of the proceeds she received from her husband's life insurance to cover college expenses, if she can afford to do so. She also may want to add income from a part-time job, help her children become excellent students so they qualify for scholarships, or limit her expenses by using a community college for the first two years of their education and state universities for the second two years.

Laura may also want to determine the amount of the lump sum she needs today to fund the $178,866 in future education costs for Jody and Sam. If Laura invests $40,000 for each child after taxes at 8 percent, what will she have when Jody is ready for college in nine years, and Sam is ready in 11 years? Will it last through college or does she need to consider saving more money now?

Determining the Lump Sum Needed to Fund College Costs

Using the table in Figure 11.4, select the yield you believe the investment would generate—for example, 8 percent—and the number

FIGURE 11.4   Multiplier Chart for Lump Sums to Fund College

Years Until College Begins	4%	5%	6%	8%	10%
1	.96	.95	.94	.93	.91
2	.92	.91	.89	.85	.82
3	.89	.86	.84	.79	.75
4	.85	.82	.79	.73	.68
5	.82	.78	.74	.68	.62
6	.79	.74	.70	.63	.56
7	.78	.71	.66	.58	.51
8	.73	.67	.63	.54	.46
9	.70	.64	.59	.50	.42
10	.67	.61	.56	.46	.38
11	.65	.58	.53	.43	.35
12	.62	.55	.50	.40	.32
13	.60	.53	.47	.37	.29
14	.58	.50	.44	.34	.26
15	.55	.48	.42	.31	.24
16	.53	.46	.39	.29	.22
17	.51	.43	.37	.27	.20
18	.49	.41	.35	.25	.18

of years until the money is needed. For instance, Laura will need $19,266 for Jody in the ninth year. The factor for nine years at 8 percent is .50. Laura then needs to invest a lump sum of $9,633 ($19,266 × .50) today to reach her goal.

Here are the costs Laura determined using an 8 percent after-tax return:

	Jody	Sam
	$ 9,633	$ 9,314
	9,386	9,165
	9,314	8,984
	9,165	8,759
Totals	$37,498	$36,222

Thus, the lump sum Laura needs for both is $73,720. By combining the lump sum method and the annual savings method, Laura should be able to determine what she needs to do to fund the college educations.

COLLEGE PAYMENT STRATEGIES

Knowing how much college will cost is one thing; meeting it is another. Here are some winning strategies for funding college.

Aggressive Tactics in Their Younger Years

The younger the child is when you start a college plan, the more aggressive you can be with the investment. For example, use growth-oriented stocks or mutual funds for children who are now under age 14. Then begin moving toward less aggressive, income-oriented investments. By the time your child is 16, the overall goal is to safeguard what you've accumulated by moving to conservative investments such as money market funds, certificates of deposit, U.S. Treasury bills, and income mutual funds.

Take advantage of the kiddie tax. The first $650 of income to your under-age-14 child is tax free because it is offset by the child's standard deduction. The next $650 is taxed at the child's rate, which is usually lower than your rate. If your rate and the child's rate are the same, it still makes sense to place enough assets in the child's name to take advantage of the first $650 of unearned income. (This is discussed in more detail in Chapter 13 Giving: How, When, to Whom, and How Much.) The table in Figure 11.5 shows the yield rates and how much you can invest before hitting the $650 or $1,300 levels of unearned income for a child.

Use a custodial account to take advantage of the kiddie tax by establishing a plan under the Uniform Gift to Minors Act (UGMA) or the Uniform Transfers to Minors Act (UTMA), as discussed in Chapter 13, Giving: How, When, to Whom, and How Much. Custodial accounts are easy to start and easy to administer. In addition, if your child's earnings from a custodial account are taxed at your child's lower rate, you may be able to accumulate college savings faster.

Other ideas to fund a college education include:

- Using the $10,000 tax-free gift exclusion, a tactic often used by grandparents. The main purpose is to reduce your estate by giving a tax-free gift of $10,000 to each child or grandchild. You

FIGURE 11.5 How Much to Invest to Take Advantage of Kiddie Tax

Yield Percentage	Maximum Investment to Earn $650/Year	Maximum Investment to Earn $1,300/Year
4	$16,250	$32,500
5	13,000	26,000
6	10,833	21,666
7	9,285	18,570
8	8,125	16,250
9	7,222	14,444
10	6,500	13,000
11	5,909	11,818
12	5,416	10,832

can time the gift so it will be used to pay for tuition, books, and other expenses.

• Having your attorney set up a 2503(c) Minority Trust. As the trustee, you will have control over the funds until the child is 21 although you can only use the benefits for the minor. Your child won't have direct access to funds until he or she is close to, or already finished, with college.

• Asking your attorney about a Crummy trust with you as trustee. This trust is named after the court case from which it originated, and is similar to the 2503(c) Minority Trust. The important difference is that the recipient of the trust—your child—may withdraw contributions made to the trust for a limited period of time in the year the contributions are made. If the funds are not withdrawn, the contribution is added to the trust principal. The trust can last as long as the trustee decides.

Investing for College

There are many investment choices available to generate funds for college education costs. The basic vehicles include:

• Money market funds;
• Certificates of deposit;

- Series EE savings bonds;
- Municipal bonds;
- Corporate or government bonds;
- Stock and bond mutual funds;
- Unit investment trusts; and
- Zero coupon bonds.

In addition, here are three investments that are primarily used for college funding:

1. *Baccalaureate bonds.* Twenty-two states offer these general obligation municipal bonds, which pay a slightly higher interest rate than other municipal bond issues. They're popular because they're perceived to be safe and because of their noncallable feature (i.e., the bonds cannot be taken away from you until maturity). These bonds are also issued in varying maturities which makes it easy to match the bond's redemption year to the year you need funds for college.

2. *College-sure certificates of deposit.* This investment vehicle is offered by the College Savings Bank in Princeton, New Jersey. The annual return is tied to an index of full college funding for first-year students at 500 private, four-year colleges and universities. This program offers FDIC insurance, the ability to keep up with college inflation, and the pure safety of an investment in certificates of deposit. It's a popular investment choice for college funding. After an initial deposit of $1,000, you can make additional deposits of as little as $250. Many states now offer similar programs.

3. *Series EE bonds.* While you can consider these for funding of college education, there are many restrictions on them that may create a lot of anxiety. First, the return on the investment is not inspiring. They pay the higher of 6 percent or 85 percent of the average return on five-year Treasury bills. Moreover, that floating rate is available only if the bonds are held for five years, so if you are the parent of a 13-year old, you will not find much consolation in EE bonds. In addition, higher income taxpayers are shut out entirely, although the phase-out ranges will be adjusted for inflation, so you may not even qualify to use them for college funding.

Grandparents who want to retain control over assets earmarked for their grandchildren's education should not invest in EE bonds. The restrictions on them force grandparents to give the money to the parent, and the parent would have to make the investment in the EE bonds.

If you do decide to purchase EE bonds as a means to finance your children's college education, remember that the bonds must be purchased in your name, not in the names of your children.

You can get more information about this type of investment by calling 800-872-6637 to obtain current rates and additional information on Series EE Bonds.

Using Your IRA to Fund College Education Costs

If you're under age 59½, you have to pay a 10 percent IRS penalty if you cash in an IRA. Between age 59½ and age 70½, you can withdraw any amount of retirement money from your IRA without penalty. However, if you need money for college education at any age, you can move your retirement account from its current investment into a life annuity from which you can take annual payments.

When you start an annuity you must take roughly equal amounts each year for five years or until you reach age 59½, whichever is later. The amounts you withdraw must be related to your life expectancy and to the amount of interest your remaining funds can earn.

If your annuity stops too soon, the 10 percent IRS penalty will become retroactive and you will have to pay it on the amounts already withdrawn.

Under the Taxpayer Relief Act of 1997 penalty-free withdrawals may be made from any IRA for qualified higher education expenses (including those related to graduate level courses) incurred on behalf of you or your children or grandchildren.

Loans

If all else fails, use the following sources of loans:

1. *Life insurance policies.* Before borrowing from a policy, check the interest rate on the cash value loan. Older policies usually

have the lowest rates. Loans against insurance policies are not subject to demand repayment. In fact, they need not be paid back at all; you simply pay the interest as long as you have the loan. Universal life policies charge you an interest rate that is close to the rate the company pays out on investments so the net effect can be a very low cost to you.

2. *401(k) plans.* If you have a 401(k) retirement plan through your employer, check to see what loan interest rates will be charged to you if you borrow from the fund. In this case, the higher the rate the better because you're really paying the money back directly into your account. Each plan has different borrowing rules, so inquire before you make the loan.

3. *Margin account.* A margin account allows you to borrow against securities you own and use the interest you pay for the loan as a deduction to lower your taxes on the securities' earnings. Be careful here. If the securities drop in value, you may get a margin call and you would have to repay some or all of the outstanding loan at that time.

4. *Government loans.* The two best known government loan programs are the Stafford Student Loan, also known as the Guaranteed Student Loan Program, and the Perkins Loan. You also may wish to investigate the lesser-known Plus Loans and Supplement Loans to Students (SLS). Other loans may be available through federally chartered agencies such as the Student Loan Marketing Association.

5. *Loans from the college.* The college your child attends may offer loans to parents who do not qualify for financial aid.

6. *Home equity loans.* These are loans you negotiate with your bank or other lending institutions using the equity in your home as collateral. The interest on home equity loans up to $100,000 is fully tax-deductible. The loans are usually available if you qualify to make the additional monthly debt payment.

Financial Aid

Now we will examine all of the previously discussed methods for college funding from a new point of view—financial aid. A critical decision you need to make is whether investments for long-range accumulation of college funds should be in your name at your tax bracket or in your child's name at the usually lower child's rate.

The tax bracket for many heirs and widowed persons does not exceed 15 percent. If you fall into this category, it may be better to keep assets in your own name. Colleges expect 35 percent of any asset in the child's name to go toward schooling, which can drastically reduce the possibility of receiving aid. On the other hand, only 5.6 percent of your assets count in this formula.

The basic rule is to save money in the child's name if there's no chance your family will qualify for aid because you'll accumulate money more quickly using the child's lower tax bracket. Then, at college time, spend it all on tuition and other college costs. If there is a possibility of receiving aid, save funds in your name because your assets are only expected to provide 5.6 percent for your child's education.

Determining your eligibility for financial aid is not easy. The tax laws are always changing and the laws covering student aid confuse lay men and professionals alike. The complete subject is beyond the scope of this book but you can get a copy of *Don't Miss Out: The Ambitious Student Guide to Financial Aid* by Robert and Anna Leider (Octameron Press) by calling 703-836-5480. Another excellent publication is *You Can Afford College: The Family Guide to Meeting College Costs* by Alice Murphey, Kaplan Educational Centers and Simon & Schuster.

Here are six other suggestions related to your quest for financial aid:

1. Don't pay a computer service for scholarship searches. Most experts agree that these services are unlikely to be of much help in your quest for financial aid.

2. Apply for financial aid if you feel there is even the slightest chance that your child is eligible. Obtain financial aid forms from your child's high school guidance counselor or directly from the College Scholarship Service (CSS). Complete the forms and mail them as soon as possible after January 1 in the year of college applicability to the College Scholarship Service, P.O. Box 6364, Princeton, NJ 08541. You will need to enclose your tax return for the previous year. CSS completes an analysis of your child's eligibility and forwards its findings to the school(s) in which you have expressed interest. The college then determines the level of awards, if any.

3. Look for colleges that have substantial endowments. These are usually schools that can provide aid in addition to work study programs or loans.

4. Apply early to receive full consideration for all available programs. Colleges review financial aid applications as they come in and the institutions often run out of money before they run out of eligible applicants.

5. Reduce your own and your child's income and assets as much as possible. Students receiving financial aid are expected to contribute 70 percent of their after-tax income and up to 35 percent of their assets each year to education. You are expected to use as much as 47 percent of your income and 5.6 percent of your assets annually.

6. Replace all consumer installment loans with home equity loans. One of the criteria for awarding financial aid is based on the net equity in your home but consumer loans are ignored when figuring your net worth for financial aid purposes; home equity loans count.

Other financial aid programs to consider are:

- *Pell grants.* While this needs-based program has been cut back in recent years, it is still worthwhile. You can obtain more information by calling the Federal Student Financial Information Center, 800-433-3243.

- *Stafford loans and Plus loans.* Stafford loans are loans of $2650 to $5500 for your child and are no longer need-based. Plus loans are for parents and under the new rules are limited to the cost of college less financial aid. Even if you have no financial aid you can apply for a Plus loan.

- *Supplemental Education Opportunity Grants (SEOG).* This is a campus-based program for students demonstrating the greatest funding need. Check with the financial officer at the college of your choice.

- *College work-study programs (CWSP).* As the name implies, this program is for students who want to earn money for college expenses by working on campus. Inquire about this program at the school's financial aid office.

- *Federal Perkins loans.* These low cost loans permit students to borrow up to $3000 a year for undergraduate studies with a maximum of $15,000 over the course of a student's schooling. Graduate study loans are also available. Uncle Sam pays interest on the loans while the student is in school and for a nine-month grace period following graduation.

- *Financial aid on the Web.* Your first stop should be the excellent Financial Aid Information Page (www.finaid.org) sponsored by the National Association of Student Financial Aid Administrators. Next, check out the Education Department's Web site (www.ed.gov/offices/OPE/finaid.tml). Then try fastWEB (www.fastweb.com), a megadatabase of scholarships. Major lenders such as Nellie Mae (www.nelliemae.com), Sallie Mae (www.salliemae.com), and many banks also offer good advice.

- *The Hope Scholarship Credit.* This is an individual credit against federal income taxes of up to $1,500 per student for qualified tuition and fees paid during the year on behalf of a student. It is available for the first two years of a student's post-secondary education. The Hope Scholarship Credit is computed on a per-student basis.

Credit rate:
- 100 percent on the first $1,000 of qualified tuition and fees
- 50 percent on the next $1,000 of qualified tuition and fees

- *Lifetime Learning Credit.* Individuals are allowed a nonrefundable credit against federal income taxes of up to 20 percent of qualified tuition and fees paid during the taxable year on behalf of yourself or any dependent. The Lifetime Learning Credit is computed on a per taxpayer basis and does not vary based on the number of students in the taxpayer's family. In contrast to the Hope Scholarship Credit, which is only available for the first two years of post-secondary education, the Lifetime Learning Credit may be claimed for an unlimited number of taxable years.

Requirements: The student must be enrolled in an eligible educational institution and must be taking undergraduate or graduate level classes to acquire or improve job skills.

Eligible expenses:
- Before January 1, 2003, paid expenses up to $5,000 of qualified tuition and fees per taxpayer return will be eligible for the Lifetime Learning Credit (i.e., the maximum credit per taxpayer return will be $1,000).

- On or after January 1, 2003, paid expenses up to $10,000 of qualified tuition and fees per taxpayer return (i.e., the maximum credit per taxpayer return will be $2,000).

The Lifetime Learning Credit that you may otherwise claim is phased out on the same schedule that is used for the Hope Credit.

- *Education loan interest tax deduction.* The Taxpayer Relief Act of 1997 also provides for the deduction of loan interest paid for the qualified education expenses for you or your dependent. The deduction is available only for the first 60 months of interest payments on qualified loans. A qualified loan is a loan to pay for qualified expenses incurred in periods when the individual is at least a half-time student.

Amounts:

- In 1999—$1,500
- In 2000—$2,000
- In 2001—$2,500

Phase Out Ranges:

- For individual taxpayers, the deduction will begin to phase out at an adjusted gross income (AGI) of $40,000 and will be eliminated at $55,000.
- For joint returns, the deduction will begin to phase out at an AGI of $60,000 and will be eliminated at $75,000.

These ranges will be adjusted for inflation after the year 2002 when they will also be rounded down to the closest multiple of $5,000.

- *Education IRAs.* The purpose of these new after-tax IRAs is to fund the qualified higher education expenses of a named beneficiary who is under the age of 18. Income will generally accumulate tax free. Only trusts and custodial accounts are permitted. Annuity contracts cannot be used.

Contributions: Annual contributions to Education IRAs are not deductible and may not:

- Exceed $500 per beneficiary, or
- Be made after the beneficiary reaches age 18.

Phase out: The $500 annual contribution amount starts being phased out at $95,000 AGI for individuals and $150,000 AGI for married joint filers. It is completely eliminated at AGIs of $110,000 for individuals and $160,000 for joint returns. No contributions can be made to an Education IRA in any year when you contribute to a qualified state tuition program on the beneficiary's behalf.

Planning for college education is one of your biggest challenges. If you allow yourself a sufficient number of years to accumulate assets, you will not feel too much strain when your children are ready to make their way onto campus.

CHAPTER 12

Long-Term Care

Long-term care refers to the medical and/or personal care services you require if you have a chronic illness or disability. You may require daily medical attention or need help with the basic activities of daily living such as dressing, bathing, and walking. Many long-term care services are provided through informal caregiving systems such as your family, friends, and relatives. Long-term care can also be provided through more formal avenues.

In a more recent phenomenon, nearly 4 million Americans are now living in retirement communities. Many of these are called continuing care or life care facilities. Some care communities are operated by nonprofit organizations while others are commercial enterprises. Care communities provide residents age 65 or older with an apartment, meals, maid service, and entertainment facilities. You must be able to live on your own when entering, but lifetime health care, including long-term skilled care, is provided as needed. Senior citizens buying into these life care communities are required to pay fairly large entrance fees as well as monthly fees thereafter.

Formal care providers include home health agencies, senior centers, area agencies on aging, and adult daycare programs, as well as nursing homes and community care homes that provide care in a residential setting.

A typical nursing home stay commonly falls into two categories: (1) short term and (2) long term. A short-term stay of one to three months that involves skilled nursing care is basically rehabilitative in nature and often follows a hospital confinement. A long-term confinement comprised mainly of maintenance or custodial care lasts an average of two-and-one-half years. The latter of the two types should concern you most.

To make an intelligent decision about long-term care you need to answer two questions: (1) Do you need it? and (2) Can you afford it?

Thereafter, you need to determine which of the many plans available meets your needs.

DO YOU NEED LONG-TERM CARE?

It is difficult to predict if you will need long-term care. The need can arise gradually as you need more assistance with the activities of daily living. Or the need can surface suddenly following, say, a stroke or a heart attack.

The longer you live, the more likely it is that you will need some kind of long-term care. Some people who have acute illnesses need nursing home care for only short periods. Others are residents for many months or years because they require 24-hour care that may not be available outside a nursing home.

According to the Mayo Clinic and the Harvard Medical School, a person age 65 has at least one chance in four of needing an average of two-and-one-half years of long-term care. At an average cost of $100 per day, this can translate into over $ 100,000 in long-term care expenses.

Note:

For most people, paying extended out-of-pocket expenses can mean financial disaster.

With people living longer than ever before, the demand for health care, including long term-care, will significantly increase. The number of people in nursing homes is expected to increase by more than 60 percent in the next 30 years. Of the people in nursing homes, 95 percent receive custodial care, 4.5 percent receive intermediate care, and only .5 percent receive skilled care.

The only Americans not exposed to the risk of nursing home costs are either so wealthy that nursing home costs are inconsequential or so impoverished that they already qualify for Medicaid. For the majority of people caught between these two groups, there is a strong possibility of a costly nursing home stay.

CAN YOU AFFORD LONG-TERM CARE?

There are only four sources of funds to pay for long-term care:

1. Medicare and Medicare supplements
2. Medicaid
3. Long-term care insurance
4. Your savings and assets

Medicare

Medicare was intended to cover short-term needs—primarily hospital and doctor bills—not custodial long-term care needs. In addition, Medicare pays only for skilled nursing care. If you're a nursing home patient, you must meet the following six criteria to qualify for Medicare:

1. The care must be provided in a skilled nursing facility. Most U.S. nursing homes, about 72 percent, are not skilled nursing facilities.
2. The skilled nursing facility must be Medicare approved. Nationwide, only 31 percent of skilled nursing facilities are approved.
3. The care must be provided within 30 days after a hospital stay of at least three days.
4. Nursing care must be at a skilled level that can only be provided by a registered nurse or a licensed practical nurse acting under a doctor's orders.
5. The care must be restorative in nature. That is, it must be designed to make the patient well. Any type of intermediate or custodial care as opposed to skilled nursing care is not covered.
6. The care must be provided continuously 24 hours a day. If you need skilled nursing or rehabilitative services only once or

twice a week, or do not need to be in a skilled nursing facility to receive skilled services, Medicare will not pay the charges. Also, even when a Medicare benefit is available, it only pays in full for your first 20 days. From days 21–100, it pays everything except $95.50 per day. After day 100 you pay for everything.

Currently, Medicare covers only 2.2 percent of the nation's nursing home costs. Medicare supplement policies generally do not cover long-term care expenses, but rather are designed to pay other costs Medicare does not cover such as hospital deductibles or excess physician charges. (See Chapter 9 for detailed information about insurance.)

Medicaid

Medicaid is a federal and state finance assistance program for certain needy and low income persons, regardless of age. Nationally, Medicaid today pays for nearly half of all nursing home care. To receive Medicaid assistance you must meet federal poverty guidelines or spend down your assets, usually on health care costs, to meet the eligibility requirements.

Many people who begin paying for nursing home care out of their own pockets spend down their financial resources until they become eligible for Medicaid. Then they turn to Medicaid to pay part or all of their nursing home expenses. One significant characteristic of Medicaid is that it covers custodial nursing home care—the kind that most institutionalized elderly people require.

Once your resources for paying for private nursing home care are depleted, the only refuge is Medicaid. Depletion of resources also means that there will be no inheritance for your children or grandchildren.

Eligibility for Medicaid depends on meeting the system's criteria. Some widowed people make Medicaid plans by structuring their income and transferring assets to fit the criteria. Medicaid planning can be controversial. Some people feel that it is improper, or unethical, to take advantage of loopholes in the system. Others feel it is unfair to divert resources intended for the poor.

Also Medicaid planning can involve risks. Some elderly people transfer all their resources to children or grandchildren only to realize that they will not need nursing home care. The result could be a serious decline in your standard of living. Additionally, Medicaid rules often change so that all the planning steps will not create the desired result of securing Medicaid eligibility. The Health Insurance Portability and Accountability Act of 1997 includes these six provisions about long-term care insurance:

1. Long-term care is classified as health insurance.
2. Individual taxpayers can deduct long-term care premiums that exceed 7.5 percent of adjusted gross income for policies that are tax qualified.
3. Deductions are limited by age:
   - 40 and under, $200
   - 41 to 50, $375
   - 51 to 60, $750
   - 61 to 70, $2,000
   - 71 and above, $2,500
4. Policies that are tax qualified also will have benefits that are received tax free based on a cap of $175 a day or $63,875 annually. Policies that were issued prior to January 1, 1997, are grandfathered and their premiums are deductible.
5. Policies issued after January 1, 1997, must meet specific standards to qualify as tax favored.
   - Benefits are triggered when the insured is unable to perform two to six activities of daily living (ADLs): bathing, dressing, transferring, toileting, eating, continence. Cognitive impairment is a separate trigger.
   - The insured's condition must be expected by a medical professional to continue for at least 90 days.
6. Showing people how to transfer assets to qualify for Medicaid is now a criminal offense subject to a maximum fine of $25,000 or five years imprisonment.

Medicaid assistance is based on the amount of your income and capital resources. The more you have, the less likely you are to qualify. Worse, state laws may make you ineligible if you have transferred more than a certain amount of assets within a specific period of time (usually 36 months), in order to protect those assets and become eligible for aid.

Most states will allow you to have assets up to $2,000 in addition to certain other exempt assets. These vary in nature and amounts from state to state. In general, exempt assets include:

- Your home
- Household goods and personal items up to $2,000
- Wedding and engagement ring
- Car of any value, if needed to go to work or receive medical care or you are handicapped; otherwise, your car can be valued only up to $4,500
- Property of any kind worth up to $6,000, if essential to your support
- Up to $1,500 in life insurance policy cash values
- A burial plot, or up to $1,500 per person for a burial plot

Transferring Assets to Meet the Resources Test

Medicaid law requires the state to delay your eligibility for benefits if you transfer assets within 36 months from the day you apply for Medicaid benefits. Thus, you can be ineligible for up to 36 months (the look back period). Before the Omnibus Budget Reconciliation Act of 1993 (OBRA '93) the look back period was 30 months, regardless of the size of the transfer. For transfers made into an irrevocable trust from which you (the transferor) cannot receive income and cannot take back any part of the trust principal, the look back period is 60 months.

What can be done about this? Remember, if you transfer assets, you are making an irrevocable transfer; you can't change your mind and get these assets back once they are gone. You may also be making what is called a taxable gift. If you do decide to transfer property to your children, grandchildren, or others, you must make your gift 36 months before you apply for Medicaid.

Each state has a published figure for the cost of private-pay care. This number can effectively raise or lower the 36-month requirement. Assume, for example, that $90,000 is transferred, and your state's cost of care is $3000 per month. The transfer in this example will create a 30-month penalty period for you. If the transfer is $750,000 instead of $90,000 and the cost of care is set at $5000 per month, the transfer will create a 150-month penalty period—a very impractical 12½ years!

If you want to leave a large inheritance to your children or you can't afford lifetime insurance benefits, here is a compromise approach: Buy a long-term care insurance policy with a three- or five-year benefit period. This policy would give you time to transfer your assets after you enter a nursing facility, 36 months or 60 months later. When the policy runs out, the assets would have been safely transferred for the required 36 months and you will qualify for Medicaid payments on any further nursing home costs.

Also, just as important, you will have entered the nursing home as a private-paying patient. While not officially acknowledged, it seems to be well-known that private-paying patients do seem to receive better care than Medicaid patients.

Once you have a grasp on how Medicaid works, you may be ready to begin Medicaid planning. This is a highly complex legal area that requires the help of professionals. Your local bar association may have a list of attorneys who practice elder law who can assist you.

Long-Term Care Insurance

This is the most desirable option for many widowed people and is described in detail later in this chapter.

Your Savings and Assets

If you can pay for your long-term health costs out of your own savings and assets, you are among a lucky few.

HOW TO SUCCESSFULLY MEET YOUR NEEDS

While no one knows for sure how rapidly long-term care costs will increase, all the experts agree that they will go up. How do you grapple with this cost picture? The following approach requires a number of assumptions on your part. However, using the data available today, they are the only realistic numbers you have to work with.

Assumptions:

- You will probably need nursing home or home health care at some point in your life.
- The costs will continue to escalate at 7 percent annually.
- The average cost today is $38,000 per year.
- You will need this coverage for a minimum of 2½ years.

Suppose you are now age 60. What will long-term care cost based on the above assumptions?

Year	Age	Inflated Cost/Year
1	61	$ 40,660
2	62	$ 43,506
3	63	$ 46,551
4	64	$ 49,810
5	65	$ 53,297
10	70	$ 74,752
15	75	$104,843
20	80	$147,048

Now you need to compare the above numbers with your own financial information. Return to Chapter 7, Retirement Planning: Making the Money Last, to determine your current resources. Will those income figures increase in the future? What about expenses? If you go into a nursing home at the age of 70, what will your total costs be? Would you choose to sell your home or continue maintaining it? Most people want to return to their home if possible but you could have the cost of long-term care in addition to home maintenance, real estate property taxes, utilities, and insurance. Suppose you can stay in your home but need home health care. All your regular expenses will remain, plus the cost of the care in your home and any special medications.

Cheryl, age 67, for example has monthly expenses of about $2,000 and monthly income is $2,500 including pension, Social Security, and investment income. Her home is paid for and she's currently in good health. Her mother just died at 94 and her father died at 88. Both required long-term care in their later years which Cheryl helped pay for. Helping her parents reduced Cheryl's assets and she has little to fall back on should she require nursing home or home health care. It seems possible that Cheryl too could eventually need long-term care.

Cheryl is a candidate for long-term care insurance available through various insurance carriers. While she can afford a policy now, as she ages her health may deteriorate and the cost of coverage will increase substantially each year she puts off buying a policy.

If she needs care at the age of 80, the annual costs could range between $75,000 and $90,000 based on a 7 percent annual increase. And it's likely she would not qualify to obtain the policy then. If she obtains a policy now, a $100 daily policy with a 100-day waiting period and lifetime benefits would cost about $78 monthly.

With Cheryl's monthly surplus of $500, she can afford it and the benefit would supplement her annual income by $36,000 should she need it. The policy should also contain a home health care rider that would pay for $50 to $100 of daily care in the home. This would add about $21 each month to the premium.

Here's how you can estimate your long-term care costs:

1. Call several nursing homes in your area and determine the long-term care daily rate. Using an average of these, multiply the rate by 365.

Daily Rate	Yearly Rate
$ 80	$29,200
90	32,850
100	36,500
120	43,800
140	51,100

2. Then, using this annual cost figure, apply the multiplier factor of 7 percent per year for the year you wish to estimate the cost.

Year	Factor
5	1.403
10	1.967
15	2.759
20	3.869

For example, the Average Daily Rate of $80 is multiplied by 365 days to derive an annual cost of $29,200. If you are age 65 now and wish to estimate what costs will be in ten years, multiply $29,200 by 1.967 to determine that the cost will be $57,436.

What If You Are Younger?

You don't need to be concerned, yet, if you are younger than age 50. However, being aware of all the ramifications of long-term care and its costs can provide you with valuable knowledge for later years.

If you're between the ages of 50 and 60, you should examine coverage now available. Here's a comparison of yearly premiums from a cross section of companies at various ages for $100 in daily benefits with a 100-day elimination period:

Age	Cost
50	$ 405
54	441
58	476
60	513
64	717
68	1034
70	1264
74	2004
78	3369

Is it worth it to buy the coverage in earlier years? There's no hard and fast rule. You have to look at your individual situation from a medical and financial point of view. For example, do you have a medical problem now that is likely to worsen as you age? Would it prevent you from acquiring the coverage? Can you presently afford to spend $700 on annual premiums, but not $2,000 in 10 or 15 years?

Buying a Long-Term Health Care Policy

There is no single plan that is perfect for everyone. The right plan for you may be completely different from the right plan for your best friend. Each company and each policy has strengths and weaknesses. To pick the policy that is best for you, you need to understand what types of coverage are available and what these plans entail.

Long-term care policies may pay for skilled, intermediate, custodial, home care, or adult day care, and each policy may define these terms differently. It is important that you understand these definitions because you receive benefits only if the care you receive is covered in the policy. Some policies make no distinctions between these levels of care. They will pay regardless of the type of care you need.

You also will have a choice in how long the benefits will last. Policy maximums limit the amount the policy will pay in benefits. Some policies state that they will pay benefits for a set number of days, months, or years. For home health coverage, benefit maximums are sometimes expressed as a stated number of visits. Other policies will pay for a certain number of units of care. Still other policies will express their maximum limits in dollars.

Benefits generally vary from $40 per day to as much as $200 per day for each day you need care covered by the policy. These benefits may last for as little as one year or for your lifetime, depending on the policy. (You may have a choice of one year, two years, three years, four years, five years, or lifetime.) Some policies pay a smaller benefit for custodial home care or adult day care.

Over time, the custodial care can be the most costly. Very few people need skilled care for a long period of time and much of the care in nursing homes is custodial. You should consider a policy that provides coverage for custodial care as well as skilled or intermediate care.

You also have your choice of elimination periods. These are waiting periods before your policy actually starts paying if you enter a nursing home or receive home health care. A waiting period can be anywhere from 0 to 100 days. Often 20 days is a popular choice. Some policies offer a 60-day waiting period.

When you are preparing to buy a policy, make certain that it does not require a prior hospital stay before you are eligible for benefits. In addition, you want to make sure that you are not required to spend time in a nursing home before home health care benefits begin.

Your policy should be guaranteed renewable. This means the policy cannot be canceled by the company as long as you pay the premiums on time. The renewability provision is usually found on the first page of the policy and describes under what conditions the policy may be canceled or when premiums may be raised. Note that the company can cancel your policy if you have misrepresented your health status on the application and the company relied on these misrepresentations to give you the coverage. Also, look for a policy that covers Alzheimer's disease. The checklist in Figure 12.1 will help you compare the policies of various insurance companies.

Companies generally require that a certain period of time pass before the policy pays for care related to a health problem you may have had when you applied for coverage. This type of health problem is called a preexisting condition. This is a condition for which medical advice or treatment was recommended by a physician and/or received by you before you signed the application. Look for a policy that does not utilize preexisting conditions.

FIGURE 12.1   Long-Term Policy Analysis Checklist

A. Benefits	Company A		Company B		Company C	
1. Daily Benefit	$_____		$_____		$_____	
	Yes	No	Yes	No	Yes	No
Skilled nursing care	____	____	____	____	____	____
Intermediate care	____	____	____	____	____	____
Custodial care	____	____	____	____	____	____
Home health care	____	____	____	____	____	____
Adult day care	____	____	____	____	____	____
2. Duration of Benefits	**Days/yr**		**Days/yr**		**Days/yr**	
Skilled care	_____		_____		_____	
Intermediate care	_____		_____		_____	
Custodial care	_____		_____		_____	
Home health care	_____		_____		_____	
Adult day care	_____		_____		_____	
3. Inflation Benefit Available						
Percent increase	_____ %		_____ %		_____ %	
Simple or compound	_____		_____		_____	
Duration of increases	_____		_____		_____	
4. What Does Policy Pay?	**Per day**		**Per day**		**Per day**	
Skilled nursing care	$_____		$_____		$_____	
Intermediate care	$_____		$_____		$_____	
Custodial care	$_____		$_____		$_____	
Home health care	$_____		$_____		$_____	
Adult day care	$_____		$_____		$_____	
Any stay in nursing home	$_____		$_____		$_____	
Years policy pays benefits	_____ yrs		_____ yrs		_____ yrs	
B. Limits or Exclusions						
Waiting (elimination period)						
Nursing home care	____ days		____ days		____ days	
Home health care	____ days		____ days		____ days	
Adult day care	____ days		____ days		____ days	
Time before preexisting conditions are covered	____ months		____ months		____ months	
Alzheimer's coverage (yes or no)	____		____		____	

FIGURE 12.1   (Continued)

Prior hospital stay required for:	Yes	No	Yes	No	Yes	No
Skilled nursing care	___	___	___	___	___	___
Intermediate nursing care	___	___	___	___	___	___
Custodial care	___	___	___	___	___	___
Home health care	___	___	___	___	___	___
Prior skilled nursing care required for:						
Intermediate care	___	___	___	___	___	___
Custodial care	___	___	___	___	___	___
Home health care	___	___	___	___	___	___

C. Costs of Policy

Monthly/annual cost w/o riders	$_____	$_____	$_____
Inflation rider	_____	_____	_____
Home health care rider	_____	_____	_____
Waiver of premium	_____	_____	_____
Any discounts	_____	_____	_____
Total Cost	_____	_____	_____

There are other features you should have in a policy. One is called *waiver of premium*. The waiver of premium clause allows you to stop paying premiums during the time you are receiving benefits. Some policies require you to be in a nursing home for a certain number of days, often 90 days, before this clause becomes effective.

Another feature is an *inflation rider*. These riders usually increase the benefits by cost-of-living increases. They may also automatically increase the policy by 3 to 5 percent per year. These benefits may be available at a simple interest basis or a compound interest basis. The inflation benefits may increase every year for the rest of your life or they may stop after a certain amount of time, 10 or 20 years for example. With long-term costs increasing at 7 percent a year, this rider is very valuable and should be considered a necessity when buying a policy. Older people should consider the simple interest feature to hold the cost down.

The inflation rider will usually add anywhere from 20 to 65 per-cent to your premium depending on what form of coverage is selected. However, without such an inflation rider, the cost of long-term care in-surance may be far greater in the future than the benefits you receive when you finally need the care.

Another feature that you should consider is a *nonforfeiture*. This is a return-of-premium feature or return-of-benefits feature. This feature returns part of what you paid in premiums if you choose to cancel your coverage after a certain period of time or if your coverage lapses be-cause you have not paid the premium. These benefits will most likely not be paid in cash but will guarantee some portion of benefits. This feature often requires that you hold the policy for 10 or 20 years.

Finally, you should choose a financially stable company. Refer to Chapter 9, Insurance: Understanding the Great Mystery, to choose a company using the rating system outlined in that chapter.

As with most methods for maximizing your inheritance, the ear-lier you begin planning for long-term care, the fewer surprises and less anxiety you'll experience as you gracefully make your way to old age.

Qualified and Nonqualified Long-Term Care Policies

A *qualified* policy offers you two federal tax breaks:

1. You might be able to write off part or all of the premium you pay. The deductible amount depends on your age. It ranges from $210 for buyers age 40 or less to $2,570 if you're 71 and up. This write-off doesn't amount to much. To get it, you have to itemize it on your tax returns. Also, it's counted as part of your personal medical expenses, deductible only to the extent that they exceed 7.5 percent of your adjusted gross income. Not many taxpayers qualify.
2. Collected benefits are guaranteed free of federal tax. All long-term care policies sold before January 1, 1997, are considered qualified. Policies sold since then are qualified only if they meet certain criteria.

A nonqualified policy, by contrast, offers no tax deductions for the premiums you pay. For most people, that's a minor item. The major item is the tax status of any benefits you receive.

Qualified policies normally pay if you cannot perform more than two of the following activities: bathing, dressing, getting to the toilet, eating, staying continent, or transferring (say, from your bed to a chair), or you're suffering from Alzheimer's or a similar brain disease. Your disability must be expected to last more than 90 days. You don't have to wait 90 days for coverage as long as it's clear that you're going to need care that long.

Now consider *nonqualified* policies. They can look better in two ways: (1) they might pay for disabilities that last fewer than 90 days, and (2) they can be triggered by a medical necessity, in addition to Alzheimer's and the life activities mentioned above. These extra benefits generally cost you more than you'd pay for qualified coverage, depending on the company.

Do you really need insurance for nursing home stays of fewer than 90 days? Often, short-term stays are covered by Medicare or Medigap. More than half of all buyers deliberately choose coverage that pays no benefits for the first 90 days or more. You might do the same. The longer waiting period holds down the price.

And when, exactly, would a medical necessity trigger your policy's coverage? On paper, this means long-term care after an injury or sickness. But insurers have different views of what is necessary. A liberal insurer might agree with a reasonable doctor who says you need care. A tough insurer may second-guess every doctor's opinion. You won't know in advance which kind of company you have.

The conclusion: You get extra benefits in some nonqualified policies but you may not need them or you may not be sure how to collect. Plus you take on the risk that you might be taxed on any benefits paid.

If you go nonqualified, look for a clause that lets you convert to qualified coverage with no medical exam.

Part Four

Prosperous Transitions

CHAPTER 13

Giving

How, When, to Whom, and How Much

Once you have financial security it may be better to give away assets and income, moving them out of your estate. However, if your estate is not large and your income needs are substantial, you need to be very cautious when making gifts. Most heirs give what they can to friends, relatives, and charity.

You may have many reasons to make gifts to others:

- It makes you feel good.
- It will often benefit others, especially your close relatives or friends.
- It can reduce your estate and consequently your federal estate taxes at your death.
- It can reduce your income taxes now.
- Your gifts can be used to provide funds to pay for future college educations for children or grandchildren.

You may find it desirable to also make gifts to charitable organizations. Reasons to make charitable gifts include:

- A compassion for those in need
- A religious and spiritual commitment on your part
- A perpetuation of one's beliefs, values, and ideas
- Support for art, sciences, and education
- A desire to share one's good fortune with others

Before you rush into a giving program, however, you need to determine if you can afford it. While it is natural and understandable that you want to make gifts, giving at the wrong time can create unfortunate results. Money can be given away but your needs still must be met. Your primary objective is to make the money last. When you have sufficient amounts of income and financial assets, then it's time to think about gifts.

Review your assets, liabilities, and cash flow (refer to Chapters 5 and 7). Will you have enough income to continue your well-being and your future standard of living? Also, run the numbers for your future retirement needs. Remember, you don't want to be a burden to anyone else at any time in the future. If the numbers show that you can afford to make gifts to children, charity, or others, go ahead and do it.

It is important to realize that when you make a gift it is absolute. Once you have given the property or money away, you cannot retrieve it. For that reason it is often wise to determine whether you are actually making a gift or a loan. If it is a loan, have a loan agreement signed between you and the person to whom you are loaning the money.

As mentioned earlier, giving can reduce your estate taxes, income taxes, and probate costs. Giving assets to save estate taxes is especially useful when the asset is likely to appreciate in value and you would like to have the growth occur in someone else's hands.

For example, Alice has more than enough income and assets to last her lifetime. She has a piece of real estate that is expected to grow in value over the years ahead. By making a gift now, she can remove that asset from her estate while also removing all the future growth at the same time.

Another advantage of giving is that you know exactly who is benefiting from your estate.

MAKING A GIFT IS A SURE THING

Unlike most gifts bestowed after your death, gifts you give during your lifetime—hence, called lifetime gifts—can be private. No one but the recipient of the gift has to know any of the details. On the other hand, property that passes under your will must be inventoried and the list may be filed with the county register of wills at which point it becomes public information. Your beneficiaries may then receive unsolicited advice from others on how to invest their money. This is generally not a problem with gifts.

Making a gift while you are alive also gives you the pleasure of seeing the recipients use and enjoy it. For example, you can watch how your son or daughter handles and invests cash. Such observation can help you make decisions about whether or when to make additional gifts either during your lifetime or at your death. Note that your gift not only provides financial security for those to whom you make the gift, but it insulates that property from claims of your creditors.

Estate taxes are not the only taxes you can save by lifetime gifts. Many gifts are given for the potential income tax savings rather than estate tax savings. For example, Mary's income puts her into the 31 percent income tax bracket. That means that 31 cents of every dollar in her top bracket will be lost to taxes.

By giving a high income mutual fund to her daughter, the income from that mutual fund is no longer taxed to Mary. Instead it is taxed to her daughter in a lower bracket. If her daughter is in a 15 percent tax bracket, the family unit realizes a 16 percent tax savings.

Giving in a Nutshell

Giving can be an important estate planning technique because it can save you estate taxes and probate costs. Giving guarantees that the party to whom you want to give your gift will receive it. It also ensures that the details of the gift will be completely private. Making a lifetime gift gives you the opportunity to enjoy the pleasure of giving to the recipient. It enables you to see how well they handle and manage the gift. And finally, gifts of income-producing property shift the tax on the income to the recipient and offer an easy way to save income taxes.

WHAT ARE THE COSTS OF GIVING?

It may not cost one cent in taxes to offer even large gifts. The reason? Before any taxes are due, you may qualify for one of the following two gift provisions:

1. An annual $10,000 per donee (i.e., recipient) gift tax exclusion (beginning in 1998 the exclusion will be indexed for inflation).
2. Use of the unified credit.

Let's see how these two gift tax reducers work.

Annual Gifts

You can give up to $10,000 in cash or other property every year to as many different people or institutions as you wish with no gift tax liability. This is called the annual gift tax exclusion. Gifts can be made to individuals, relatives or not, or any other party such as a charity or a club.

For example, Jane is a 65-year-old widow with three nephews, Bill, Ed and Alex. She gives each nephew $10,000 in cash or other property each year. This means she removes $30,000 each year ($10,000 × 3) from her estate at no federal estate or gift tax cost to her. If Jane remarries, she and her new husband can agree to split the gift and the amount then doubles. Together they can give up to $60,000 ($20,000 to each) to Jane's three nephews.

Because Jane's life expectancy is about 20 years she can avoid estate taxes on approximately $600,000 ($30,000 × 20), if she continues the gift-giving program. The annual exclusion over time can remove massive amounts of property from estates.

Unified Credit

Federal estate tax law provides a single tax credit called the unified credit. This is a dollar-for-dollar reduction for any gift or estate tax due. The credit in 1999 is equal to an exemption of $650,000, while the credit is actually $211,300.

For example, assume Robin makes a $660,000 gift to her son. The computation would be as follows:

Gift	$660,000
Annual Exclusion	10,000
Net Gift	650,000
Tax on Net Gift	211,300
Unified Credit	211,300
Net tax due	-0-

The unified credit you use during your lifetime will reduce any credit available against any estate or gift tax at your death. For estate taxes in Robin's case, there will be no credit left for her estate for 1999. She can still make gifts of $10,000 per year to a particular person or entity without incurring taxes but she has used up the total $211,300 unified credit.

Donors must file a gift tax return on or before April 15 following the end of the calendar year in which the gift is made if it exceeds the annual exclusion. (See Chapter 14, Estate Planning: Passing Along Your Wealth, for a more complete description of the Unified Credit.)

WHEN IS THE BEST TIME TO MAKE A GIFT?

As far as the $10,000 annual gift exclusion is concerned the best time to make a gift is now. The exclusion is a noncumulative opportunity. You either use it or lose it. However, whenever stocks or other assets which can fluctuate widely in value are being considered as gifts, you should give them away when the asset is valued as low as possible. In making any gift decision, carefully consider both your current and long-term financial security.

It is extremely important for you to focus on the circumstances of your financial situation before making a gift. Do not give away any asset if it will reduce your standard of living or financially endanger your comfort level. You should focus on the impact of the gift on your income and your capital needs as well as your need for liquidity. Again, refer to Chapter 7, Retirement Planning: Making the Money Last, to determine whether you are in position now—or will be in the future—to make gifts.

WHAT GIFTS TO GIVE

The type of gift or property to give depends on your circumstances and objectives. It may be good to give income-producing property if you are in a higher income tax bracket than the person to whom you are giving the property. Properties which are likely to increase in value substantially—such as life insurance, common stock, antiques, art, or even real estate—are prime candidates.

The future appreciation of these types of properties can be removed from your estate now. The gift should be made when the gift tax value, and therefore the gift tax transfer cost, are the lowest. Property which has already appreciated can be considered if the sale of such property was contemplated anyway and the recipient is in a lower income tax bracket than you. Property with somewhat low gift tax value and high estate tax value, such as life insurance, makes an excellent gift. It's not a good idea to give away property showing a loss because the recipient cannot deduct your loss. You should sell the property, take the deduction for the loss yourself, then make a gift of the cash proceeds.

Another type of property which should be considered for giving is property owned by you in a state other than your state of residence. Do this to avoid ancillary probate at the time of your death.

Present Interest and Crummy Trusts

Under gift tax laws, you, the donor, must be giving a present interest in property or cash in order to qualify for the $10,000 annual exclusion. This means that the recipient must have complete access to the funds which might be very unsettling if you are contemplating making gifts to a minor child. There are, however, a few ways around this concern.

Several years ago the Crummy family (yes, that was their name) wanted to make gifts to their family members and qualify for the annual gift tax exclusion while restricting access to the funds. In order to accomplish this, they created trusts. The language in the trust document allowed the beneficiaries to withdraw funds gifted to the trust within a limited period of time. If the funds were not withdrawn, they became trust assets.

This provision became known as a Crummy withdrawal power. The tax court ruled the gifts qualified for the annual gift tax exclusion because the beneficiaries had a present power to withdraw the funds.

Another feature of the Crummy trust is referred to as 5-in-5 powers. They permit withdrawal of $5,000 or 5 percent of the trust balance, whichever is greater. Your attorney can draft a document which accurately reflects your interest. If you are interested in pursuing this, talk to your attorney about a Crummy trust.

Other ways of making gifts to children include the Uniform Gift to Minors Act (UGMA) and the Uniform Transfers to Minors Act (UTMA).

Complex giving techniques include Section 2503(b) trusts and Section 2503(c) trusts. Setting up these trusts can be fairly complicated and both require the services of a competent attorney familiar with these trusts.

CHARITABLE GIVING

There are many different reasons for making gifts to charitable organizations. You can give cash or checks, securities, a residence, a farm or ranch, a family business, or personal property like life insurance, works of art, precious stones, precious metals, gold, and silver.

Note:

You can give almost anything to charity.

While it may not sound very charitable, you need to consider your tax situation when contemplating gifts to charity. Many charitable trust arrangements are attractive based on tax planning and financial grounds alone.

Factors to Consider When Making Charitable Gifts

Charitable trusts are accepted and enforced in all states. The law provides that there must be a definite charitable purpose in the gift; i.e., religious or educational. The common law of most states will make a gift void and thus a continuing part of your estate if the trust does not (1) end, and (2) distribute assets within a time period measured by the lives of living beneficiaries, plus 21 years.

Federal income tax law permits you a deduction for gifts made to qualified charities subject to certain limitations. In addition, there are deductions for estate and gift tax purposes for transfers to qualified charities. State income, gift, and inheritance tax laws also provide for charitable deductions.

When you make a tax-deductible donation, the IRS is interested in the organization that benefits from that donation. You will not be able to reduce your taxable income if the group is not on the list of qualified organizations. You can obtain a copy of this list from the Internal Revenue Service (publication #78).

Generally, your deduction is safe if you give your property to any of the following: governments (federal, state, or local), domestic trust foundations with charitable or similar purposes, and some, but not all, domestic veterans or fraternal organizations. To be sure that your deduction is valid, ask for proof that the organization has been granted tax exempt status. The group should be able to provide you with a copy of a ruling letter from the IRS granting the exempt qualified status.

The IRS also wants to be sure that your gift is made with a charitable intent. Any correspondence with the charitable organization should state your willingness to make the donation to the charity. If there is any hint that the contribution is being made for business purposes, your deduction could be disallowed.

Regulations on charitable contributions can be complex. If you play by the IRS rules, however, there are substantial benefits both for you and for your favorite charity.

Tax Deduction Limitations

Because all gift giving has tax deduction limitations, let's quickly examine the playing field:

- Deductions for your contributions of cash or ordinary income property to public charities are limited to 50 percent of adjusted gross income. The deduction is based on the cost of the property or the amount of the cash donated.
- Deductions for your contributions of appreciated property to public charities are limited to 30 percent of your adjusted gross income. The deduction value of your contribution is based on the fair market value of the property at the date of the gift.
- Deductions for your contributions of tangible personal property, unrelated to the charitable purpose of the donor organization, are limited to the cost of the property.
- Deductions for your contributions of cash or ordinary income to private foundations, war veteran organizations, fraternal lodges, and certain other organizations are limited to 30 percent of your adjusted gross income.
- Deductions for contributions of appreciated property to private foundations and organizations are limited to 20 percent of your adjusted gross income.

Be aware of the alternative minimum tax on gifts of appreciated property. Under the 1986 Tax Reform Act, the untaxed portion of appreciated capital gains property contributed to a charity is treated as a tax preference item. This means that if you are subject to the alternative minimum tax, the charitable contribution deduction is limited to the cost of the property.

There is some relief. Each taxpayer has a substantial exemption from the alternative minimum tax. If you are filing jointly, the exemption is $45,000 per year; for a single taxpayer the exemption is $33,700. The exemption is fully phased out, however, for taxpayers with an alternative minimum taxable income of $304,300 or more on a joint return, or $243,700 for a single taxpayer.

CHARITABLE GIVING THROUGH TRUSTS

Charitable strategies involving trusts are complicated and require an attorney, financial planner, or accountant with special expertise in this field. There are several types of trusts and each has its own special features and rules. These vehicles do, however, offer considerable flexibility in structuring contributions to meet your financial needs. They allow you, in part, to divide an asset into its income and ownership aspects and to give away only one component.

Charitable remainder trusts, of which there are several varieties, allow you to give a future interest in an asset to a charity while keeping an income stream for yourself. These types allow you to transfer assets to a trust with the stipulation that you receive income for a specified period. Property in the trust is transferred to the charity at the end of the trust term.

You can choose one of two options: (1) a charitable remainder annuity trust which provides a fixed amount of annual income, or (2) a charitable remainder unit trust which remits a fixed percentage of trust income annually.

The sale of property held by the trust has no immediate tax effect on either you or the trust. Charitable remainder trusts are mainly exempt from federal income tax. Because of this exemption, many people transfer appreciated assets to a charitable remainder trust prior to the sale of the asset. You are liable for taxes only on the payments you receive from the trust.

The trust will not pay taxes on capital gains because the asset is irrevocably dedicated to charity. This can work to your financial benefit. Also, gifts to a charitable remainder trust provide a charitable income tax deduction now. By transferring appreciated assets to such a trust, you can lower your current income taxes, avoid capital gains and estate taxes, and accomplish your charitable goals.

You can even structure a trust to give you a higher level of income than you are currently receiving from your assets. For example, Sylvia is a 65-year-old widow with a $350,000 home and $500,000 in other assets. Of this $500,000, she has $300,000 in stock yielding only 4 percent. If she sells the stock she will incur a sizeable capital gains tax. But the charitable gift of that stock to a remainder trust could increase her retirement income and her children's inheritance while also benefiting a charity of her choice.

Here is how it would work. The trust sells Sylvia's stock tax free and reinvests the securities, generating a greater income. The trust agreement provides for Sylvia to receive an annual income of 5 to 10 percent for the rest of her life. She also receives immediate tax deductions of approximately $95,000 (from IRS tables), and she can use part of her improved cash flow to buy life insurance. At her death, the life insurance would more than replace the value of the gift (see Wealth Replacement Trust below). When Sylvia dies, the charity will get the assets in the trust.

Wealth Replacement Trust

While a charitable remainder trust can help accomplish your current financial objectives, it may not please your heirs. You may be concerned that your surviving family members are slighted by your gift to charity. Using the concept of wealth replacement, you no longer need to choose between your favorite charity and your family.

This charitable giving strategy offers an attractive annual income, provides you with a current income tax deduction, and reduces your estate taxes. Plus, it protects your family's inheritance. You may be able to accomplish all of these objectives by creating a wealth replacement trust in conjunction with a charitable remainder trust. A wealth replacement trust can be funded with life insurance that pays its proceeds upon the death of the person named in the policy. The premiums for a life insurance policy can often be paid with the tax savings generated by the current income tax deduction from the charitable contribution. Enough insurance can be purchased to replace the value of the assets left to the charity as part of the remainder trust.

Charitable Lead Trusts

Another trust strategy you can use is called a charitable lead trust. Securities or other assets are placed in a trust that pays all of its income to a charity for a fixed number of years. When that period is up, the trust assets go to a beneficiary you have previously named. The tax impact here is that you get a charitable deduction now for the present value of the monies that the charity will receive over the ten-year period.

The part of the gift that is left to your beneficiary in the future is subject to gift tax, but this tax will usually be low because the IRS puts a greatly discounted value on such gifts. The benefit here is that you can make a large future gift to your beneficiary with a fairly low gift tax cost.

Suppose you put $100,000 into a charitable lead trust for ten years leaving the assets to your children after the charitable interest runs out. Using IRS tables, a ten-year income stream is valued at 61 percent of the value of the trust property. So $61,000 is the amount of your charitable gift and income tax deduction. The gift to your children is valued at only $39,000.

The benefit here is that your children will eventually get the full amount of the gift ($100,000) and the gift tax you pay is still based on only $39,000. Additionally, if the assets increase in value, the gift tax does not increase. Thus, if the $100,000 you donated to the trust grows to a value of $200,000 when your beneficiaries take it, you will still pay a gift tax on only $39,000.

Gifts for an IRA

You might consider making a gift of $2,000 per year to your younger adult children to fund an IRA account. For example, if your son is age 21 and working for a company making $23,000 per year, he is allowed to make the full $2,000 contribution. Because his company doesn't have a pension plan and his income is below $25,000, he can take the full $2,000 deduction. He could also use the nondeductible Roth IRA.

Let's assume that you continue to make a gift of $2,000 per year until your son is age 27. He then marries and his income combined with his wife's income and their company pension plans eliminate their IRA deduction at that time. Here's a look at the benefits of this program:

Annual deposit	$2,000
Number of years for deposit	6
Assumed interest rate	8%
Accumulation value after 6 years	$14,672

Now allow the lump sum accumulation of $14,672 to continue to grow at 8 percent until your son reaches age 59½:

Starting deposit	$14,672
Number of years to age 59½	32
Assumed interest rate	8%
Accumulated value at age 59½	$440,632

All of this was achieved with six years of gifts of only $2,000 each. In addition, your son will be able to take a $2,000 tax deduction in each of those six years. If the Roth IRA is used, no tax deduction is allowed; however, the accumulation and proceeds are all tax free.

Making Small Gifts Count

There is another approach to this idea. You may start a savings account for children or grandchildren in order to teach them the value of saving money for the future. If you have a young adult child or grandchild who is getting married or beginning a career, this is another way to help him or her learn the value of investing. Open an IRA account in the young person's name. Make the first contribution and encourage regular investments. Note that he or she must be over 18 and have earned at least as much as the contribution in order to obtain the tax deduction.

Looking back over investment history there is evidence that even a small investment over time can grow to a large value. For example, 40 years ago a $1,000 investment in one of the oldest and largest growth mutual funds in America would be worth $152,000 today with all distributions being reinvested. That is a gift with tremendous leverage. Subsequent investments pay out handsomely, too. If your young adult added only $500 per year for those 40 years, the fund would have had an additional $495,000. That is a total of $645,000 from a $21,000 investment. Naturally, we are talking about long periods of time.

Most younger people would like to have the cash right now and here is a way they can get some of it. Your contribution to their IRA is probably tax deductible to them. A gift to them of $1,000 will result in a minimum $150 reduction in federal taxes. That would provide some extra spending money now. If they are in a 28 percent tax bracket it would provide $280 in extra spending money. Remember that the IRA account must be in their name. You have to give the money to the young adult and they must make the investment.

Two other areas for considerations are a Roth IRA and Education IRAs. A Roth IRA permits contributions of up to $2,000 per year. While there is no tax deduction allowed for the contribution, the earnings and future withdrawals are tax free. This is a very powerful tool to use for future retirement planning. The Education IRA permits nondeductible contributions of $500 per year per beneficiary under age 18. Distributions are exempt from taxes and penalties when used to pay qualified education expenses.

Done well, giving can yield wonderful tax saving benefits to you and the receiver.

CHAPTER 14

Estate Planning
Passing Along Your Wealth

*Y*ou've had to deal not only with the grief of your spouse's or parent's death, but also the difficulties associated with settling the estate. Now, you may wish to put your own estate in order. Doing so will ensure that when you die your heirs will receive what you want them to have when you want them to get it with a minimum of expense, estate taxes, and administration.

Estate taxes—which are at a maximum rate of 55 percent—can be the largest tax expense you will ever face. Your estate is everything you own—all that you've accumulated during your lifetime including what you've inherited.

Note:

Lack of proper planning could mean loss of over half of what you, your spouse, or parent spent a lifetime building.

Estate planning creates a structure by which to manage your property while you're alive and to provide for its desired distribution upon your death. Without a plan, the estate you wanted to leave may end up being much smaller than you anticipated.

Please don't think of this chapter as a replacement for professional advice. It is intended to be a guide, to show you some of the available

233

strategies, and provide you with basic concepts. However, estate planning is highly complicated and the rules change frequently. Before implementing any estate plan strategies, seek the advice of an attorney, accountant, or financial planner qualified in estate planning. You can determine whether you already have an adequate estate plan by answering the questions in Figure 14.1.

ESTATE PLANNING IS DEFINITELY FOR YOU

To handle the distribution of your own estate, you can do nothing or you can prepare and sign a will and/or establish trusts. Here are six good reasons why estate planning is good for your financial well being:

1. You decide who will receive your assets or portions of assets.
2. You decide in what amounts and when your chosen beneficiaries will receive those assets.
3. You decide, either through will or by trust, who will be the executors and trustees of your assets.
4. You can reduce estate taxes and avoid probate or administration fees.
5. You can select a guardian for minor children.
6. If you own a business, you can plan for its orderly maintenance or its disposal.

If you have no estate plan state laws determine who gets your assets and when they get them. Without a plan the court will appoint a guardian for minor children and an administrator for your estate. To maintain control over these issues, you must act in advance of death.

Five Steps to Estate Planning

The *first* step in estate planning is vital and personal—you need to decide who will receive your assets and when those individuals or institutions should receive them. You'll have to address the following four questions:

1. If you have children, should they share equally or do any of them have special needs that require more financial help?

FIGURE 14.1 Estate Planning Questionnaire

If you answer "No" to any of the following questions, you are a good candidate for estate planning.

1. Do you have a will?

2. Do you know the value of your estate?

3. Are you comfortable with the executors and trustees you've selected?

4. Have you executed a living will or health care proxy in the event of catastrophic illness or disability?

5. Have you considered a living trust to avoid probate?

6. If you have a living trust, have you retitled the appropriate assets in the name of the trust?

7. Does your will name a guardian for your minor children?

8. Do you have the right amount and type of life insurance?

9. Do you have an irrevocable life insurance trust to exclude insurance proceeds from being taxed as part of your estate?

10. Have you created trusts for family gift giving?

11. If your estate is large enough, does it take advantage of the estate tax exemption?

12. Are you currently making gifts to take advantage of the annual gift exclusion?

13. To maximize future estate tax savings, have you made gifts of assets that are likely to appreciate?

14. Have you considered a charitable trust that could provide both estate and income tax benefits?

15. If you own a business, do you have a management succession plan?

16. Do you have a buy-sell agreement for any interest you hold in a family business?

17. Have you considered a gift program involving your family-owned business?

18. Is your estate plan current and does it take into account all your personal wishes and all the tax-saving strategies of which you are aware?

2. Do you have grandchildren? If so, how should they enter into the picture?

3. Do you have a life-long friend or other relative whom you would like to include?

4. Do you want any charities to play a role in your inheritance plans?

The *second* step is to consider which assets will go to which parties. For example, if you own a home or other real estate, do you want all the beneficiaries to share equally or would such an arrangement be too cumbersome? Can all of your beneficiaries appropriately handle a cash bequest? If not, perhaps a trust vehicle with a trustee designated to distribute the cash over a period of time would be better than an outright bequest.

The *third* step is to decide when the beneficiaries should receive the assets, considering the age of each heir and his or her ability to manage assets. If your beneficiaries are young or immature, perhaps you'd prefer that the assets be distributed over time as your heirs mature so they can handle all the assets you intend to pass on to them.

The *fourth* step is to consider the drawbacks and the advantages to using trusts in your situation. Perhaps you want a reliable trustee to remain in control of the assets if the size of the inheritance might affect the beneficiaries' work ethic or personality. Or, maybe you should make gifts now to reduce the size of your estate and to prepare your beneficiaries for asset management.

The *fifth* step involves several other planning issues that you need to consider, such as finding the right attorney, a process that is covered in detail in Chapter 16 Choosing Professional Advisers, and understanding probate and making plans to simplify it, a subject that is discussed extensively in Chapter 6. You will want to use as many legal methods as you can to reduce estate taxes.

Why You Need a Will

A will is an essential part of any estate plan and the primary document by which to transfer your wealth when you die. If you die intestate (without a will), state law will control the distribution of your property.

Before you see your lawyer about drafting a will, you must make eight crucial decisions:

1. *Naming an executor.* The executor is your personal representative after your death. The person or institution you designate is responsible for managing your estate and distributing the assets as you have directed. The executor has to conserve the assets, prepare them for distribution to your beneficiaries, pay taxes, and file government documents.

    Choose your executor carefully. You may wish to designate a family member, trusted friend, or associate. If your estate is complex, it may be best to name a professional adviser or an organization such as a bank as executor or coexecutor. Some of the advantages and disadvantages of naming personal or institutional executors are listed in Figure 14.2.

2. *Creating trusts.* Your will directs how your estate will be distributed and can provide instructions for creating trusts to achieve your long-term goals—such as providing funds for an elderly parent or funding for the education of children or grandchildren. You will have to choose one or more trustees when you create a trust and you must take even greater care in choosing a trustee than you did choosing an executor because the trustee's duties may last much longer than the executor's.

3. *Designating guardians.* To protect your minor children and ensure they will be cared for by people you trust, you will want to name a guardian in your will. You'll want to give careful thought to choosing a guardian(s) whose ideas about children and child-rearing are similar to yours. Remember to speak to the person(s) you want to name as guardian(s) and get his or her consent before designating them in your will.

4. *Waiver of probate.* You can insert a provision in your will that waives the legal requirement for your executor to be bonded. In the absence of a will, the court will require a fiduciary bond to guarantee replacement of any funds embezzled or diverted by the executor. The cost of the bond must be borne by the estate.

5. *Specific bequests.* You may use your will to make explicit bequests of jewelry, heirlooms, furniture, or cash to specific individuals. In the absence of a will, you cannot be certain that your written or oral instructions will be followed.

FIGURE 14.2   Executors: Financial Institutions vs. Individuals

Naming a Financial Institution as Executor

Advantages:

- They are specialists in handling estates and trusts.
- They have no emotional bias.
- They are usually free of any conflict of interest with you or your beneficiaries.
- They remain in the same location and never go on vacation.
- They never get sick or die.

Disadvantages:

- The staff usually has little familiarity with your family.
- They may have high administrative fees.

Naming an Individual as Executor

Advantages:

- Familiarity with your family situation.
- No or low administrative fees.

Disadvantages:

- Lay people may not understand estates and trusts.
- Emotional bias might keep an individual from acting impartially.
- There may be frequent scheduling conflicts.
- An individual may not be able to provide service if he or she is incapacitated or otherwise unavailable.

6. *Avoiding additional expenses.* Sometimes it is necessary to sell assets to pay death taxes and expenses of probate. In such a case, you can avoid additional expenses by stating in your will that your executor may sell assets for such a purpose without having to publish a notice of sale in the newspaper.

7. *The law of intestacy.* A will avoids having your assets distributed under your state's intestacy law which will automatically pass property to certain relatives. Intestacy laws have been drafted

to be fair in an average situation but you may not want your assets to go to some family members, or perhaps not in the amounts the intestacy law mandates. Rather, like most people, you probably want to choose the people who will benefit from your estate.

8. *Peace of mind.* Although it cannot be measured in dollars, you will benefit from peace of mind when your estate is in order. Eliminating that emotional burden promotes your well-being and that of your family.

Avoiding Probate

Avoiding probate is a high priority in estate planning. Probate, the process to prove your will is genuine and to administer it under the jurisdiction of a court, is a public procedure. This means that anyone who wishes—including creditors, former spouses, and sworn enemies—can go to the courthouse, look up a will admitted to probate, and learn what assets are available in the estate. In addition, probate can be time-consuming and expensive. Thus, avoiding probate should be one of your primary estate planning goals.

The basic techniques for avoiding probate are listed in Chapter 6, but another method deserves further discussion here: the living trust. A living trust is a legal document that resembles a will. It can contain all kinds of instructions for managing your assets if you are disabled, as well as directions for distributing your holdings when you die. Once you've set it up, you have to transfer the legal title to any assets to be placed into the trust to the trust's name.

You still control the assets in a living trust and you don't need to file a trust tax return or pay taxes out of the trust providing you declare the trust's income yourself and pay taxes on it as an individual. You are, in other words, the trustee for your own assets. However, when you die the assets in the trust don't go through probate. Thus, if you've covered all your assets by the techniques outlined in Chapter 6 or by a living trust, your estate will avoid probate.

Consult an attorney about drafting a living trust, and make sure it dovetails with your other estate plans. Also, remember that avoiding probate and avoiding estate taxes are two entirely separate matters.

Estate Tax Reduction Strategies

While federal income tax rates have dropped during the last ten years, estate tax rates have remained high. The top marginal estate tax rate can be as high as 55 percent and hidden surtaxes can take the rate up to 60 percent. This only applies to federal estate tax; you may also be liable for state and inheritance taxes as well as administrative costs. You can see the Unified Federal Gift credits available in Figure 14.3. The Estate Tax Table in Figure 14.4 shows the tax rates.

Unified Federal Gift and Estate Tax

Many widowed persons do not have to worry about estate tax because everyone is exempt up to the first $650,000 (for 1999) of lifetime gift and death benefits combined. This means, in effect, that the tax on the first $650,000 of assets in an estate—$211,300—is given to you as a tax credit. Also, without touching your $650,000 lifetime exemption, you can give away up to $10,000 each year to as many people as you like free of gift tax.

Do you need to worry about estate taxes? Is your net worth over $650,000? Go back to Chapter 5 where you listed your assets and liabilities and take a look at your net worth. Don't forget to include personal use assets such as your home, automobile, camper, and your IRA account or pension plans. These items of value are included automatically in your assets for estate planning purposes.

Consider adding to your total net worth any inheritance that you are aware you will receive within the next few years. Also, if you own a life insurance policy, the proceeds will normally be included in your estate at death. Life insurance benefits will not be included if someone else owns the policy; that is, if someone else has the right to choose beneficiaries. Thus, a $250,000 life insurance policy you omitted from your net worth may become a $250,000 asset in your estate when you pass away.

Perhaps your estate is over $650,000 or the current growth of your assets will put you over $650,000 soon. Most individuals are quite surprised at the size of their estate. Previous law exempted the first $600,000 of value from federal estate tax but that amount hadn't been raised for years meaning that inflation had effectively reduced it. The new law will raise the exemption to $1 million by 2006. That's the good news.

The bad news is that the increase takes place over nine years, beginning in 1998, and most of it occurs in the last three years (2004, 2005, and 2006). For the exact schedule, see the table in Figure 14.3.

If your net taxable estate is $650,000 or less, there will be no federal estate tax at your death in 1999. However, if your estate is close to or above $650,000, read on. The estate will be subject to a marginal tax rate beginning at 37 percent. You can find your estate tax rate in the table in Figure 14.4.

ESTATE TAX PLANNING STRATEGIES

Set Up an Irrevocable Life Insurance Trust

If you own life insurance policies when you die, the proceeds can be included in your taxable estate. Ownership is determined by who has the right to name or change beneficiaries. You can correct this problem by transferring ownership of the policies to a trust. However, if you should die within three years of the transfer, the proceeds will be added back into your estate for estate tax purposes.

This procedure can be used for current life insurance or new purchases of life insurance. In either case, the trust owns the policies and pays the premiums. At your death the proceeds are paid into the trust, are not included in your estate, and are tax free.

The trust can then provide benefits to your desired beneficiaries or it can buy assets from your estate by exchanging cash for estate

FIGURE 14.3 Unified Federal Gift and Estate Tax Credits

Year	Unified Credit	Exemption
1999	$211,300	$650,000
2000, 2001	$220,550	$675,000
2002, 2003	$229,800	$700,000
2004	$207,300	$850,000
2005	$326,300	$950,000
2006	$345,800	$1 million

FIGURE 14.4 The Estate Tax Table

Taxable Estate	Federal Estate Tax	Marginal Tax Rate (Tax on the Next Dollar)
$ 650,000 or less	-0-	37%
750,000	$ 55,500	39%
1,000,000	153,000	41%
1,250,000	255,500	43%
1,500,000	363,000	45%
2,000,000	588,000	49%
2,500,000	833,000	53%
3,000,000	1,098,000	55%

assets. The estate thus has the cash to pay estate taxes and the trust has assets which it can pass on to your children.

For example, Mary Kelly now has an estate of $1.55 million. When her husband died she received most of his pension benefits in a lump sum, but she transferred his IRA to her IRA, thus deferring income taxes on his IRA.

When Mary dies, her estate is facing estate tax of $363,000 plus federal income tax of $27,000 on her IRA account—a total of $390,000. Her current income is approximately $105,000 a year.

Mary had her lawyer set up an irrevocable life insurance trust and transferred some income-producing assets into it. The trust purchased a life insurance policy on Mary's life and pays the premiums. When Mary dies, the $390,000 tax-free proceeds of the life insurance policy flows into the trust which the trust will exchange for assets in the estate. These funds will be used by the estate to pay its taxes. The assets in the insurance trust will ultimately go to the named beneficiaries— Mary's children—as they would have through her estate, but now the estate tax can be paid with discounted dollars from the insurance policy.

Annual Gift Program

You can take advantage of the annual gift tax exclusion to reduce estate taxes, while passing assets onto your family or anyone you choose. Thus, if you have two children, four grandchildren, and a favorite charity and you wish to give each $10,000 a year, you could give away $70,000 each year, reduce your estate by $70,000, and incur no gift taxes.

For example, Roger has an estate of $2.5 million. If he dies today, the federal estate tax will be approximately $833,000, even with his $650,000 exemption. Over the next five years, Roger decides he will give $10,000 a year to each son, daughter, son-in-law, daughter-in-law, and four grandchildren—a total of $80,000 a year. Assuming the value of his estate has not changed, in five years its worth will have decreased from $2.5 million to $2.1 million. If Roger dies in five years, the estate tax will be $588,000—a savings of $245,000.

Moreover, the savings to Roger's estate is probably greater than $588,000 because the earnings on the money, had it been left in his estate, would be taxable at his death. Further, if these assets had grown in the estate, Roger's estate tax problem would have been even higher than originally suggested. Thus, Roger gave away $80,000 of assets a year and passed on the income as well as the appreciation of those assets.

If you want to qualify for the annual exclusion, the law requires that you give a present interest in the property to the recipient. This means the person receiving the property must have full and complete use of, and access to, the funds.

Direct Payment of Medical or Tuition Bills

Here's a little known estate tax strategy. If you pay a child's medical and tuition bills directly to the institution entitled to payment, the funds are treated as a gift that is tax free. This tax-free gift is in addition to the regular $10,000 limit per year.

Thus, Marge, a widow with a large estate, not only gives each grandchild $10,000 a year but also pays each grandchild's college tuition of $6,300 a year. This removes $16,300 per grandchild from Marge's estate. If she left the money in her estate at her 50 percent estate tax bracket only half of it would go to her heirs after taxes.

The Crummy Trust Provision

This is named after the Crummy family which wanted to set up trusts that would limit the beneficiary's access to the funds but still qualify for the annual gift tax exclusion. The trust was written so that the beneficiaries had a limited time to withdraw funds that had been transferred to the trust. If the funds were not withdrawn within the specified time period, they remained as part of the trust.

Because the beneficiaries had the current ability to withdraw the funds, the money qualified for the annual $10,000 gift exclusion. When the funds were not withdrawn, the original goal of keeping the funds in the trust was accomplished. This became known as the Crummy trust provision or Crummy withdrawal power.

Obviously, if you use a Crummy trust provision, you risk that the beneficiary could withdraw the funds within the limited time period. However, if you make known your desire that the assets are to remain in the trust, the beneficiary may acquiesce to your wishes.

Giving Assets That Are Appreciating

You can save the most in estate taxes by giving away assets that have or will have the highest growth potential. For example, suppose you own a stock valued today at $30,000 that over the next three years is expected to grow in value to $70,000. If the projected appreciation actually occurs, you will have moved a $70,000 asset out of your estate. Note that any amount you give away to one person in excess of $10,000 per year counts as part of your lifetime gift/estate exemption.

Therefore it may make sense to use some of the first $650,000 in your estate to make current gifts. The estate and gift tax system is a combined system, hence the title Unified Federal Gift and Estate Tax. Thus, the first $650,000 of taxable gift creates no gift tax just as the first $650,000 of an estate creates no estate tax. However, you are only allowed to claim a total of $650,000—for example, a combination of $325,000 in gifts and $325,000 in estate values.

You can use the total $650,000 exemption during your lifetime or at death, whichever you desire, but not both. Sometimes it may make sense to use up all or a portion of the $650,000 in gifts during your lifetime.

Suppose you have a property worth $650,000 that is growing at a high appreciation rate. If you give it away now and it's worth $1 million in five years, in effect you've moved an additional $350,0000 out of your estate—the $650,000 the property was worth at the time you gave it away plus the $350,000 that it grew in value. Of course, if you do that, there will no longer be a $650,000 exemption available to your estate when you die.

Charitable Giving

This subject was covered extensively in Chapter 13, but it's worth mentioning again here because it's a valuable estate planning technique.

The premise is simple: direct gifts to charity are fully deductible. Thus, if you share your estate assets with a charity you will save estate taxes. If you give your entire estate to a charity, there will be no estate taxes at all.

You can also make gifts to charity and to those close to you personally by setting up a charitable remainder trust. This trust will pay income to your beneficiaries at your death for a specific period of time, after which the assets pass to the charity. There are many variations on this theme. For example, you can make a gift to your charitable remainder trust during your lifetime with the provision that income be paid to you until death when the trust proceeds will pass to the charity. Using this device can provide income tax benefits and estate tax savings.

You can also set up a charitable income trust. In this situation, income goes to the charity for a period of time then the remainder passes to your beneficiaries. This kind of trust would also provide estate tax benefits.

Using Generation-Skipping Techniques

If you have a large estate, due to the number of times assets are passed from generation to generation, skipping a generation by transferring property to your grandchildren or great-grandchildren is an effective method of avoiding estate tax liability. However, if you choose this method, you could be subject to the Generation-Skipping Transfer Tax (GSTT) which is designed to eliminate the tax advantages of jumping over several generations without paying taxes on the generations skipped. There is a $1 million exemption available, but this is a fairly complex planning strategy and if you decide to pursue it you should consult competent counsel.

OTHER ESTATE PLANNING CONSIDERATIONS

Suppose you became so incapacitated that you are unable to make your own health care decisions. Whom would you want to decide for you? A *living will* allows you to select the person to whom you want to grant this responsibility while you're still healthy.

A living will is a legal document stating your desire that extraordinary artificial techniques should not be used to prolong your life when death is imminent, loss of mental capacity is substantial, incurable, or irreversible, and there is no hope of recovery. Valid in most states, a living will can help your family, doctors, hospitals, and other caregivers to follow your wishes.

The Supreme Court has decided that no parent, sibling, adult child, or friend will be allowed to make life-determining decisions for you unless you have previously provided clear and convincing evidence that their actions carry out your express wishes. Consult with your attorney about the proper wording and your state's requirements for a living will. Once the document is prepared, make certain you understand each term before signing.

Many states have authorized by specific law the use of *health care proxies*. A health care proxy is broader and more flexible than a living will because it gives the person you name authority over many types of health care, not just those relating to life sustaining techniques. The proxy allows you to appoint someone to make any and all health care decisions on your behalf if you are unable to make your own, unless you limit the authority in the document. Health care proxies are often used in addition to living wills. However, sometimes a proxy is written broadly enough to take the place of a living will

As long as you remain able, you can continue to make your own decisions, you can refuse any health care treatment merely by objecting, and you can revoke, orally or in writing, the power of attorney you gave.

Anatomical Gifts

The subject of anatomical gifts is an uncomfortable issue for many people. Whether you are for or against them, you should know how to make such a gift or protect yourself if you don't want your body used in this way.

The Uniform Anatomical Gift Act (UAGA) provides that people over age 18 may at death donate their entire body or any one or more of its parts to any hospital, surgeon, physician, medical or dental school, or various organ banks. Organ gifts can be made for educational research, therapy, or transplant purposes. However, neither your body nor any of its organs may be donated if you have objected to such a gift in writing.

Durable Power of Attorney

Durable is the key word here because it means that the power you have given your agent to act in your behalf with respect to financial matters is not affected by your disability or incapacity. Each state has its own special wording that must be used to make the power durable.

A well-drawn durable power of attorney is often as important as a will. If you have a durable power, your family won't need to petition a court for appointment of a guardian to handle your assets in the event you become incapacitated. If you currently are experiencing a physical disability or illness that could lead to permanent or long-term incapacity, you should seriously consider a durable power of attorney.

Springing Power of Attorney

You may have run across the term *springing power of attorney,* so named because it takes effect only in the event you become disabled or incapacitated. The definition of disability or incapacity is extremely important in any power of attorney. Some states provide a definition or you can provide one in the document which specifies that one or more physicians must examine you to certify that you are incapacitated.

The Ethical Will

An ethical will is not meant to be a legal document, although many people consider it just as important. An ethical will passes on to your beneficiaries a spiritual legacy. Ethical wills can take any form you wish—a written document, tape recording, videotape, or combination of these. They can cover any and all subjects you wish including instructions, apologies, praise, thanks, love and appreciation, or any other thoughts you have.

Letter of Instructions

This is a private, formal, nonlegal document in which you give specific instructions which cannot or should not be included in your will. Often it will contain:

- The location of key documents
- Funeral and burial instructions because your will may not be located until after the funeral
- How you'd like your obituary to read
- Advisers to contact and how to reach them
- Friends you'd like notified
- Instructions regarding specific care of certain children or parents
- Other personal information you feel would be helpful

You can write a letter of instructions, seal it, and place it in an envelope marked "To Be Opened in the Event of My Serious Illness or Death." Then tell your heirs where you put the envelope. A sample letter is provided in Figure 14.5.

Estate planning is not a do-it-once process. The major elements of wills and trusts can be set into place but they need to be reviewed periodically to ensure that everything fits your present situation. There are other reasons to review your estate plan:

- *Changes in family situations* such as birth or adoption of children or grandchildren, marriages, divorces, and deaths.
- *Changes in financial situation* including drastic increases or decreases in the size of your estate.
- *Changes in the tax law.* The estate tax laws are modified constantly. Competent counsel can help you determine whether your estate plans meet new or amended laws.

Last, any other changes in your life may merit a review of your estate plan.

FIGURE 14.5   Personal Letter to My Family

Dear Family,

I am writing this letter to supplement my estate plan and arrangements. I hope by explaining my objectives on paper it will help you handle my estate and investment matters and make other important decisions.

I cannot foresee what will happen between the time I write this and the time you read it. Therefore, my thoughts should not be followed inflexibly, but tempered by consideration of the circumstances existing as I write and how they may have changed since then.

1. Instructions about my funeral, last rites, burial services, cemetery, etc. _____
   _____

2. Directions about my medical and nursing home care, etc. _____
   _____

3. My wishes about life support systems. _____
   _____

4. My wishes about organ donor transplantation. _____
   _____

5. People I would like my family to consult about medical, legal, and financial
   matters. _____
   _____

6. My suggestions about investment philosophies for each of you. _____
   _____

7. Goals that I consider important for our family. _____
   _____

8. Special investments or comments for my heirs. _____
   _____

9. Other considerations._____
   _____

Date: _____

    Signature: _____

CHAPTER 15

The Financial Aspects of Remarriage

*M*ost widowed individuals thrust into singlehood miss various aspects of married life. Often loneliness can lead to ill-timed remarriage, sometimes with negative results. You need to be cautious about remarriage, both emotionally and financially. In this important chapter we will deal with the emotional and financial factors to consider before remarrying. If you are an adult child and your parent is a surviving spouse, the information in this chapter may provide you with the framework to counsel your parent.

There are many things for you to assess when contemplating remarriage. Certainly, you should not think about taking a new partner until you feel you've said goodbye to your deceased spouse. No one can replace your departed mate and the other person in a new relationship deserves to be considered as an individual in his or her own right.

One of the most important issues is your children. Most people think only young children have feelings about a parent's remarriage. However, adult children often find it hard to accept their parent's need for companionship, a sexual relationship, and sharing. Because children tend to think of parents as asexual creatures, your offspring may frown on your remarriage plans.

Note:

Grown children often feel threatened financially by a new spouse, fearing that your funds might be diverted from them in favor of the new partner.

More than likely, your children truly are concerned about you, about your new mate's motives, and about your financial and emotional involvement. However, if you feel your new relationship is worthwhile and you want to marry, ask your children to consider and accept your needs. If you do not receive their approval, you may find yourself in conflict with them. If they cannot accept your situation, your conflict with them may remain unresolved.

There are also other factors for you to consider about remarriage. These include your respective backgrounds, the other relationships that come with you into the marriage, what habits each of you bring, and any differences in financial assets that could become a cause for estrangement.

MONEY TALK

Money can be a major source of tension in a marriage so you'll need to talk about how you want to spend your money as a couple, whether you want joint, separate, or combination checking accounts, or any special savings accounts. Decide what important things you will save for and how you will allocate your salaries fairly if you're going to be a two-paycheck couple and one person earns substantially more than the other.

Some newly remarried couples pay household bills using a ratio based on earnings which means that each partner contributes to the household in proportion to the income he or she earns. For example, if one partner earns $50,000 a year and the other earns $100,000, the partner earning $50,000 might contribute one-third and the other partner might contribute two-thirds toward household expenses. The funds left over are each person's private money to spend or save as he or she wishes.

Most remarrying couples are less willing to merge funds completely, not because they lack confidence in their new partners, but because each person has become accustomed to running his or her own finances. No matter how money was handled in your first marriage, you may have to be flexible and do things differently this time around.

Financial Considerations before Remarrying

Here's a quick rundown of thirteen major points that need to be covered before you proceed down the aisle again:

1. Do your respective wills need to be updated or substantially changed?
2. Do you have trusts that need beneficiary changes or new language because of your new relationship?
3. Do you want to change beneficiary designations on life insurance policies?
4. Do you have other kinds of insurance coverage that overlap; for example, if there are two automobiles, can you place both of them with the same carrier, thereby achieving a discount?
5. If you both have health insurance, can one of you go on the other's policy to reduce overall cost?
6. How will your assets be titled? Will yours remain in your name? Will you own anything jointly?
7. Does your estate plan need to be revised? Note that when you remarry you regain the marital deduction. You may wish to consult your attorney about creating a marital deduction trust.
8. How will any pension benefits be affected? Do either of you lose any or all of them upon remarriage?
9. What effect will your remarriage have on Social Security benefits?
10. Do you need a prenuptial agreement?
11. How do each of you view your assets and your current giving programs in relation to your respective sets of children? This is a delicate area; for instance, your spouse-to-be may feel that money is going to your children that should be used for the benefit of the marriage.
12. Review liability insurance policies to reflect the new joint net worth especially if both of you are bringing substantial assets to the marriage.
13. Does your intended have debts that you would have to assume or share jointly?

Community Property States

There are eight community property states: Arizona, California, Idaho, Louisiana, Nevada, New Mexico, Texas, and the state of Washington. If you live in one of these states, property you owned before marriage or acquired after marriage by gift or inheritance is considered separate property; it is yours. However, all property acquired by any other means after marriage is considered to be community property and each spouse may be said to have a one-half interest in all community property regardless of who is the titled owner.

Before you remarry, you will want to evaluate how each of you will hold your property in a community property state. (In noncommunity property states property acquired after marriage can be titled individually or jointly.)

Prenuptial Agreements

Experts agree that a prenuptial agreement is virtually indispensable if you're planning a second marriage. Although second timers swear it won't happen to them, statistics show second marriages run a high risk of failure. Such an agreement is designed to preserve the separate properties of the spouses-to-be for distribution to their respective families in event of divorce or either spouse-to-be's death. Here's what a prenuptial agreement can do:

- Define your property rights and those of your spouse after the marriage.
- Avoid having your state's law applied if you or your spouse dies without a will.
- Set out any rights of your new spouse with respect to the estate of your first spouse.
- Establish the rights of the spouses-to-be to each other's property in the event they divorce.

Other Advantages

Such an agreement gives both of you control over what you want, not what various state laws or others decide. Creditors in a bankruptcy action will go after any asset. Assets can be protected by establishing them as separate in a prenuptial agreement.

Usually a surviving spouse can claim part of the deceased spouse's estate (right of election law). This claim can be waived or modified. Prenuptial agreements supersede both inheritance and right of election laws. Having your second spouse limit or waive claims on property, gifts, or inheritance may be necessary to protect the rights of your children from your previous marriage, not only from unfair property dispositions but also from the stress occurring from litigation.

Most states require that prenuptial agreements be fair when made and not unconscionable at the time of enforcement. Before signing a prenuptial agreement, you and your spouse-to-be should each have your own attorney, and each should disclose fully to the other all assets and income.

Some people ignore premarital planning because they don't want to consider the possibility of failure; others may have more practical reasons. For example, wealthy widowed persons may not wish their fiancé to know the full extent of their net worth, which is necessary for a prenuptial agreement.

Note:

You may think it's awkward to discuss a prenuptial agreement in the glow before the wedding but having one may prevent grief later on.

Many widowed individuals don't like to think about the topic, but the discomfort of approaching it before remarriage may be far less than the misery you may experience if you don't approach it at all. In the long run, a prenuptial agreement is a great anxiety reducer.

Marriage Tax Penalties

It's unfortunate, but if both partners in a marriage are age 65 or over, they will usually pay more taxes on a joint return than the combined tax they would pay if they were single. The couples affected most by this are the ones with fairly equal but moderate incomes. Often, as single taxpayers they would be in the 15 percent tax bracket. When they marry their joint income moves them into the 28 percent bracket. One remedy is to move your investments into tax-deferred or tax-free areas such as annuities or tax-free bonds.

Occasionally the opposite can happen. Let's say you earn $28,500 a year and your new spouse earns no income. As a couple you will now be in the 15 percent tax bracket. In this case, the couple with unequal incomes benefits from marriage and filing jointly.

Furthermore, if your income plus one-half of your Social Security benefits exceed a certain level—$25,000 for single people or $32,000 for a married couple—as much as 85 percent of the Social Security receipts are taxable. Two singles can receive a total of $50,000 of taxable income before any of their Social Security benefits are taxed. Thus, combining your incomes on a joint return may force you to pay tax on Social Security payments that would be completely tax free if you hadn't remarried.

Another tax penalty of remarriage regards losses available on rental properties. Rental real estate is classified by the IRS as a passive activity and falls under the passive gain/loss rules. The rules provide that up to $25,000 of passive losses from rental real estate can be deducted each year against income from nonpassive sources such as wages and investments.

If the single person's income is above $100,000, the $25,000 is reduced using the following formula:

(Adjusted Gross Income − $100,000) × 50% = Reduction Amount
    At $150,000 AGI, the passive loss deduction is completely lost.

Here's an example of how this might affect a remarriage. Jim has an adjusted gross income of $120,000. His passive loss is reduced by $10,000 [($120,000 − 100,000) × 50%]. Barbara, his fiancé, has an AGI of $30,000 and thus does not lose any of the deduction. Once married however their combined AGI is now $150,000 and they lose the entire $25,000 deduction:

$$(150,000 - 100,000) \times 50\% = \$25,000$$

To remedy this situation look for ways to reduce the AGIs or sell the real estate properties and place the proceeds into other investments with tax-deferred or tax-free features.

Standard Deduction Penalty

For 1998, two single people have a combined standard deduction of $8,500 versus $7,100 for a married couple filing jointly. If both singles are over age 65, the combined standard deduction is $10,500 compared to $8,500 for the married couple.

Other tax penalties include:

- IRA phase-out ranges. For two singles the combined range is $50,000–$70,000. For a married couple filing jointly it is $40,000–$50,000.
- Personal exemption phase-out ranges. Personal exemption in 1998 equaled $2,700 for each exemption claimed. The exemptions are phased out as income increases above certain levels. For two singles, the combined range is $249,000–$494,000. For a married couple filing jointly it is $186,800–$309,300.

Estate Planning upon Remarriage

Once you've remarried you may need to review some of the following estate planning concepts with an estate planning attorney.

Use of the Marital Deduction

The marital deduction is a powerful estate planning tool. Any assets passing to a surviving spouse pass estate tax free at the time of the first spouse's death (assuming the surviving spouse is a U.S. citizen). Therefore if you are willing to pass all your assets to your surviving spouse, there will be no federal estate tax at that time.

However, this doesn't solve the estate tax problem—it only defers it. If your surviving spouse does not remarry, he or she will not be able to take advantage of the marital deduction at death. Therefore the assets transferred from the first spouse will be subject to tax in the estate of the second spouse.

One solution to this problem is to set up an irrevocable life insurance trust that holds a second-to-die life insurance policy on the two of you. At the second death, the life policy provides to your named beneficiaries a replacement amount to offset the estate taxes. (See the irrevocable life insurance trust description later in this chapter.)

Qualified Terminal Interest Property Trust (QTIP)

The QTIP trust is often used by remarrying couples as a method to ensure that their respective assets will be distributed according to their individual wishes at death.

Typically, each spouse establishes a QTIP trust as part of his or her will. Both spouses stipulate that when one dies a predetermined part of the deceased's assets will be held in trust for specified beneficiaries, usually managed by the survivor and a cotrustee. The survivor receives the income from the trust and with the cotrustee's approval can even tap the principal to uphold his or her standard of living. The beneficiaries of the trust cannot be changed and they receive the full assets of the trust after the second spouse dies. Note that upon the surviving spouse's death, the assets in the trust pass as indicated in the will of the first spouse. Seek expert legal help to set up this type of arrangement.

The Irrevocable Life Insurance Trust

If you own life insurance policies at your death, the proceeds are included in your taxable estate. Ownership is usually determined by who has the right to name the beneficiaries of the proceeds. The way around this problem is not to own the policies when you die. Instead, create an irrevocable life insurance trust. The trust owns the policies and pays the premiums. When you die, the proceeds pass into the trust and are not included in your estate. The trust can be structured to provide benefits to your surviving spouse and/or other beneficiaries.

Be sure to get professional advice before setting up one of these trusts. A properly structured trust could save you more than 50 percent in estate taxes on any insurance proceeds. Thus, a $1 million life insurance policy owned by an irrevocable insurance trust could reduce your estate taxes by over $500,000.

QTIP Charitable Trust

A QTIP charitable trust has proven to be an excellent method to make a deferred gift to a charity and still make the entire estate available for the financial security of your surviving spouse—all without any gift or estate taxes. A modification of this plan permits you to benefit your children as well as your spouse and the charity.

For example, if you establish a living revocable trust it would provide that:

1. you would receive all the income for your life;

2. at your death, the trust would continue and all income would be paid to your surviving spouse for life;
3. at the death of the surviving spouse, the trust property would pass to a charitable remainder trust that would pay a 10 percent annuity to your daughter for her life; and
4. the trust property would pass to a designated charity at the death of the daughter.

When you die, the value of the trust qualifies for an estate tax marital deduction at the election of your executor. And when your spouse dies after you, the value of the charitable remainder trust is deductible for federal estate tax purposes. Again, this technique requires the expert assistance and draftsmanship of an attorney experienced in estate plans and charitable giving.

Planning with Your New Spouse

While your finances should not control your happiness, the road ahead will be smoother if you discuss and plan your financial life before you enter into remarriage. In finances as in love, it is often what spouses don't tell each other that hurts. Whether your new marriage should end by death or divorce, you may pay plenty for lack of knowledge. Every estate lawyer has file drawers full of stories about the anguish and expense bequeathed to clients by spouses who died without putting their affairs in order.

Secrecy among mates complicates the chore of settling an estate, yet many newly remarried couples are reluctant to talk to their new spouses about their assets. Some partners assume that their mates will not understand finances or are not interested in them; others just don't trust their partner when it comes to money.

Partners who may be fearful of divorce often think it is necessary to conceal assets, and considering one out of four remarriages fail, the fear is understandable. Nevertheless, it is tough to hide major assets from a sharp divorce lawyer.

Perhaps the main reason people don't like to talk about their assets is that they don't like to talk about death. The fact remains that in most successful marriages the partners share with each other information about all their assets. Being knowledgeable also facilitates each spouse's financial strategies and planning for their respective children and grandchildren.

While you may not share your new partner's assets, you certainly should be aware of them. The last things you need to encounter are financial surprises upon the death of your new partner.

THE TAXPAYER RELIEF ACT OF 1997

This new tax bill enacted a number of thresholds and phase-outs that affect married couples more than singles. Here's a brief recap of the most notable provisions:

- *Student loans.* Under the new law, interest on student loans will be deductible during the first five years that payments are required. Taxpayers will be able to deduct up to $1,000 next year, with the amount climbing to $2,500 by the year 2001. However, the deductions phase out for incomes between $40,000 and $55,000 for singles and $60,000 and $75,000 for married couples. For example, two new graduates collect their degrees and go to work for $39,000 each. If they remain single they can deduct $2,000 between them next year; if they marry, they get no deduction.

- *Roth IRAs.* Married workers cannot contribute to a Roth IRA if their joint income is more than $160,000. However, single partners making $80,000–$110,000 each could contribute.

- *Child credit.* The $500 credit ($400 in 1998) for each child under 17 is reduced by $50 for each $1,000 that income exceeds a certain limit: $110,000 for married couples, $75,000 for singles and heads of household. Thus, if two singles, each with one child, were making $70,000 each, they would be entitled to credits of $400 each next year. However, if they married, their credit would drop to zero.

- *Education IRAs.* Contributions to new IRAs for education expenses are phased out through a complicated formula that effectively eliminates contributions by singles at $110,000 of income and married couples at $160,000. Two singles each making $80,000 could make a contribution for each child, whereas if the same two were married, they could make no contribution.

- *Capital gains.* The new law creates a special low capital gains rate of 10 percent for lower-income taxpayers. The rate applies to incomes up to $41,200 for married couples and up to $24,650 for singles. For two singles with incomes of $24,000 each, some capital gains would qualify for the 10 percent rate. If they married, their gains would be taxed at 20 percent.

CHAPTER 16

Choosing Professional Advisers

You can probably do your own planning for many of the topics discussed in this book, while some will require a professional's expertise. Previously, reference has been made to the importance of retaining competent experts—an attorney, financial planner, accountant, insurance agent, or banker. Plan to build on your strengths and don't let your weaknesses frustrate you. Hire competent help and surround yourself with other people's knowledge. The basic rule is: Build on your strengths and let other people help you in areas in which you are weak.

If you don't already have advisers, let's look in detail at how to choose the right people to work on your behalf.

FINANCIAL PLANNERS

Anyone can call himself or herself a financial planner and there is no shortage of people who do. Your challenge is to find a qualified planner who understands your problems, whose fees are within the range of your pocketbook, and who demonstrates professional experience and credentials.

First, look for planners who have some or all of the following three credentials:

1. Certified Financial Planner (CFP)
2. Chartered Financial Consultant (ChFC)
3. Accredited Personal Financial Specialist (APFS)

Certified Financial Planner (CFP)

The Institute of Certified Financial Planners defines a qualified CFP as a person with competence, experience, and intelligence in the complex profession of financial planning. Certification is awarded to those who have passed six comprehensive half-day tests over a two-year period, have three years' experience, offer client references, and provide proof of a college undergraduate degree. CFPs complete a financial planning curriculum that must be registered with, and approved by, the International Board of Standards and Practices of Certified Financial Planners. CFPs also are required to have 15 hours of continuing education per year, and many CFPs belong to the Institute for Certified Financial Planners. CFPs must abide by a professional code of ethics.

The CFP designation is the oldest financial planning credential in the United States and the one that's best known by consumers. Advanced programs are available to CFPs for specialties in the financial planning field leading to a master's degree.

You can call the Institute of Certified Financial Planners at 303-751-7600 to request a list of qualified planners in your area. (Also see the resources list later in this chapter.)

Chartered Financial Consultant (ChFC)

This highly regarded certification is issued through the Society of Financial Service Professionals (formerly American Society of CLU and CHFC) located in Bryn Mawr, Pennsylvania. Most planners who carry this certification come from practices heavily involved in insurance.

The comprehensive course of study which is held in high esteem by professionals within and outside the insurance industry takes several years to complete and consists of ten two-hour exams. Several master's degree programs are also available.

Accredited Personal Financial Specialist (APFS)

Issued by the American Institute of Certified Public Accountants, this designation is awarded to accountants who are members in good standing of the American Institute of Certified Public Accountants, have valid and unrevoked Certified Public Accountants certificates, complete a one-day exam, and have 750 hours experience in personal financial planning in the three years preceding application.

Six references are required along with a written statement of the Certified Public Accountant's intention to comply with reaccreditation standards. APFS practitioners are required to have 24 hours of continuing professional education annually that are directly related to personal financial planning.

Other Designations

Occasionally you may see or hear other designations for financial planners. These are less meaningful in your search for a competent professional but you should know what they are:

- *LUTC Fellow* means the planner has completed a series of sales courses offered by the Life Underwriter Training Council located in Washington, D.C.
- *Registered Investment Adviser (RIA)* may sound impressive but most anyone can become one and the title is no guarantee of competence or skill. The designation means only that people who give investment advice are required to be on file with state and federal agencies, pay a fee, and complete many forms.

  Once approved, registered investment advisers must make available a form called the ADV to potential clients. This form discloses detailed information about the advisers, such as how they operate, how they're paid, and what their contracts include.

A good financial planner will have a wide range of knowledge and experience to help you integrate all the financial pieces into a comprehensive plan. Such a professional will be knowledgeable about all the subjects covered in this book and will be able to work with other professionals to make sense out of your situation, coordinate your plans and strategies, and help you move toward your financial goals.

FINDING A FINANCIAL PLANNER

When you're ready to choose a financial planner, ask your friends, your attorney, and your accountant if they can recommend a trusted adviser. Then call some financial planning companies—most are listed in the yellow pages under financial planners—and ask them to send you information about their firm and a copy of the ADV form. Also refer to the resources list in Figure 16.1. Plan to interview two or three planners.

Look for any personal chemistry between you and the planner, assess if the planner is good at drawing out your ideas, and if he or she can make financial terms understandable. Ask for client and professional references, then call the references and ask a lot of questions. Remember, you have to trust the planner with a lot of personal information.

Here are ten questions to use when you're interviewing a planner:

1. What's your background, education, and experience? How do you keep yourself current with new laws, products, and so forth?
2. How do you get paid? Are there conflicts between your interests and mine? Are you fee only?
3. My urgent concern is _____; have you handled such problems before? How do you tackle them?
4. What experience do you have working with clients whose income and situation are similar to mine?
5. Are there other people in your office who would be working on my plan or do you handle all of my concerns yourself? Are there other resources you might tap in complex areas such as tax planning, individual stock selection, or insurance policy valuation or estate planning?
6. Can I see a copy or a sample of a written financial plan?
7. If you sell insurance and investments, what companies do you work with? Will you tell me your commissions on each product you recommend?
8. If you don't sell financial products, can you recommend specific investments and insurance policies and can you help me obtain them at a good price?
9. What continuing services will I receive after the initial plan and what will they cost?
10. Have you ever been reprimanded or disciplined by any regulatory or industry bodies?

FIGURE 16.1   Associations of Financial Planning Professionals

American Institute of Certified Public Accountants
1211 Avenue of the Americas
New York, New York 10036-8775
800-862-4272

> CPAs who have earned the accredited personal financial specialist (APFS) designation.

Society of Financial Service Professionals
270 Bryn Mawr Avenue
Bryn Mawr, Pennsylvania 19010
800-392-6900

> Insurance agents and planners who hold the Chartered Life Underwriter and Chartered Financial Consultant designations.

Institute of Certified Financial Planners
3801 E. Florida Avenue, Suite 708
Denver, Colorado 80210-2544
800-322-4237

> Financial planners holding the CFP designation.

International Association for Financial Planning
Two Concourse Parkway, Suite 800
Atlanta, Georgia 30328
800-945-4237

> Financial planners who have met the specific qualifications of membership.

National Association of Personal Financial Advisers
1130 Lake Cook, Suite 105
Buffalo Grove, Illinois 60089-1974
800-366-2732

> Fee-only financial planners who can provide a useful interview form.

American Association of Retired Persons
601 E Street, NW
Washington, D.C. 20049
202-434-2277

> Provides a 12-page guide, *Facts About Financial Planners.*

Fees and Commissions

Financial planners can be compensated by commissions, fees, or a combination of the two.

- *Commission only.* These are advisers who receive commissions from life insurance or security companies for insurance and investment sales.
- *Fee only.* This is a common method by which planners are compensated either hourly or by a set schedule such as 1 percent of your assets or net worth.
- *Fee and commission.* Here the planner charges a fee, usually less than a fee-only planner, and also receives commissions from those products sold to the client.

Note:

Choose a planner who is compensated in a way that matches your needs.

If you have a small sum to invest for a grandchild, for example, you don't need a complete financial plan. If you have a complicated estate, need a detailed cash flow analysis, or your requirements for advice are ongoing, you may want a highly qualified planner in your corner.

Once you start working with a planner, how do you tell if he or she is treating you properly? Everyone has heard anecdotes about the life savings of a lonely widow being invested in the Brooklyn Bridge, Florida swampland, pyramid schemes, and other swindles.

In fact, most dishonest schemes are more subtle; they make money for some people and dance around the gray areas of the law. For a good financial planner, the term *honesty* suggests more than truth. It includes fairness, good faith, and complete disclosure. It means looking at the good news as well as the bad. It means knowing all of the important facts and presenting them in an understandable way, not just through several pages of small type.

How do you know who is honest and who isn't? Ask yourself:

- Is my adviser totally independent of any and all investment products or companies? Was that information offered to me or did I have to ask for it?

- Does my adviser focus more on my money than on my concerns and well-being?
- Does my adviser provide full disclosure of fees, costs, and compensation?
- Does my adviser build long-term client loyalty?

Building a long-term working relationship with a financial adviser who has your complete interests at heart will be invaluable to you. For example, a widow was concerned about one of her investments. The problem was that she'd been receiving what looked like a fantastic yield on shares of a Government National Mortgage Association (Ginny Mae), a pool of mortgages just like the one you have on your home.

She didn't realize, because her adviser hadn't told her, that when she received the monthly payment from the Ginny Mae, she received both principal and income, not just income. Thus, what seemed to be a 14 to 15 percent return on her investment was really only 6 or 7 percent plus the erosion of her principal. If she had been told that she'd be receiving principal as well as interest earlier, she could have planned to reinvest the principal rather than deplete it through spending.

Finally, a comprehensive financial planner will sit, figuratively, at the hub of your other advisers, coordinating, explaining, and tying up all loose financial ends. Choosing your financial adviser carefully may have a significant impact on your ability to make the money last.

ATTORNEYS

There are attorneys and there are attorneys. Which one is best for you? Do you need one? Perhaps you already have an attorney, one who was employed by your spouse, drafted a will, or helped settle on a house. Do you continue with that attorney or find someone else?

Unless you are prone to lawsuits, you won't need a lawyer often. Each time you do, your needs can be very different from the time before. Here are six tasks for which you may need an attorney:

1. Drafting your will, a trust, a living will, and a durable power of attorney.
2. Settling an estate.
3. Assisting in the aftermath of an auto accident or a crime.
4. Helping you if you must appear if court as a witness.

5. Defending or prosecuting a civil suit.

6. Dealing with tax issues, real estate transactions, and estate planning.

You can see from this list that your needs can range from a criminal lawyer to a trial lawyer or an attorney who specializes in estate planning.

The following are sources for finding an attorney:

- Ask your accountant.
- Ask your financial planner.
- Ask your friends who have had a similar problem.
- Call the local bar association.
- Ask attorney friends who knew your spouse.
- Call the legal reference service or legal aid, both of which can be found by calling the information operator in your town.
- Ask at clubs to which you belong and your religious institution.
- Consult Sullivan's Lawyers Directory or Martindale Hubbard law directory, both of which can be found at your local library.

When you are soliciting referrals for attorneys, be as specific as you can. You want to use several referral sources. You may rule some out completely but eventually you will notice that several names are mentioned over and over again. Once you have three to five names you can investigate each one.

Talk to the lawyer on the phone or in person. Ask right away what the charges are for an initial visit or a phone conversation. Remember, you're hiring someone to do a particular job for you and the person you retain will be working for you as well as with you. Here's a list of questions to help you get started when interviewing an attorney.

Regarding fees and billing:
- How much do you charge?
- Do you require a retainer? If so, how much?
- Do you charge for phone calls?
- On what do you base your fee?
- How often will I be billed?
- Will I be charged if I talk to your secretary?
- Are there any other fees or charges?

Regarding practice specifics:
- Will you be working with me exclusively or will other members of your firm be involved?

- Do you practice in the local courts?
- Do you specialize? If so, what is your specialty?
- What other kinds of work do you do?
- In what states are you admitted to the bar?
- How large is your firm and how many people work for you?
- How did you become interested in law or in your particular specialty of law?

Regarding specialized services:

- Do you do your own financial analysis for your clients?
- Does your firm provide accounting as well as legal services?
- Have you worked with widowed persons? If so, how many and under what circumstances?

It's a good idea to meet with all the lawyers you will interview within several days. That way your impression of each individual will be fresh in your mind. Once you've interviewed at least two lawyers, compare your notes and opinions of them. You may find you have additional questions that you want to ask over the phone.

Be ready to make a decision once you feel you have enough information. If you let it drag out over a long period of time, the impressions you got from your painstaking work will become hazy and you'll have to start all over again.

ACCOUNTANTS

The answers to the following seven questions will let you know whether you need an accountant:

1. Is your estate large?
2. Do you have many liabilities?
3. Do you own or operate a business?
4. Are there many tax consequences in your financial situation?
5. Do you believe your financial situation is complex?
6. Do you own stocks and bonds or tax shelters?
7. Do you need help in filing tax forms, preparing estimated taxes, etc.?

If you answered yes to any of these questions or if your attorney is weak in tax and financial knowledge, you may want to hire an accountant. The individual you retain should work for you and report to you. Then, if you decide to change lawyers or financial planners at a later time, you will not have to change accountants as well.

Smaller accounting firms generally charge about 30 percent less per hour than large ones and some people feel they get better and more reasonable service from a smaller firm. Others think their interests are best served by one of the larger, better-known firms. You want an accountant who can help you rethink your tax situation in light of any new tax laws, who can guide you through financial transactions, and who can tell you which tried-and-true tax-savings strategies are good and which aren't. You also want your accountant to tell you about new tax-savings opportunities that won't put you at risk and to alert you to tax traps in financial dealings in which you're already involved.

Ask for recommendations from friends, neighbors, members of clubs you belong to, or other advisers. Word of mouth is by far the best way to find the right accountant. Give additional weight to recommendations from those whose financial situations are similar to yours. Also ask your banker or attorney for recommendations. They are financial professionals who probably know some of the best tax accountants in the area.

Once you've received recommendations, select three or four possible candidates and schedule interviews as you did with attorneys. Ask about fees and all the other matters relative to your situation. A competent tax professional will want to see copies of the income tax returns you filed over the past few years, as well as any other important papers involved in your financial situation.

Once you've narrowed down the candidates, make your final decision. Professional qualifications and fees being equal, the final choice is a personal one—select an accountant with whom you feel comfortable.

INSURANCE PROFESSIONALS

There are approximately 250,000 life insurance agents eager to receive your business. The problem is finding one who is well trained, represents a variety of financially strong companies, has personal and business integrity, and is interested in your long-term well-being.

Ask your other professional service providers who they use. Attorneys, accountants, trust officers and financial planners generally employ quality life insurance professionals—Chartered Life Underwriters—whose educational credentials in the life insurance field are on par with their own. Chartered Life Underwriters receive this designation from the Society of Financial Service Professionals in Bryn Mawr, Pennsylvania, and have completed ten semester courses and ten examinations over five years.

If the agent whom you are interviewing has passed the ten advanced courses, it indicates two things: (1) the individual is committed and capable of taking and passing such exams, and (2) the agent is committed to learning more in order to serve you better. The agent has, in effect, worked to become qualified to serve as your insurance consultant.

Further, if the prospective agent is a member of the National Association of Life Underwriters (1922 F Street, Washington, D.C. 20006) it indicates a willingness to help promote and strengthen the insurance industry as well as abide by standards set by the best agents in the world.

A key question to ask prospective insurance consultants is, "Are you a member of your local life underwriters association, and if so, have you held offices there?" An affirmative answer indicates the individual's dedication to the life insurance profession.

Here are eleven questions for evaluating insurance agents:

1. What is your educational background?
2. Do you represent one company or many?
3. How long have you been in the business?
4. Can you provide references?
5. Are you obligated to complete continuing education requirements?
6. Are you licensed to sell securities?
7. Do you owe money to any insurance company?
8. Have you ever been terminated by an insurance company for reasons other than not making quota?
9. Have you attended or taught life underwriting training courses?
10. Do you have a particular expertise in the insurance industry?
11. Do you have experts you can call upon for advice in those areas outside your specialties?

Once you've collected answers to these questions, the well-qualified agent will become readily apparent, and if you are comfortable working with him or her, the choice of agents will be easy.

PROPERTY AND CASUALTY INSURANCE AGENTS

This professional is often overlooked whenever financial advisers are chosen. However, a good P & C agent can provide valuable services to you when it comes to protecting your home and automobile.

Those who have demonstrated comprehensive professional knowledge through course study and testing in addition to that required for state certification can use the designation Chartered Property Casualty Underwriter (CPCU) after their names.

The P & C agent's primary role is to protect your assets from sudden, devastating loss due to a natural disaster, lawsuit, fire, or other misfortune. The American Institute for Property and Liability Underwriters can provide a list of agents in your area.

BANK TRUST OFFICER

A bank trust officer is often useful to surviving spouses seeking confidential, honest assistance with their financial plans. Because the bank will not die or become incapacitated, it can be relied upon to provide competent, professional services for as many years as you and your heirs might need its services.

You may need the services of a trust officer in the following situations:

- Your spouse's will named a bank trust department to oversee your assets, left under their care; or,
- You want the services of a bank trust department to be trustee of a trust you have, be executor of your or your parents' will, or provide management services related to paying for health costs should you be incapacitated.

In some situations, the bank trust department acts solely as custodian of the trust assets. The bank holds the assets but someone else outside the bank manages them. In these cases, the bank will charge a custodial fee but not a fee to manage the assets.

If the trust department is managing assets in a trust for you, you will receive monthly or quarterly statements detailing all the relevant financial data. Trust departments have historically provided rather low returns on investments due to the their pronounced conservatism. However, you can have the bank provide custodial and accounting services and have your investments handled by outside professional money mangers.

If you are considering a trust department, investigate the fees you will pay and who your trust officer will be. Developing a relationship of mutual trust and interest can be highly valuable. Ask a lot of questions about all the services the trust department can provide, how the services are implemented, ongoing costs, and how the bank can interrelate with other members of your financial team.

One final note: Ask to see the investment results of their typical portfolio and any mutual funds offered through the trust department. Some trust departments do a very creditable job, while others do not.

Too many surviving spouses and inheritors trust luck or the yellow pages to lead them to competent financial advisers. The only method of rating professionals is to ask questions. A successful technique is to make your financial planner the coach of the financial team of which you are the owner. The planner's role is to find all the other advisers for you—with you having the final word on who joins the team.

Finding and building long-term relationships with financial advisers is an important step in your quest to maximizing your inheritance.

CHAPTER 17

Frauds and Scams

Protecting Yourself

D o not take lightly any warnings you hear about swindles that are perpetrated on unsuspecting people, especially if you are newly widowed. There are far too many instances in which the unsuspecting have been burned financially. While you may feel aware and alert, you probably have many other things on your mind at this stage. If you find yourself listening to someone who supposedly was a good friend of your spouse or parent whom you never met who has a terrific investment for you, beware.

TYPES OF CON GAMES AND SCAMS

There are many variations of the con games that follow. Once you understand the basics, it should be fairly easy to spot similar actions.

Granny Fraud

Widows and elderly women are usually the prey in this "bank examiner's" con game. Here's one version:

1. A phony bank examiner or bank official telephones the potential victim at home to ask for help in catching a dishonest teller who is looting the victim's account.

2. As instructed, the victim calls who he thinks is a police officer at a certain number (sometimes 911). The phony police officer asks the victim to withdraw funds from the bank and meet him at a designated spot (often a parking lot near the bank).

3. The victim withdraws a large sum of money from bank, keeping the reason a secret as instructed.

4. The victim meets the police official who shows his badge and gives a receipt in return for the money. He tells the victim he will call with further information.

5. Hours later the victim may be told all is going well but a further withdrawal is needed. Often, the victim does so, turns money over again, and never hears from the police or the bank examiner again.

The Pigeon Drop Scam

In this age-old con, one person mentions to you that someone has found a lot of money. Within minutes another person joins in saying he is the one with the money and doesn't know what to do with it. Soon, you are promised a piece of the action if you'll drive to your bank and withdraw your funds so that a so-called expert friend of one in the group could compare bills to see if the found money is counterfeit. Most victims never see their money again.

Phantom Banks

One of the newest scams going on right now is that of phantom banks. These scams target the wealthy and elderly with ads for prime bank notes promising returns far beyond current market rates. Using official-sounding names and upscale addresses, these banks are not really banks but fake companies existing only on paper. For example, a bank in Rochester, NY, supposedly affiliated with a bank in the former Soviet Union, sold millions of dollars of phony CDs. The number of these phantom banks is on the rise according to regulators.

Diamonds

Diamond scams come back into vogue every few years. These hustlers sell stones by mail, over the phone, or via road show investment seminars. A typical operation will promise huge profits. In reality the diamond peddlers are the only ones to make money. You, the customer, ordinarily will pay more than retail price, although you are led to believe you're paying much less. When it comes time for you to sell your diamonds, you will probably receive only a fraction of what you originally paid. Note that the appraisals that accompany these stones are often not reliable because the appraiser is in on the con.

Ponzi Schemes and Pyramid Games

The pyramid pitch tends to be made person-to-person or via a chain letter with the scammers and scammees constantly changing as people buy in, cash out, or go bust. Other types of swindles are more straightforward—crooked people prey on credulous ones. Such schemes are often national in scope and involve the use of 800 numbers and mass mailings.

Airplane is a big-money variation on the pyramid game which should be familiar to anyone who has received a chain letter with a request for $1 and the promise of many dollars to come. It also goes by the alias *friends helping friends*. A captain is at the apex of a four-tier pyramid. Below the captain are two cocaptains. Below them are four more players, and below them, at the base, are eight empty squares. Newcomers pay the captain $1500 to buy one of the eight squares. In theory, each captain collects $12,000 total from eight new passengers—eight times his or her own initial investment of $1500. Everybody in the pyramid is responsible for bringing in new players.

After all of the eight bottom squares are sold, a captain cashes out and flies away. The pyramid then splits in two with the two cocaptains now on top of their own pyramids. Once again at the bottom of each are eight new empty seats to be sold at $1500 per square. In theory, entrants eventually move up to a captain's chair and collect, too.

For a pyramid scheme to work, the number of players has to keep doubling and that is impossible. If you start with the number 1, then double it and continue to double it each day, in 30 days you will end up with 1,073,741,824.

In a Ponzi scheme a relatively small number of influential people in a community are approached and offered an opportunity to invest with a high guaranteed return. The schemes today are often high-tech and sophisticated sounding. Soon, other investors are approached and sold into the scheme often through referrals obtained from the initial investors. A portion of the money received from the second set of investors is used to pay large profits to the original groups. As word spreads about the high paybacks, more investors put up even larger sums of money. Some of this money is then used to recycle the fake profit payments and as word continues to spread, more investors are pulled into the circle. At some point, the operators quietly pack up and leave town—with all the money.

The Perfect Forecaster

It works like this. You receive a phone call from a person who says he is an investment forecaster. He doesn't want you to invest a cent. However, he will demonstrate his skill in picking stocks (or most anything) by giving you the name of a stock that he feels will have a significant price increase. And sure enough, the price goes up.

A second phone call follows the pattern of the first. He simply wants to share his expertise with you and prove that a certain stock will go down (or up). His pitch is that his forecasts, or his firm's, will help you decide whether his outfit is the kind of firm you might some day want to invest with. Sure enough, the stock again follows his prediction.

At the third call you're pretty much a believer and the perfect forecaster looks good. You not only want to invest but you want to invest enough (at his subtle urging) to make up for what you missed out on the first two recommendations. What you do not know is that the perfect forecaster started with a list of 400 people. In the first call he told 200 that the price would go up and the other 200 were told that the price would go down. When it went up, he called back the first 200 who had been given the correct forecast. Of these 200, he again split the group, with 100 forecasted up and 100 down. By the third phone call he had 100 eager investors—who all lost their money.

Other Con Games

A con artist may call telling you that your spouse or parent ordered a product or a service—maybe even a gift for you—and ask when he or she can deliver it (or perform the service) and pick up your payment. They usually ask for cash. Or a person may come directly to your home with a C.O.D. package containing an inexpensive item (often a

Bible). Other times they will want to start performing some service and then demand payment.

A con artist also may pretend to be a city inspector who claims there is something seriously wrong with your home, such as plumbing, wiring, or furnace. He then will tell you that some vital area of your house must be shut down until repaired but he has a friend who can fix it quickly and cheaply.

GUIDELINES TO PROTECT YOURSELF

Investigate anyone who wants to make house repairs at bargain prices, or offers to sell you anything or invest your money. Don't give out information about yourself over the telephone. Ask callers for their names, their companies' names and phone numbers, and say you will call back. Check the numbers in the telephone directory to ensure that they're working numbers for the companies the callers said they represent.

Listed below are nine general guidelines you can use to protect yourself from being taken:

1. Learn to say no, especially in the face of a pressured hard sell.
2. Deal with reliable local dealers, service providers, and merchants.
3. Never buy on a sales representative's first visit to your home.
4. Don't be afraid to ask questions because you fear the other person will consider your inquiries dumb.
5. Avoid buying anything sight unseen.
6. Read and understand contracts before signing.
7. Check with someone you know who is familiar with the product before you buy it.
8. Stay within your income; do not be oversold.
9. Suspect a phony if any of the following apply:
   • You're asked to sign your name right now.
   • The prices are too good to be true.
   • The salesperson discredits others who sell similar products.
   • A cash payment is necessary or the contract has vague or tricky wording.

The National Futures Association (800-621-3570) provides an excellent booklet titled *Investment Swindles: How They Work and How to Avoid Them.* It is free to the investing public.

The traditional advice—to check on a company through a better business bureau or consumer-protection agency, or with consumer groups located where the company is headquartered—is much more unreliable. There is often a lag between the time people start getting scammed and the point at which consumer-protection agencies get the word and start putting out warnings. A dirty company can look clean when you call consumer authorities to check on it.

Also, don't be sure you'll short circuit a scam by requiring the names of previous satisfied customers. Sometimes scammers give fast, prompt service to the first dozen or so "customers" and then supply their names to anyone who asks for references. Everyone gets scammed from then on.

If you think you've been cheated, don't be silent. Complaining may help you and others. If you don't take action, the shady practices will be allowed to continue. Check out a company with consumer groups and ask for references before buying. At the very least, this slows the process down and gives consumers time to think. Scammers tend not to keep bothering people who say they'll do some checking.

Call the National Fraud Information Center's hotline at 800-876-7060 (Monday through Friday, 10 AM to 4 PM, EST) if you think you're being scammed. The service will give you advice on reporting a scam and the process for recouping your loss. They will give you advice on evaluating a mail or phone deal before you lose any money. You will also hear warnings about the newest scams taking place nationwide. Free education materials will be sent to you upon request.

CHAPTER 18

Preparing for Incapacity

It is estimated that over the next twenty years the number of persons over the age of 65 will increase dramatically. We can expect to live longer. We can also expect to face growing concerns over how to deal with property and health care decisions when our ability to care for ourselves is significantly impaired through advanced age or illness.

In response to this change in demographics, a body of law has developed that concentrates on the needs of older Americans. Called *elder law,* it centers mainly on the interplay between elders' personal finances; public programs such as Social Security, Medicare, and Medicaid; and the need for long-term care.

Elder law encompasses an area called *advance directives.* Advance directives are written documents that ensure your wishes concerning physical and financial matters will be carried out if you lose the capacity to make such decisions for yourself.

If you don't have advance directives and become incapacitated,

- you can expect extraordinary medical costs.
- medical authorities can and may even be required by law to extend your life for years—at your expense.
- your next of kin may have to make stressful decisions about your physical well being without your guidance.
- the effect upon your finances can be disastrous.

If no one has the authority to pay the rent or mortgage, you could possibly lose your residence. You can lose all your medical coverage and life insurance if no one pays the premiums. Without costly and time-consuming court guardianship proceedings, no one can act for you quickly in a financial emergency.

The information presented in this chapter is not intended to be legal advice. The services of an attorney specializing in elder law should be employed when setting up any advance directive.

The most widely used advanced directives are:

- Health care power of attorney
- Living will
- Do-not-resuscitate order
- Durable power of attorney
- Revocable living trust

HEALTH CARE POWER OF ATTORNEY

A power of attorney is a document in which you give another person the authority to act on your behalf. The person you give the power to is normally called the agent or attorney-in-fact.

The health care power of attorney—also known as the medical power of attorney, health care proxy, and durable health care power of attorney—is a special kind of power of attorney activated only in the event of your incapacity or incompetence. The power requires hospitals, nursing homes, doctors, and other health care providers to obey your designated agent's decisions as if they were yours. In most states no adult, not even spouses, can make medical decisions for another person without this power. While as a practical matter your physician may listen to your next of kin, why take the chance?

The document must include the word *durable*. Note that powers terminate in the event you become incompetent unless they include the word *durable*.

The health care power can be structured to give your agent as little or as much authority as you choose, but generally it authorizes your agent to make all decisions regarding your health care, including:

- to use or withhold life support and other medical care.

- whether to place you in or take you out of a health facility such as a hospital.
- decisions not specifically covered by a living will.

The power of attorney can also give the agent these rights:

- to deal with Medicare, public benefits, and private insurance companies.
- to review your medical records.

The health care power of attorney does not:

- give any authority with respect to financial matters, administering involuntary psychiatric care, or sterilization.
- generally cover medical treatment that would provide comfort or relieve pain, which means that a health care proxy cannot refuse pain relief on your behalf.

The durable health care power of attorney generally only takes effect when two physicians, including your physician of record, certify that you are not capable of understanding or communicating decisions about your health. It applies as long as this condition continues.

You should have a number of original copies of the durable health care power. You should file one with your primary physician, your pharmacist (so information about your medication can be exchanged without worry about invasion of your privacy), and your agent, and save one copy for hospital use.

Should you require hospitalization, make sure your agent knows in advance to have the documents placed in your records at the hospital in case you can't do so at admission.

LIVING WILLS

The person named in your health care proxy becomes involved if you are unable, even temporarily, to make a health care decision. The person named in your living will only becomes involved if you are near death.

A living will is an advance directive that describes your end-of-life wishes concerning life-sustaining medical treatment and procedures in the event you become incompetent or unconscious. The living will allows you to describe the physical conditions that trigger the document's provisions, as well as the types of treatments and/or procedures to be avoided. It only becomes effective as the final statement of intent when the person who executed it is unable to make or express his or her own decisions concerning medical care.

A living will can be drafted in general terms, such as "to withhold or withdraw any and all procedures that delay death"; or it can be drafted to be specific about authorized and unauthorized procedures.

Decisions about medical treatments during one's final days are deeply personal and should be based on your values and beliefs. Because it is impossible to foresee every type of circumstance, you may wish to consider the following:

- Your overall attitude toward life and death, including the activities you enjoy and situations you fear
- Your attitude about independence and control, and how you feel about losing them
- Your religious beliefs and moral convictions, and how they affect your attitude toward serious illness
- Your attitude about illness, dying, and death
- Your feelings about physicians and other caregivers
- The impact of your decisions on family and friends

If you have a particular medical condition or may develop one, discuss it with your doctor. Find out what may happen, and what treatments might be used, including life support treatments. Try to be as specific as possible so that little, if any, decision needs to be made by the people trying to carry out your wishes. For instance, phrases like *heroic measures,* which could mean any of a number of medical procedures, are hard to follow.

Instead list specific wishes, such as about:

- Cardiopulmonary resuscitation
- Major surgery
- Mechanical breathing/respirator
- Dialysis
- Blood transfusions
- Hydration
- Artificial nutrition
- Pain medications

DO-NOT-RESUSCITATE (DNR) ORDER

A do-not-resuscitate order is a document that prohibits medical personnel from providing medical assistance measures to revive you in the event your lungs or heart stop functioning if you are near death.

The same information concerning resuscitation may also be in your living will. However, if you want to cover only this situation, you can have the DNR order. A DNR order only applies when the heart stops beating or the lungs stop breathing. It does not prevent other treatments from being offered or given. (That is where the living will serves its function.)

DURABLE POWER OF ATTORNEY

Once a person becomes legally incompetent the only way to arrange for the management of that person's property is to follow a court proceeding to have a conservator or guardian appointed. This often time-consuming and expensive procedure may also be very unpleasant for the heirs. A more effective and simpler alternative is to have the individual prepare a durable power of attorney.

Often when the court appoints a guardian, it is an attorney who has little idea how you want your life managed. The guardian may end up just paying bills, rather than making appropriate decisions that might incur liability. In addition, a court-appointed guardian requires compensation from your estate, adding another cost.

Not only is a guardianship likely to be more expensive than creating a durable power of attorney, appointment of a guardian also entails public disclosure of personal matters and financial information.

One way to avoid having a court-appointed guardian is by using a durable power of attorney. A durable power of attorney is often used for business and other affairs. Because it contains the magic word *durable*, it does not terminate if you become unable to communicate or otherwise incapacitated. However, it does terminate on your death.

Powers can be effective immediately or, if your state law allows it, can be springing; i.e., the power "springs" to life when a certain event or events described in the power occur. For example, it could be stated that the power only becomes effective if and when you, the principal, become incapacitated.

The document can give your agent the power to determine when you are incapacitated. This doesn't mean your agent can just declare you incapacitated. The agent must ask your doctor to certify incapacity. An effective provision would be to permit the agent to determine incapacity with the confirming agreement of two physicians, one of whom is your attending physician. If you do not provide any instructions, a court may have to make the determination.

To be sure your agent has the necessary powers to take care of unforeseen matters, it is wise to include a general list of important specific powers in addition to the ones specified in the state statute. Unless these powers are specifically mentioned, the agent's actions may be limited to only the matters covered in the statute. Consider giving your agent some of the following powers:

- To change your domicile to a state where Medicaid rules are more favorable
- To access your safe-deposit box
- To disclaim an inheritance and/or insurance proceeds (This can be useful for estate and Medicaid planning, unless prohibited by state law.)
- To authorize preparation of tax returns, sign tax returns, sign powers of attorney, and settle tax disputes in case of an IRS audit
- To handle claims and deal with and collect proceeds from health and/or long-term care insurance carriers; to take loans from life insurance policies or to accelerate any death benefit, and even to sell the coverage (possibly using a viatical settlement)
- To make gifts or continue a gifting plan that can be used to systematically reduce the size of an estate and thus reduce the estate tax or to qualify for Medicaid
- To revoke or amend the power of attorney itself.

Consult with a local attorney before signing any power of attorney to be sure of the correct wording and effectiveness in the state in which you live.

If you execute a durable power of attorney, you may wish to execute up to six originals because many companies or organizations insist on having an original for their files. Also, go to all financial institutions you deal with and get copies of their power of attorney forms. Although each of these companies should eventually accede to your form, they are likely to give your agent a needless hassle if your power is not on their form. They can also be expected to hassle over a power executed more than a few years ago, so it is best to re-execute this document every few years.

Many attorneys recommend that you include the notarized signature of your agent or agents on your power. It is the authenticity of that signature upon which the person to whom the power of attorney is presented will be relying.

REVOCABLE LIVING TRUST

Revocable living trusts are covered in the chapter on estate planning. However, for purposes of this chapter, you need to be aware of another alternative to guardianship through the creation of a revocable living trust.

A revocable living trust offers a number of advantages, but as an advance directive it can serve you well. If you become incapacitated and cannot function for any reason, the trust through its successor trustee will immediately take over and thereby eliminate the need for a guardian and any disputes with respect to assets in the trust. This in no way should be construed to replace a living will (the terms *living will* and *living trust* are often mistakenly used interchangeably).

Avoiding guardianship should be considered as only one of many benefits of using a revocable living trust.

ADDITIONAL INFORMATION

Advance directives often vary from state to state and you should have an attorney write and/or review all your documents. Check the yellow pages for elder law attorneys in your area or call the local bar association. Be sure the wording and execution of your documents conform *exactly* to the state law where you reside. If you change your residence to a different state you should have an attorney review your documents for that state's laws.

If you spend time in several states, be sure the documents meet the requirements of each state. Or, create a separate document for each state conforming to each state's laws. Although many states have reciprocity agreements that honor out-of-state documents, the advantage of using a directive for each state is that familiarity with the state-approved form may prevent delays in validation. A costly delay may occur while lawyers, nurses, doctors, or technicians work to understand unfamiliar forms.

You may wish to have more than one agent in the event the first one is unavailable when needed, or refuses to serve. Make sure your order of preference is clearly documented and that each agent can act on his or her own.

The forms and execution requirements for each state's advance directives can be obtained through several sources, including:

- The Cancer Information Center, 800-422-6237
- Choice in Dying, 800-789-7455, www.choices.org (there is a small charge)
- Most hospitals and medical facilities

The table in Figure 18.1 shows where to keep your documents. Do not keep them in a safe-deposit box, because then you can't get to them when they are needed.

FIGURE 18.1   Where to Keep Your Advance Directives

The Original(s)	Copies	Type of Document
You and your attorney	Your agent and any alternate agent	Durable power of of attorney
Your agent(s) and your attorney	Your primary physician, pharmacist, nursing home, hospital	Durable power of attorney for health care
Your personal physician, your designated decision maker	Next of kin Any other relatives	DNR Living will

Telephone Number Resource Directory

American Association of Retired Persons — 202-434-2277

American Psychiatric Association — 202-682-6000

American Society of Certified Public Accountants — 800-862-4272

American Society of Appraisers (ASA) — 800-272-8258

Best Fares (for up-to-date travel deals) — 800-880-1234

Discount Brokerage Firms
- Jack White — 800-233-3411
- Kennedy Cabot — 800-252-0090
- Quick & Reilly — 800-221-5220
- Charles Schwab — 800-435-4000
- Waterhouse — 800-934-4410

Car Buying Services
- Autoadvisor — 800-326-1976
- American Car Buying & Leasing — 800-223-4882
- Carbargains — 800-475-7283

Car Pricing Services
- Car Price Network Consumer Reports — 800-227-3295
- Auto Price Service — 800-933-5555

Checks at a Discount
- Checks in the Mail   800-733-4443
- Image Checks   800-562-8768

Consumer Credit Counseling Services   800-388-2227

Consumer Loan Advocates   708-615-0024

Credit Bureaus
- Equifax   800-685-1111
- Experian   888-397-3442
- Trans Union   800-645-1533

Department of Veterans Affairs   800-827-1000

FDIC   800-934-3342

Federal Reserve Bank of Washington   202-874-4000

Institute of Certified Financial Planners   800-282-7526

Internal Revenue Service
- Blank forms   800-829-3676
- Problems & resolutions   800-829-1040
- Refund hotline   800-829-4477

International Association of Financial Planning   800-945-4237

Medicare and Medigap   800-638-6833

National Association of Claims Assistance Professionals   708-963-3500

National Association of Personal Financial Advisors   800-366-2732

National Association of Securities Dealers (to check out your broker) 800-289-9999

National Association for Self-Employed   800-232-6273

National Center for Retirement Benefits (to be sure your
 lump sum payout is correct)   800-666-1000

National Fraud Hotline   800-876-7060

National Insurance Consumer Helpline (they can answer your
 insurance questions)   800-942-4242

Rating Services
- A.M. Best (Insurance)   908-439-2200
- Moody's   212-553-0377
- Standard & Poor's   212-208-8000
- Weiss Research (Insurance)   800-289-9222

Securities and Exchange Commission   800-732-0330

Small Business Administration   800-827-5722

Stock Search International (find out what your old stocks are worth)   800-537-4523

Veribanc (bank safety rating)   800-443-2657

APPENDIX B

Second Singlehood®

During my years of work with widowed individuals, I have come to recognize the array of potential financial disasters that can beset them. To deal with these issues, I have developed a comprehensive personal and financial advisory service to assist widowed people.

Second Singlehood® is a personal money management service providing service in all financial aspects for widows and widowers. Our service can help you in the areas of taxation, money management, financial planning, estate planning, claims processing, personal planning, and elder care planning.

Like physicians who concentrate on maintaining the patient's physical and mental health, we focus on helping you to achieve your desired level of financial health and well-being. We can assist you in coordinating investment strategies and finding the best solutions to your financial problems.

We maintain an extensive list of professional references whom you can contact and we welcome your inquiry into our professional background. If you're interested in receiving additional information about this program, please contact us at:

Second Singlehood®
c/o Jarratt G. Bennett
3600 Chain Bridge Road
Fairfax, VA 22030
800-663-0717

$\mathcal{B}$IBLIOGRAPHY

Other Publications and Reference Books

Brothers, Dr. Joyce. *Widowed*. New York: Ballantine Books, 1992.

Colgrove, Melba, PhD., Peter McWilliams and Harold H. Bloomfield. *How to Survive the Loss of a Love*. New York: Prelude Press, 1993.

Foehner, Charlotte, and Carol Cozart. *The Widow's Handbook: A Guide for Living*. Golden, CO: Fulcrum, 1988.

Gates, Philomere. *Suddenly Alone: A Woman's Guide to Widowhood, Divorce, and Loneliness*. Gridiron Publishers, 1999.

Grollman, Earl A. *Living When a Loved One Has Died*. Boston: Beacon Press, 1995.

Kubler-Ross, MD, Elizabeth. *On Death and Dying*. New York: Collier Books, 1997.

Kushner, Harold S. *When Bad Things Happen to Good People*. New York: Avon, 1992. *On Being Alone*, AARP Fulfillment, 601 E Street, NW, Washington, D.C. 20049.

Loewinsohn, Ruth Jean. *Survival Book for Widows*. Washington, D.C.: AARP; Glenview, IL: Scott, Foresman, 1984.

Magee, David S., and John Ventura. *Everything Your Heirs Need to Know: Organizing Your Assets, Family History and Final Wishes*. Chicago: Dearborn, 1999.

Neeld, Elizabeth Harper, PhD. *Seven Choices*. Centerpoint Press, 1997.

Parkes, Colin Murray, and Robert S. Weiss. *Recovery from Bereavement*. Jason Aronson, 1995.

Rando, Theresa A. *How to Go on Living When Someone You Love Dies.* New York: Bantam Books, 1991.

Richards, Susan. *Protect Your Parents and Their Financial Health.* Chicago: Dearborn, 1999.

Schiff, Harriett Sarnoff. *Living Through Mourning: Finding Comfort and Hope When a Loved One Has Died.* New York: Viking, 1987.

Temes, Roberta. *Living with an Empty Chair.* New York: Irvington, 1991.

Ungar, Alan B., CFP. *Financial Self-Confidence, A Woman's Guide for the Suddenly Single.* Lowell House, 1997.

Viorst, Judith. *Necessary Losses.* New York: Crest, 1996.

Westberg, Granger E. *Good Grief.* Philadelphia: Fortress, 1962.

Worden, J. William. *Grief Counseling and Grief Therapy.* New York: Springer, 1991.

Index

A

A.M. Best Company, 151
AARP, 170
Accelerated death benefits, 148–49
Accidental death benefits, 12, 34
Accountants, 14, 84, 271–72
Accredited Personal Financial
    Specialist (APFS), 265
Administrator/administratrix, 87
Adjustable-rate mortgage, 177–78
Advance directives, 283–90
    do-not-resuscitate (DNR) order,
        287
    durable power of attorney,
        287–89
    health care power of attorney,
        284–85
    living wills, 285–86
    placement of, 290
    revocable living trust, 289
    state-to-state variations, 289
Advisers, professional, 263–75
    attorneys, 82, 84, 269–71
    bank trust officer, 274–75
    estate settlement and, 84–85
    financial planners, 263–69
    insurance professionals, 272–73
    property and casualty insurance
        agents, 274
Affidavit procedure, 94
Airplane pyramid game, 279
Alternate valuation date, 100
Alzheimer's disease, 215. *See also*
    Long-term care

American Association of Retired
    Persons, 267
American Council of Life Insurance,
    153
American Institute of Certified Public
    Accountants, 267
American Legion, 13
American Society of Appraisers, 161
Anatomical gifts, 246
Annual cash flow planning sheet,
    73–74
Annual renewable term insurance,
    143–44
Annual savings chart, college
    expenses, 188
Annuity claims, 35–36, 37–38
Assessments, 172
Assets, 67, 76, 88
Associations
    of financial planning
        professionals, 267
    group life insurance through, 29
Attorneys, 14, 82, 84, 269–71
    durable power of attorney and,
        287–89
    sources for finding, 270
Automobile insurance, 12, 29,
    158–60
Average rate of return, 109, 110

B

Baccalaureate bonds, 192
Bank cards, 16–17
Bank-related matters, 12, 14

Bank trust officer, 274–75
Beneficiary/beneficiaries, 14, 32, 88,
    236
    of annuities, 37–38
    Crummy power, 88
    minors named as, on life
        insurance policy, 150
    qualified plan benefits and, 85
    savings bonds and, 86
Bequest, 88
*Best's Agent Guide to Life Insurance
    Companies, The*, 152–53
Bodily injury auto insurance
    coverage, 159
Bonding, of executor/personal
    representative, 94
Building codes/permits, 181

C

Cancer care policies, 29
Cancer Information Center, 290
Capital gains, 260–61
    dividends, 116
Capital needs worksheet, 141–42
Car insurance, 158–60
Cash, immediate demands for, 10,
    15–16, 18–19
Cash flow statement, 66–67, 71–77
    actual vs. estimate, 75–76
    cash flow control plan, 76–77
    shortages, 75–76
Cash reserves, 67–68
Certificates of deposit, 12
Certified Financial Planner (CFP), 264

Certified Professional Personal Property Advisors, 161
Charitable giving, 225–28, 245
    considerations, 225–26
    tax deduction limitations, 226–27
    trusts and, 227–28
Charitable lead trusts, 229
Chartered Financial Consultant (ChFC), 264
Chartered Life Underwriters, 273
Chartered Property Casualty Underwriter, 274
Checking accounts, 10, 11
Child care, 10
Child credit, 260
Children
    as beneficiaries on life insurance, 150–51
    education of. *See* College expenses
    estate planning considerations and, 234, 236
    gifting, 134
    life insurance on, 150
    Social Security benefits for, 49, 53
    Social Security numbers for, 123–24
    veterans benefits for, 59
Choice in Dying, 290
Citizenship test, 130
Civil Service Retirement System annuities, 57
COBRA, 11
Codicil, 88
Coinsurance, 157
College Costs Book, The, 184
College cost worksheet, 186
College expenses, 183–98
    determining, 185–89
    direct payment of bills, 243
    investing for, 190, 191–93
    life insurance and, 140, 144
    payment strategies, 190–98
College Savings Bank, 192
College Scholarship Service (CSS), 195
College-sure certificates of deposit, 192
College work-study programs, 196
Collision coverage, 159
Community property states, 254
Comprehensive (auto) coverage, 159
Comprehensive major medical insurance, 158
Condominiums, 171–72, 173
Con games. *See* Frauds and scams
Consumer protection, 181
Contingent beneficiary, 32
Continuing care facilities, 201
Contractors, home improvement, 179–82
Convertible ARM, 178
Cooperative apartments (co-ops), 172, 173
Cost-of-living increases, 116

Credit, 16–17, 25
Credit insurance, 12
Credit life insurance, 17
Credit life policies, 28
Creditors, 15
Crummy power, 88
Crummy trust, 191, 224, 243–44
Custodial accounts, 190
Custodian-to-custodian transfer, 131

D

Death certificates, 10, 32
    foreign, 14
Debt, 15
    outstanding, 11
    payments, rearranging, 75
Decedent, 88
Decreasing term insurance, 144
Deductibles, major medical insurance and, 157
Deductions, 124
    education loan interest tax deduction, 198
    marital, 257
    mortgage interest, 167
    standard deduction penalty, 256–57
Dental insurance, 158
Department of Veterans Affairs, 58
Dependents, claiming, 129–30
Devise, 88
Diamond scams, 278–79
Digest of Education Statistics, 184
Disability. *See* Long-term care
Disability income insurance, 154–55
Disability insurance benefits (Social Security), 52–53
Disclaimer (qualified), 88
Dividends, 116
Divorce, pension benefits claims and, 41
Do-not-resuscitate (DNR) order, 287
Don't Miss Out: The Ambitious Student Guide to Financial Aid, 195
Duff and Phelps Credit Rating Company, 152
Durable health care power of attorney, 284
Durable power of attorney, 247, 269, 287–89

E

Education Department web site, 197
Education IRAs, 198–99, 260
Elder law, 283
Election against the will by the surviving spouse, 100
Elective share statute, 100
Emergency funds, from life insurance, 34
Employee benefits, 11, 18

claiming, 38–39
government, 56–57
group disability insurance, 155
group term insurance, 145
retirement plan distributions, 131–33
Employee claims benefit letter, 39
Estate
    defined, 88
    planning. *See* Estate planning
    settlement. *See* Estate settlement
Estate planning, 233–49
    anatomical gifts, 246–47
    avoiding probate, 239
    durable power of attorney, 247, 269, 287–89
    ethical will, 247
    letter of instructions, 248–49
    remarriage and, 257–59
    springing power of attorney, 247
    steps, 234–36
    tax reduction strategies, 240
    techniques, 99–100, 241–45
    Unified Federal Gift and Estate Tax, 240–41
    will, 236–39
Estate settlement, 81–101
    debts and claims, 96
    distribution of estate, 98–99
    estate income/expenses record book, 79
    executor/personal representative, 81, 93–101
    no will or no executor named, 93
    official documents needed, 82–83
    probate, 85–88, 90, 237, 239
    reading of will, procedure following, 83–86
    terminology, 87–92
Estate tax, 96–98
    Form 706, 97
    installment payment of, 100
    life insurance and, 147–48
Estimated taxes, 127–29. *See also* Taxes/tax planning
Executor/personal representative, of estate, 81, 93–101
    basic responsibilities of, 94–99
    executor/executrix defined, 89
    financial institution as, 238
    naming, 237
    postmortem planning techniques, 99–101
    responsibilities, of, 94–95
    waiver of fees, 100
Exempt property award, 100
Expenses, cash flow control plan and, 76–77

F

Fair market value, 89
Family settlement agreements, 100

fastWEB, 197
Federal Employees Group Life Insurance claims, 56–57
Federal Employees Retirement System annuities, 57
Federal Perkins loans, 196–97
Federal Personnel Guide, 57
Fiduciary, 89
Finances, organization of, 11, 65–79
   cash flow statement, 66–67, 71–77
   considerations after loss of spouse/parent, 4–5
   estate income/expenses record book, 79
   file headings, 66
   net worth, determination of, 65–66, 67–71
   storage of valuable documents, 77–79
Financial aid, for college expenses, 194–95, 197
Financial Aid Information Page, 197
Financial institutions, notifying of death, 13–14
Financial planners, 263–69
   credentials of, 264–65
   estate settlement and, 84
   fees and commissions, 268–69
   finding, 266–67
Five-year averaging, 43–45
Fixed-rate mortgage, 176–77
Food stamps, 53
Form 706, 97
Formal care providers, 201
Forms 1040/1041, 97
Forward averaging, 132–33
401(k) plans, borrowing on, for college expenses, 194
Fraternal orders, 29
Frauds and scams, 34, 277–82
   con artists, 280–81
   diamond scams, 278–79
   granny fraud, 277–78
   home improvement contractors and, 181
   perfect forecaster, 280
   phantom banks, 278
   pigeon drop scam, 278
   Ponzi scheme, 279–80
   protecting yourself against, 281–82
   pyramid games, 279
Friends helping friends pyramid game, 279
Funeral
   expenses, 14–15, 32
   instructions, 248, 249

G

General obligation municipal bonds, 192
Generation-Skipping Transfer Tax, 245

Gift/gifting, 89, 134, 219–31, 242–43
   annual, 222
   appreciating assets, 244–45
   charitable, 225–28, 245
   Crummy trusts, 224
   costs of, 221
   exclusion, 190–91
   splitting, 89
   timing of, 223
   unified credit, 222–23
Government benefits, 13
   see also Social Security; Veterans benefits
   employee benefits, 56–57
Government loans, for college expenses, 194
Granny fraud, 277–78
Gross income test, 129
Group disability insurance, 155
Group life insurance, 28, 145
Guaranteed issue policies, 29
Guardian
   for incapacitated adult, 287, 289
   for minor children, 89, 237
Guide to Social Security and Medicare, 54

H

Harvard Medical School, 202
Health care power of attorney, 284–85
Health care proxy, 246, 284
Health insurance, 38, 155–58
Health Insurance Portability and Accountability Act of 1997, 205
Home Equity Conversion Information Kit, 170
Home equity loans
   college expenses and, 194
   home improvements and, 181
   interest deductions, 124
Home improvement contractors, 179–82
Home ownership, 165–82
   buying process, 175–78
   home improvement contractors, 179–82
   life estate, 174–75
   refinancing, 166–69
   renting option, 178–79
   reverse mortgages, 169–70
   selling process, 170–74
   tax advantages of, 165–66
Homeowners insurance, 160–61
Homestead allowance, 100
Hope Scholarship Credit, 197
Hospital insurance, 54–55, 156
Housing, 16. *See also* Home ownership; Rental residence

I

Incapacity
   home ownership and, 174

preparing for. *See* Advance directives
Income, 109, 111, 114–19
   determining future income projections, 116–17
   employment, 114–15
   interest and dividends, 116
   IRA, 115–16
   master income worksheet, 118
   Social Security, 115
   wages unpaid at death, 86
Income tax
   see also Taxes/tax planning
   accelerated death benefits and, 149
Incoming mail system, 10
Independent College 500 Index, 184
Indexed annuities, 37
Index rate, 177
Inflation, 106–7
   factors, 112
   income/retirement analysis adjusted for, 107
Inflation rider, 213–14
Inflows, 71–72
Inheritor's capital needs worksheet, 141–42
Installment refund, 36
Institute of Certified Financial Planners, 267
Insurance, 139–62
   automobile, 158–60
   COBRA, 11
   credit life, 17
   disability income, 154–55
   disability insurance (Social Security), 52–53
   group disability, 155
   health care, 155–58
   homeowners, 160–61
   liability umbrella, 161–62
   life insurance. *See* Life insurance
   long-term care. *See* Long-term care insurance
   Medical Information Bureau, 153–54
   mortgage, 12, 28, 144
   professionals, 272–73
   risk, 139–40
   supplemental income (Social Security), 53–54
   survivor insurance (Social Security), 48–52
Insurance Activity Index, 153–54
Insurance agent, 14
Insurance claims
   sample letter, 31
   tracking form, 30
Insurance Information, 145
Insurance Quote, 145
Insurance trust, 90
Interest payments, 124
   life insurance claims and, 32
Interest rate, 177–78

Internal Revenue Service (IRS), 137
  see also Taxes/tax planning
  estate settlement and, 97
  insurance policies and, 32, 147
  notifying of move, 125
International Association for
  Financial Planning, 267
inter vivos trust, 85
Intestate, 90, 238–39
Investing, for college expenses, 190,
  191–93
Investment assets, 67–68
*Investment Swindles: How They Work
  and How to Avoid Them,* 281
IRA(s), 12
  education IRAs, 198–99, 231,
    260
  funding college education with,
    193
  gifts, 229–30
  income, 115–16
  rollovers, 41, 42–43, 44–45,
    130–31
  Roth IRA, 231, 260
  surviving spouses and, 130–31
Irrevocable life insurance trust, 258
Irrevocable transfer, 206
IRS. *See* Internal Revenue Service
  (IRS)

J–K

Joint return test, 130
Joint tenancy with right of
  survivorship (JTWRS), 85
Key Communications Group, 57
Kiddie tax, 190, 191

L

Labor unions, 13
Lawyers/legal assistance, 82, 84,
  269–71
Leases, property, 179
Legacy, 90
Leider, Robert and Anna, 195
Level term insurance, 144
Liabilities, 67, 90
Liability insurance
  contractors and, 181
  umbrella, 161–62
Life annuity with guaranteed, time-
  specified payments, 35–36
Life care facilities, 201
Life estate, 174–75
Life expectancy tables, 111
Life insurance, 11–12, 28–36, 140–53
  accelerated death benefits,
    148–49
  amount of, 140–43
  borrowing on, for college
    expenses, 194

on children, 150
choosing a company, 151–53
claiming, 28–36
comparing types of, 146–47
contestable periods, 34
documentation needed, for
  estate settlement, 83
emergency funds, 34
exchanging policy, 147
funeral expenses and, 32
irrevocable life insurance trust,
  241–42
lost policies, 28
minor as beneficiary, 150
ownership of, 147–48
probate and, 85
sale of policies, 75
suicide and, 34
taxes and, 36, 135, 137
term, 143–45
whole life, 145–46
universal life, 146
variable life, 146
veterans, 58
viatical settlements, 149–50
Lifetime Learning Credit, 197–98
Life Underwriter Training Council,
  265
Liquid investments, 68
Living trust, 85
Living wills, 246, 269, 285–86
Loans, college, 193–94, 260
Long-term care, 108, 201–15
  insurance. *See* Long-term care
    insurance
  Medicaid, 204–7
  Medicare, 203–4
  savings and assets and, 207
Long-term care insurance, 207,
  208–15
  buying a policy, 210–14
  estimating care costs, 209
  qualified and nonqualified
    policies, 214–15
Lump sum distributions, 35, 43–45
LUTC Fellow, 265

M

Mail system, 10
Major medical insurance, 157–58
Manufactured homes, 171
Margin account, 194
Marginal tax bracket, 126–27. *See also*
  Taxes/tax planning
Marital deduction, 90, 257
Marriage tax penalties, 255–57
Mayo Clinic, 202
Medicaid, 53–54, 108, 204–7
  transferring assets and, 206–7
Medical bills
  auto insurance coverage of, 259
  direct payment of, 243

paid by estate, 125
Medical care, long-term. *See* Long-
  term care
Medical expense insurance, 157
Medical Information Bureau, 153–54
Medical power of attorney, 284
Medicare, 54–56, 158, 203–4, 215
  HMOs, 56
  hospital insurance, 54–55
  medical insurance, 55–56
MediGap policies, 158, 215
Member of household test, 130
Membership organizations, 13
Minority Trust (2503[c]), 191
Money market fund, 16
Moody's Investor Service, Inc., 152
Mortgage
  broker, choosing, 168–69
  insurance, 12, 28, 144
  obtaining, 176–78
  refinancing, 166–69
  reverse, 169–70
  tax advantages of, 165–66
Mourning, do and don't actions
  during, 7–18
Multiple listing service, 176
Multiplier chart (college funding),
  189
Murphey, Alice, 195

N

National Association of Insurance
  Commissioners, 153
National Association of Life
  Underwriters, 153, 273
National Association of Personal
  Financial Advisors, 267
National Association of Student
  Financial Aid Administrators, 197
National Fraud Information Center, 282
National Futures Association, 281
National Service Life Insurance, 58
Negative amortization, 178
Nellie Mae, 197
Net worth, 67–71
  statement, 65–66, 71
Nonforfeiture, 214
Nonprobate holdings, 85
Nonqualified policies, 214–15. *See
  also* Long-term care insurance
Non-refund life annuity, 35
Nursing homes, 108, 201–2
  Medicaid and, 204–7
  Medicare and, 203–4

O

Office for Inheritance Tax, 83
Office of Servicemen's Group Life
  Insurance, 59
Outflows, 71

Outgoing mail system, 10
Owner-employee, retirement program and, 44

P

Pell grants, 196
Pension plans, 107
    claiming benefits, 39, 41–43
    lump sum distributions and, 131–33
    nonservice-connected death pension, 59
    Pension Search Program, 42
Perfect forecaster, 280
Period certain only annuity, 35
Personal letter to family, 249
Personal representative, of estate, 93–101
    basic responsibilities of, 94–99
    postmortem planning techniques, 99–101
    responsibilities, of, 94–95
    waiver of fees, 100
Personal use assets, 67
Phantom banks, 278
Phone log, 10, 21
Physician expense insurance, 157
Pigeon drop scam, 278
Plus loans, 196
Points, 167
Ponzi schemes, 279–80
Power of appointment, 90
Prenuptial agreements, 254–55
Primary beneficiary, 32
Principal, 91
Probate, 85–87
    avoiding, 239
    defined, 90
    information needed, 86
    waiver of, 237
Professional advisers. *See* Advisers, professional
Property appraisals, 161
Property and casualty insurance agents, 274
Property damage liability, 159
Pyramid games, 279

Q

QTIP, 91, 257–58
    charitable trust, 258–59
Qualified disclaimer, 100
Qualified domestic trust (QDOT), 91
Qualified Medicaid Beneficiary program, 55
Qualified plan benefits, 39, 41–43, 85
Qualified policies, 214–15. *See also* Long-term care insurance
Qualified retirement plan rollover, 131

Qualified terminable interest property trust (QTIP), 91, 257–58

R

Railroad retirement benefits, 55
Real estate. *See* Home ownership; Rental property
Reciprocal wills, 91
Recordkeeping, 10
Refinancing a mortgage, 76, 166–69
    analysis, 167–68
    mortgage interest deductions, 167
Registered Investment Adviser (RIA), 265
Regular medical expense insurance, 157
Relationship test, 130
Remarriage, financial aspects of, 251–61
    community property states, 254
    estate planning, 257–59
    financial considerations before, 253
    financial planning, 259–60
    marriage tax penalties, 255–57
    prenuptial agreements, 254
    Taxpayer Relief Act of 1997, 260–61
Rental property, 75, 124
Rental residence, 178–79
Resource directory, 291–92
Retirement communities, 201
Retirement planning, 105–22
    average rate of return, determining, 109, 110
    income, 109–11, 114–19
    inflation and, 106–7, 112
    interest and dividends, 116
    IRAs, 115–16
    long-term care, 108
    Social Security. *See* Social Security
    worksheets, 113, 117–18, 120–21
Retirement plans
    distribution of, and taxes, 131–33
    lump sum distributions and, 131–33
    rollovers and, 131
Reverse mortgages, 76, 169–70
Revocable living trust, 289
Right of dower, 91
Risk, 139–40
Rollover, 132–33
Roth IRAs, 231, 260

S

Safe deposit box, 12, 77–79
    will enclosed in, 84
Sallie Mae, 197
Savings accounts, 10

Savings bonds co-owned, 86
Scams. *See* Frauds and scams
Scholen, Ken, 170
Second Singlehood, 293
Second surgical opinion, 156
Second to die policies, 29
Section 303 stock redemption, 100
Select Quote, 145
Self-directed IRA, 41
Self-employed, pension benefits and, 44
Series EE bonds, 192–93
Service-Disabled Veterans Insurance, 58
Servicemen's Group Life Insurance, 58
Shrinkage, 91
Simplified net worth statement, 69
Single premium deferred annuity, 37
Small estate procedure, 94
Social Security, 13, 47–56, 61–63, 107, 114, 134–35, 136
    claiming benefits, 50–51, 52
    delaying benefits, 62
    disability insurance benefits, 52–53
    early benefits, 61
    Medicare, 54–56
    supplemental income benefits, 53–54
    survivor insurance benefits, 48–52
Society of Financial Service Professionals, 267
Specific bequests, 237
Springing power of attorney, 247
Stafford loans, 196
Standard deduction penalty, 256–57
Standard & Poor Corporation, 152
Step-up in basis, 92
Storage, of valuable documents, 77–79
Student loans, 260
Suicide, 34
Supplemental Education Opportunity Grants, 196
Supplemental income benefits, 53–54
Support test, 129
Surgical expense insurance, 156
Surviving spouse
    Social Security benefits, 49
    tax status, 125–26
Survivor insurance benefits, 48–52
Survivorship life policies, 29

T

Taxes/tax planning, 123–37
    on annuities, 38
    claiming dependents, 129–30
    double-checks before filing returns, 133
    education loan interest tax deduction, 198

Taxes/tax planning *(continued)*
  estate settlement and, 96–98. *See also* Estate planning
  estimated taxes, 127–29
  filing status, 125–26
  gifting and, 134
  inheritance, 83
  home ownership and, 165–66
  insurance and, 12
  IRA beneficiaries, 130–31
  IRS settlements, 137
  life estates and, 175
  life insurance proceeds and, 36, 135, 137
  lump sum retirement plan distributions and, 43–45, 131–33
  marginal tax bracket, 126–27
  marriage tax penalties, 255–57
  planning tips, 123–25
  qualified long-term care policies and, 214
  Social Security benefits, 134–35, 136
  standard deduction penalty, 256–57
  surviving spouse tax status, 125–26
  worthless securities, 134
Taxpayer Identification Number and Certification request (Form W-9), 33
Taxpayer Relief Act of 1997, 260–61
  education loan interest tax deduction and, 198
  IRA withdrawals for college expenses, 193
Tax shelters
  annuities, 37
  variable life insurance, 146
Telephone log, 10, 21
Telephone number resource directory, 291–92
Tenancy by the entirety, 85
Ten-year averaging, 43–45
Term life insurance, 143–45
Term Quote, 145
Testate, 92
Totten trusts, 86
Transfer on death accounts, 86
Travel accident policies, 28

Trust(s), 82, 92, 237, 269
  charitable, 227–29
  Crummy, 191, 224, 243–44
  department, of banks, 274
  irrevocable life insurance, 241–42, 258
  life insurance and, 32, 90, 147–48, 151
  qualified domestic trust (QDOT), 91
  qualified terminable interest property trust (QTIP), 91, 258–59
  Totten, 86
  2503(c) Minority Trust, 191
  wealth replacement, 228
Trustee, 92
Tuition, direct payment of, 243
2503(c) Minority Trust, 191

U

Underinsured motorists coverage, 159–60
Unified credit, 92
Unified Federal Gift and Estate Tax, 240–41
Unified Tax Credit, 98–99
Uniform Gift to Minors Act (UGMA), 190, 220
Uniform Transfers to Minors Act (UTMA), 190, 220
Uninsured motorists coverage, 159
United States Government Life Insurance, 58
Universal life insurance, 146
Use of alternate valuation date, 100

V

Variable annuities, 37
Variable life insurance, 146
Veterans benefits, 13, 57–60
  claiming, 60
  dependency and indemnity compensation, 59
  education assistance, 59–60
  life insurance, 57–58
  nonservice-connected death pension, 59

Veterans Group Life Insurance, 58
Veterans Reopened Insurance, 58
Veterans Special Life Insurance, 58
Viatical settlements, 149–50

W–Y

Wages
  see also Income
  unpaid at death, 86
Waiver of premium, 213
Waiver of probate, 237
War Orphans and Widows Educational Assistance Act, 13
Wealth replacement trust, 228
Weiss Research, Inc., 152–53
Whole life insurance, 145–46
Widowhood, 4–5
Will(s), 11, 82, 92, 236–39, 269
  ethical, 247
  living wills, 246, 269, 285–86
  no executor named in, 93
  reading of, simplified procedure following, 83–86
  reciprocal, 91
  reviewing, 15
William M. Mercer, Inc., 54
Work area, 9
Worker's compensation, 29
Worksheets
  average rate of return, 110
  college costs, 186
  estimated taxes, 129
  future expense, 113
  inheritor's capital needs, 141–42
  interest and dividend conversion, 117
  long range retirement planning, 120–21
  master income, 118
Work study programs, 195, 196
World Wide Web, financial aid (college) and, 197
Yearly renewable term insurance, 143–44
You Can Afford College: The Family Guide to Meeting College Costs, 195
Your New Retirement Nest Egg: A Consumer Guide to the New Reverse Mortgages, 170